what some

Safe Landings

A very personal and poignant account of a family's military service—both the triumphs and the tribulations. Full of anecdotes that include pomp and protocol that had changed little from the time of the Civil War until their entry into military life in 1960—a way of life that is now gone forever. The many colorful events could have happened to any of us, and that is what makes *Safe Landings* so engaging, so readable, and so instructive today. Once you wade into the McGraw saga, you can't put it down!

—Colonel Larry Gordon (USA, Ret.),
author, *The Last Confederate General:
John C. Vaughn and His East Tennessee Cavalry*

For all those people who have said, "Life is just not fair," here's your instructional guide on how to handle it. In *Safe Landings*, Fran McGraw's intentions were to openly and honestly share hers and Jim's life experiences as a gift to their family. However, she has unintentionally created a guidebook for future generations on how to successfully handle life's up and downs. It is down to earth, practical, and an enjoyable read. Thanks for sharing it with me ... it brought back many fond memories of our forty-plus years of friendship.

—Captain Hank Collins,
Shotgun 46, 1965–1966

Fran McGraw takes the reader on a journey of her life's joys and tribulations with humorous, sad, serious, and lighthearted stories. In the process she rekindles so many memories. A memorable read.

—Gary D. Varner,
author and storyteller

Fran McGraw's book, *Safe Landings* reads like a novel. It has a hero and a heroine who overcome financial challenges in their youth, endure numerous lengthy separations and frequent relocations related to military service and Jim's insatiable desire to fly with a second career as a civilian pilot. While doing all this they raised two well-adjusted, successful children and maintained an enviable relationship. Reading Safe Landings gave me a better understanding of the sacrifices made by those in military service and their families in keeping the world a safer place.

—Betty Hay, longtime friend.

A family's love story, both the good times and the not so good, with a wonderful outcome that continues to get better and better.

—Henry Armstrong, friend and coworker.

Safe Landings

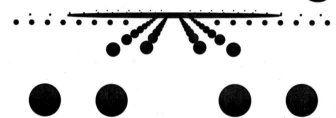

Safe Landings

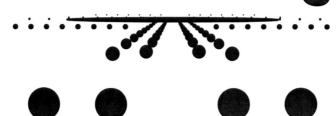

Memoirs of an Aviator's Wife

Fran McGraw

TATE PUBLISHING & *Enterprises*

Published by Tate Publishing & Enterprises, LLC
127 E. Trade Center Terrace | Mustang, Oklahoma 73064 USA
1.888.361.9473 | www.tatepublishing.com

Tate Publishing is committed to excellence in the publishing industry. The company reflects the philosophy established by the founders, based on Psalm 68:11,
"The Lord gave the word and great was the company of those who published it."

Book design copyright © 2009 by Tate Publishing, LLC. All rights reserved.
Cover design by Amber Gulilat
Interior design by Stephanie Woloszyn

Published in the United States of America

ISBN: 978-1-61566-563-1
1. Biography & Autobiography / Personal Memoirs
2. Family & Relationships / Marriage
09.12.08

Prayer When Homesick

Coming to you now, God, is sort of like coming home...and that's just where I'd like to be! You know how much I miss those I love, how I long for everything that is familiar and "home" to me. It's hard on a man to be homesick, but you know that's exactly what's with me now! God, help me understand the simple, human ache that's inside me. It's good just to have you here though—for you're a close part of my life—you are one of my loved ones too. God, let me use this empty feeling as a tiny way to thank you for all you've given me in my life—for all the wonderful people I so love, for the swell memories and the good things I now miss so much. Yes, thanks God, for giving me so much that I can be homesick! It means I have much for which to keep myself good and to trust into your care and keeping all that I love. Yes, my God, thank you for all I love! Amen.

To our descendants—
as many as there may ever be—
with the hope that if they read our story,
they'll say, "Wow, they had some rough
turbulence along the way, but
they managed to make safe landings!"

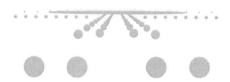

Acknowledgments

To longtime friends, to new friends, to friends that seemed to have just slipped away, to distant cousins, Zane and Jenna, and to *all* my family, thank you for your help and encouragement.

To my dear husband, whom I have adored for more than fifty years, thank you for your patience, especially when you awakened in the middle of the night and found that I was not in bed beside you, but upstairs in the office typing away. Thanks for keeping the bed warm!

Contents

"Bess 'Um Heart"

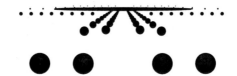

Saying good-bye to family and friends in eastern New Mexico and the Texas Panhandle would have been much harder had I known it would be three and a half years before Jim and I would see them again. *Six months maximum until we'd be back in Texas,* we thought, *probably at Fort Hood or at least Fort Sill, Oklahoma.*

We said good-bye to my folks at the farm near Fort Sumner, New Mexico. I was the fourth of six children; only my youngest sister was still at home.

Daddy hugged Jim and me. "Take care of each other," he said as he pulled a big white handkerchief from his hip pocket and blew his nose.

"Okay," I whispered.

Mother hugged us for a long time and managed only, "Be sure to write." By this time I needed a handkerchief. I knew they would miss us no less than if I were an only child.

Jim backed the car out of the tree-lined gravel driveway and turned onto the typical unpaved farm road. We waved until we no longer saw them. Jim looked at me, patted me on the thigh, and said, "Bess 'um heart." I smiled through tears. He was sweet, and I loved him so.

Back at Jim's folks' home in Amarillo, Texas, I couldn't tell for sure if Pop understood we were leaving. He'd been sick for so long after his stroke. Mom certainly knew we were leaving, and it was difficult for her. She rambled on, masking her feelings.

"I don't understand why the army is sending you all the way to New Jersey when Fort Sill is so close or even Fort Hood," she fussed. "I don't like you going into the army. Dad was in World War I, and he's been sick ever since he was gassed in France with that old mustard gas, and Ben Jr. got food poisoning in World War II and almost died. You know I don't believe in war, and I didn't raise my sons to be soldiers. America should mind its own business and stay out of everyone else's."

"I'm sorry, Mom, but that's the way it is," Jim responded. "I'm going to be in the army for at least two years, maybe longer if I into get flight school."

"Now you know I don't like airplanes," she raised her voice. "If God had intended you to fly, he would have given you wings."

I knew she must be proud of Jim because of all the photos on her living room wall, and I knew Pop was proud of his son. Unable to talk anymore, he stared at Jim as if trying to understand what was going on. His pale blue eyes were moist as he reached out with a partially paralyzed hand to pat Jim on the back.

When we were ready to go, Mom hugged us and came alongside the car, talking nonstop as she always did, but somehow this time it seemed rude to just leave like we always did while she was still talking. We knew she would rather have us close by. "You and Pop will be okay," Jim assured her. "Junior's next door. He'll help you." Knowing that Ben Jr. lived next door made it easier for us. Ben and Juanita were at work. We'd said our good-byes the night before.

"You kids be sure to write," she called as we backed out of her gravel driveway. She waved, still talking, and closed the gate. We waved until she turned away.

My eyes were moist as we left Amarillo, Texas, that bright, brisk morning on Saturday, October 1, 1960. We had been married three years, and I was two months pregnant with our first child. With our little Shetland sheepdog, Kelly, we headed to Fort Monmouth, New Jersey, where Jim would attend the U.S. Army's Signal Corps Officer Basic Course. He'd been commissioned a ROTC second lieutenant upon graduation from college in May and had received orders to report for active duty by October 10. On our way now, we were excited! The future we had worked for was beginning.

Cutting the wedding cake

We traveled in our new, cram-packed Plymouth up through Stillwater, Oklahoma. Jim wanted me to see where he had spent his first two years of college, and especially the football stadium where he'd played two years on a football scholarship for then Oklahoma A&M. I marveled at the campus's beauty with the white pillars on red brick buildings among magnificent trees. There was grass everywhere and even a large pond. The contrast to the campus in New Mexico where we'd met was stark; nevertheless, we loved Eastern New Mexico University and had fond memories of our time there. We decided his transfer to ENMU was meant to be because we'd met there! That subject flooded us with memories of how we'd met on the dance floor the next evening after I'd come to college as a freshman, and that later I had to get someone else to teach me how to jitterbug to get more of his attention! And, right there on the dance floor, we discovered we were both Methodists. Our church background was very important to both of us, and it helped move our relationship right along.

"You've never been on a turnpike, have you?" Jim asked as we traveled toward Tulsa and got on the Will Rogers Turnpike.

"No," I answered. "It's my first. I may have lots of firsts on this trip."

"That's right. Oh, I'm so excited, Frances. We're finally on our way!"

I smiled and nodded. He patted me on the thigh and said, "We're going to have such a wonderful life!"

We spent that first night in Joplin, Missouri. As I tried to sleep, I realized I was farther from my parents than I'd ever been. But that was okay; I knew I was exactly where I was supposed to be. I snuggled closer to my husband.

Jim had traveled a lot and was much more aware of the world. He was always able to answer my questions. An athlete, his competitive spirit kept him ready for what came, and I was amazed at how quickly he responded to situations. All wasn't perfect, however. I had a hard time understanding that he wanted to be in control, but expected me to keep things in order so he could be in control! But once we were on our way, I was sure all our problems were behind us. Army pay, though not great, would be better than what we'd had, and we looked forward to other benefits. I loved him and loved being with him.

During these long hours of driving, we reminisced and laughed about things we hadn't talked about for a long time—things that happened while we were dating, like the night the car battery died and we had to walk a couple of miles into town, only to discover the first place we could find a phone was at a motel. Then, when he called his friend Eldon Wetsel to come pick us up, Eldon brought the entire football team with him! There had been only five minutes to spare when we arrived back at my dorm before my dorm mother would have to call the Dean of Women! We talked about the time I discovered the beer in his car and promptly told him that drinking would not be a part of my life! He had promptly responded, "Baby if you want me, you'll take me with my beer." Almost in tears I said okay, because somehow I knew I did not want to lose this special guy. We had talked long and hard after that about what we expected in a marriage. He had already taken a class in marriage and the family. That next semester I enrolled in the course.

On the second day we crossed the Mississippi River. My wide eyes amused Jim, and he delighted in showing me things he'd seen before. Unfortunately, that night somewhere in the middle of Illinois, we were miserable. The only motel we found that allowed pets was on the corner of major crossroads. Eighteen-wheeler engines stopping and starting kept us awake most of the night. Then the next morning, I opened a bar of soap, a new deodorant soap called Dial. Adding to my sleepless misery, my queasy stomach couldn't handle the smell.

"Bess 'um heart," Jim said as I struggled. I could not tolerate the soap for a very long time.

America's new interstate highway system was beginning to take shape, and we allowed the finished portions to spoil us. We listened to the World Series as we traveled across corn-fields of Indiana and into Amish country. We spent one night in Ohio with Sonya and Howard Rose—Sonya was maid of honor in our wedding. We then traveled along Lake Erie and saw Niagara Falls near Buffalo, New York. That evening in Utica, we had dinner with Jim's niece, Jana, and her in-laws in a lovely older home and neighborhood that until then I could have only imagined. Needing to make up some time, we drove on to Schenectady and finally found a motel that did not have a "No Pets Allowed" sign. Jim returned to the car and said it would cost $20 to spend the night. The most we'd ever paid for a motel before was $12.

The next morning we traveled through Vermont and into New Hampshire, where we stopped in a small town for a ham-burger. We couldn't believe our eyes when we were given plates with a bun, a piece of hamburger, and a bottle of ketchup.

"Could we have some mustard, lettuce, tomato, and onion, please?" Jim asked.

"This is the way we serve hamburgers here," the unsmiling waiter responded.

I whispered to Jim that folks up here didn't seem as friendly as they were back home. Not whispering, Jim responded, "No, they're not as friendly as they are back home."

Midafternoon found us at my brother's home at Pease Air Force Base near Portsmouth, New Hampshire. Doyle was now a captain. He and his wife, Marilou, loved showing off their little boy, Keith, who was almost one year. They showed us the Atlan-tic Ocean, and took us to see antique shops in Maine. We saw lighthouses and countryside that we'd seen only in movies. We fell in love with New England–style clam chowder!

I stayed at Doyle's for a few days while Jim went on to New Jersey to find an apartment and sign in at Fort Monmouth. Because I had a copy of Jim's official orders with me, Doyle helped me get my military ID card. Marilou then introduced me to shopping in the Base Exchange and Commissary.

"In the Air Force, it's called a BX," Doyle explained, "and in the Army it's called a PX for Post Exchange. You know the air force has bases and the army has posts, but both have commissaries."

"Oh, I see," I responded, realizing I'd had my first lesson in military life. I also learned that every time I wrote a check I'd need to put Jim's service number, 05409703, on it. It became like a tattoo on my mind, especially the last four. Seeing how military families lived was good, and I adored Doyle, Marilou, and little Keith, but I missed Jim. The every-morning-queasy-stomach didn't help.

When Jim returned for me, we traveled south into Massachusetts and took the beltway around Boston. October in New England was indescribably beautiful! We'd never seen anything to match the autumn burst of colors. On to Connecticut and New York, Jim's travel plan skirted New York City. We crossed the Hudson River entering New Jersey. Jim delighted in showing me the huge bridges, the city's skyline, and things he'd seen on his trip down. We did not delight in the traffic and thought it unbelievable. *Who are all these people?* I wondered. *Where are they going, and what are they doing?* My mind drifted back to the dirt road by my folks' farm, where we rarely saw more than half a dozen cars a day.

25 Melrose Terrace, Long Branch, New Jersey

Our small apartment on Melrose Terrace in Long Branch fit our needs, and the rent was exactly the $87 quarters allowance the army gave a second lieutenant. On the outside the place appeared to be just another single residence on the street, but the inside had been made into three apartments, two on the main floor and one in the basement. At the front entrance, a hallway had been made from a part of the living room, and it separated the two apartments. Ours was fashioned from the original two bedrooms on the east wing separated by the bathroom. We enjoyed this original bathroom, but the kitchen was small and was separated from the small living area by an accordion-style folding door that didn't move too well. For me, it was great to be a housewife. I enjoyed cleaning, cooking, and sewing, and at last I had time to make that cherry pie with the lattice-work pastry top! I had it in the oven when Jim came home one evening. He had a hug and even a bigger smile for me when he smelled it. When it was time to take it out, the rack, which had not been placed in the oven properly, tipped. My beautiful cherry pie landed upside down on the floor! I burst into tears.

"Oh, no, Frances!" Jim exclaimed, but always quick to react, he grabbed a fork from a drawer, knelt on the floor, and took a big bite. He grinned and said, "This is the best cherry pie I've ever had!" He made me feel better. I loved him!

One lesson learned: each time we move, check the oven racks before baking.

The larger apartment became available just before Thanksgiving, and we were able to move from apartment B to apartment A. When the couple there was moving out and we told them we were moving in, the wife gave me a shiny cookie sheet. She explained that the previous occupant had left it with her saying that army folks always leave something nice for the next family that moves in and now she wanted to leave it with me. *What a wonderful gesture among army wives,* I thought. Of course I planned to leave it when we left, but the hassle of moving caused me to forget it, and the movers packed it away. I still have it; I use it fondly, and I keep it shiny.

We enjoyed the larger, original kitchen, living room and bedroom, but the bathroom had been put off the kitchen in what was probably a pantry that seemed to have been added as afterthought. *It was cold.*

The ocean was very near our apartment, and I enjoyed standing on the pier to watch and listen to the waves. I also loved the New Jersey countryside, especially the Colt's Neck apple orchard area.

Winter in the northeast that year was one of the worst ever. I saw my first white Christmas, and the little tree Jim so painstakingly picked out was elegant with blue lights and angel hair. Jim was like a child at Christmastime; this first one away from our families was no different, *and* we were homesick. The worst time for us was Christmas Eve candlelight services at the Fort Monmouth Chapel. I loved singing, but as candles were lit and lights dimmed, I couldn't sing "Silent Night" for the tears that welled in my throat. We held the hymnal together, and Jim put his arm around me. We missed our families, but we grew closer and needed each other more than ever.

Chance of a Lifetime

After the basic course, Jim took the Signal Corps Supply course that finished in March. During that time, he applied for U.S. Army Flight Training. He passed the written and physical tests. I was certain he would soon be assigned to helicopter training at Fort Wolters or fixed-wing training at San Marcos, both in Texas. But in order to apply for flight school, he had to "extend indefinitely," rather than remain on active duty just two years. When his name appeared on the indefinite list at the Pentagon, he was told he would soon receive orders because the army needed fifty second lieutenants in Europe! Although dismayed at flight school being put on hold and the thought of being away from our families for so long, *not to mention our child not being born in Texas,* we decided to accept the chance of a lifetime to live in Europe.

"Frances, Ben and Mary Lou want us to come for dinner tonight," Jim announced as he came in one evening after Christmas.

"Well, okay, but I have dinner started."

"Can it keep? They really want us to come tonight."

"Sure," I said as I began putting things away. It seemed strange to me that even our good friends would invite us on a weeknight. Jim was quiet until just before we arrived at their apartment.

"Frances, I got orders for Italy today. I have to go by myself for two years."

Not believing my ears, I turned to look at him. He kept his eyes straight ahead. The word shock meant something to me for the first time in my life.

"Oh, Jimmy," I gasped. "Why?" Nothing had or has ever hit me as hard as the thought of our being apart for two years, *let alone not being together when our first child was born!*

"Well, the reason, I was told," Jim began as if from memory, "is that America has a serious gold flow problem, and the politicians in Washington think it's too costly for soldiers to have their dependents accompany them overseas. They call it the dependent travel ban." He helped me from the car and up the stairs to our friends' apartment.

Ben answered the door, took one look, and said, "She knows." Mary Lou came forward and hugged me tightly. I didn't cry as we talked together about the terrible injustice of the situation, but once Jim and I were home and together in bed, the tears came. I sobbed all night, long, aching sobs. Jim tried to be strong as we held each other tighter than ever.

The next day, Jim learned that I could go to Italy—*as long as we paid my way!* He made arrangements with a high-interest finance company to borrow the money and settled down to making plans for the journey along with figuring out how to pay the money back.

Euphoric is the only way to describe our feelings when President Kennedy announced, soon after his inauguration in January 1961, that he was doing away with the dependent travel ban and reinstating accompanied tours overseas because soldiers and their families should not be expected to bear the burden of the gold flow problem. We happily began getting our affairs in order for the trip that would take us to Verona, Italy. The thought of not being together had put things in perspective for us. It wasn't so hard to think about being away from our families now. We had each other. We were together.

Leaving the USA

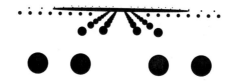

The Green Portfolio

Friday morning, March 17, 1961, we left Fort Monmouth after Jim made stops at various facilities on post. He had a form that was checked off at each place, proving he had no open accounts so that he was cleared to leave. The form was left at headquarters when he signed out. Clearing post was a ritual upon leaving any military facility.

We had four suitcases, one red plaid garment bag, one green portfolio, and two overnight kits that all together I hoped wouldn't weigh more than the one-hundred-sixty-five-pound limit on baggage that Jim kept reminding me about. We drove to Staten Island and took the Brooklyn Ferry across the harbor. It was terribly cold, but we left the car and walked to the top deck where we could see the Statue of Liberty and Manhattan Skyline. We watched the ships anchored in the harbor awaiting port entry. Their many different flags revealed they were from all over the world. What a sight to see!

In Brooklyn, we drove around for an hour trying to find the tiny pet shop at 78 Henry Street where we would leave Kelly to be sent to Europe on a commercial airline. Once there, a very gracious man took Kelly and explained what getting a small dog to Europe involved, which included a tidy sum of money. It was hard to leave her; we didn't know when or where we'd see her again.

It was St. Patrick's Day with much "wearing of the green," and we enjoyed hearing the Irish songs on the radio. After leaving our car at the Brooklyn Army Terminal from where it would be shipped to Italy, we took a taxi—*whee*—to the New York Port Authority Bus Terminal. We *just barely* had time to catch the 4:30 p.m. bus to Fort Dix and McGuire Air Force Base in west-central New Jersey.

"Frances, help me keep up with this," Jim said as he clutched the green portfolio containing the official orders for his assignment in Europe. "If we lose my orders, we're in trouble. We can't afford to lose our health records either—especially yours. Hey, let's put a copy of my orders in your purse. That way if something happens to this, then we'll have one copy. Let's make that two copies."

"Okay," I said. I sure didn't want to have any problems that would keep us from going on to Europe. He'd need the orders for in-processing at his new assignment.

The bus trip was a comfortable two-hour journey—we'd expected three. We arrived at Fort Dix a bit weary but in good spirits. In the passenger terminal, we picked up my passport and other papers Jim was expecting that verified his Southern European Task Force (SETAF) assignment. We took a taxi to the passenger hotel where we registered and then rushed to the dining room before it closed. There we met a Lieutenant Renegar, his wife, and five children who were also on their way to Verona, Italy.

After I repacked so we could get along with two bags until take-off time, Jim checked our luggage in and was informed that we had to get rid of any flammable items, such as lighter fluid and hairspray. We were upset; we'd purchased ours just that afternoon! We went to our room and after satisfying ourselves that we still had everything with us, settled down to our last night in our beloved USA.

We both slept well, and as I aroused I laced the strings through the plastic grommets on both sides of my maternity girdle while still flat on my back. As the baby grew larger, the extra weight caused pressure on a nerve, and my right leg had collapsed a few times. After a couple of falls, the doctor at Fort Monmouth prescribed the girdle for me. I was over six months along, and it was the perfect relief—as long as I put it on while flat on my back each morning before getting out of bed! The girdle wouldn't come off again until after I'd made my last trip to the bathroom before crawling into bed each night. *I'm really getting big,* I thought to myself.

"Frances, I'm so excited!" Jim exclaimed when he'd finished brushing his teeth. "We're flying to Europe today! I can't wait to get started!"

"I'm excited too," I responded, breathlessly, as I swung my legs off the bed and trotted to the bathroom.

At breakfast we joined the Renegars and admired their well-behaved children. They were pleased to learn we were going on the same airplane all the way to Italy together.

"I'm feeling kind of tired right now," I said as we left the dining room. "I'm going back to the room to lie down."

Jim frowned. "Aw, come on, I thought we'd walk around the base some."

"I'm sorry, honey, but I need to lie down. You go ahead."

"Okay. Here's a room key. I'll see you later," he quipped as he turned and left.

My feelings were pretty close to the surface, and I wished Jim could be a little more sensitive now that I couldn't keep up with him as I always had. I knew he loved and cared about me and the baby, but he didn't seem to understand that I was beginning to slow down. We'd always been able to do everything together. We loved sight-seeing and exploring new territory, but now all I wanted to explore was the bed.

Jim was back when I awakened and was sitting on the side of the other twin bed, his elbows resting on his knees, hands loosely clasped.

"How're you feeling?"

"Hmm, much better."

"Good. You know, it's kind of scary...leaving the United States."

"Uh huh, but it's exciting too. I just hate to think about being away from our families for so long. I can't believe we'll actually be in Italy for three years. I just don't think we will be."

"Sure we will. That's what the army's sending me over there for, three years. I just hate to wait that long before I get to go to flight school." He lay back on the pillow, put his arms behind his head, and crossed his legs, "I'll have to take care of myself so I can pass the physical again."

"Yes, you will."

"Can you imagine, Frances, three years before we see our friends again?"

"I know, but we'll make new friends. And just think about all the things in Europe we'll get to see—things I've never even dreamed of seeing!"

"Yeah, it's exciting, but I'm afraid this trip will be hard on you," he said, seriously.

I knew he was telling me he was sorry about leaving so abruptly earlier.

"Well, so far I'm okay, but I need my rest. Do we have everything together, ready to go?"

"Yep, it'll be easier with only two bags and this green thing." He picked up the portfolio with so many important papers in it. "This is neat. First time I've seen a zipper like this." He moved the toothless zipper up and down, up and down.

The hotel shuttle bus took us to the passenger terminal. We

watched MATS (military air transport) planes land and take off, and we were thankful we were together when we saw other couples parting. At 3:40 p.m., flight number 427 for Frankfurt, Germany was announced. We rushed to gate number three, carrying overcoats, overnight kits, magazines, and the valuable green portfolio. We were ushered to the plane and settled comfortably inside the four-engine C-118 aircraft. Within minutes, we were rolling down the runway and listening to a life preserver demonstration. With seat belts fastened (and a lump in my throat), we were soon airborne. Jim enjoyed my comments and expressions about my first flight. I had butterflies as we saw from the air where we had lived and watched as America slipped away beneath us. The weather was an excellent fifty degrees and the flight smooth. The hostess passed out gum and candy, served coffee, and helped make everyone comfortable.

Within an hour we were served our evening meal of hot roast beef, mashed potatoes, mixed vegetables, salad, bread and butter, milk, and ice cream. Although Jim had flown before, this was also his first meal in the air. Soon we were over Canada, and night was coming quickly. We flew over cities and villages that were beautiful from the air. At nine fifteen the aircraft landed gently on the ice-covered runway at Harmon Air Force Base, Newfoundland. In the terminal we enjoyed hot chocolate and coffee and talked with other passengers. The most prominent topics were the seven degree-Fahrenheit temperature and the snowfall gauge that measured *189.1 inches of snow to date!* We were soon in the air after a smooth take-off in spite of the icy runway. It was much too dark to see anything outside, so we read for a while and finally fell asleep. Unfortunately, airplanes aren't much for sleeping, especially if you're "fat in the middle" and can't curl up.

Dawn came somewhere over the middle of the North Atlantic. There's nothing quite like seeing the sunrise on top of clouds—pink, gold, and crimson against the blue sky. It wasn't long before we were served breakfast with choices of waffles, bacon, cereal, fruit, toast, and milk.

"How do they prepare all this on an airplane?" I asked Jim.

"They send out for it," he answered, grinning.

I wrinkled my nose at him and jabbed him with my elbow. "Oh, you … you always have to tease me."

"Hey," he said, grabbing my elbow, "you're teasable." He was fun, and I loved him. The soft look with a bit of mischief in his brown eyes assured me he loved me too.

At approximately seven o'clock Harmon Air Force Base time (and twelve noon Germany time), we began seeing splotches of land. The aircraft commander announced we were over Scotland. The original flight plan was to land at Prestwick, Scotland, but the weather was excellent so we pushed on over England, the English Channel, and Holland. Then at two o'clock that afternoon, we circled over wooded areas near Frankfurt, Germany, and landed at Rhein Mein Air Base. After another smooth landing and the "glad to have had you aboard" speech from the hostess, we stepped from our home of the past *twenty hours* onto German soil. It was cool and misty. We went by bus to the large, modern passenger hotel. U.S. Air Force servicemen took care of each person's official orders or passport, but all other employees of the hotel were German civilians. *What good English they speak,* I thought. We were shown to our room, where I immediately laid my weary "selves" down on a firm, comfortable, even if *another* twin-sized bed, and slept for three hours.

While I slept, Jim learned that military officials in Verona didn't know we were coming at that particular time. A telegram had to be sent to confirm orders so we could make reservations for the trip down. This would take until eight o'clock Monday, so we were told to make ourselves comfortable and make use of the hotel facilities. We looked around the hotel and went to the cafeteria for dinner. We were quite hungry and all of a sudden realized this was only our second meal of the day! After dinner we went to our room where we bathed, relaxed, and settled comfortably in our twin beds.

We were up early, went directly to the cafeteria for a hearty breakfast, and passed some time in the BX Annex in the hotel. I bought a "Mother-To-Be" magazine. At eight o'clock we learned that it would be nine o'clock *Tuesday* morning before we could leave Rhein Mein for Italy. We wondered how we could spend the day. The cost for renting a car seemed reasonable, so we decided to see the countryside and the city of Frankfurt. A red-orange Volkswagen was delivered, and we set out upon the Autobahn, a nice highway that looked like the new interstate highways back home. We understood none of the direction signs except arrows pointing toward Frankfurt; however, most of the traffic signs, such as men working, road narrows, railroad, etc., were simple silhouettes of those things and were easy to understand.

Spring had begun to touch the countryside. The grass was green, fruit trees were beginning to bloom, and here and there farmers and their families toiled in the fields. We'd left the States still brown with winter, so it was a joy to see springtime. It dawned on us that the next day was, indeed, the first day of spring.

Jim had directions to the Army Post Exchange in downtown Frankfurt that had seemed easy enough, but in the hustle-bustle of this strange city where we couldn't understand words on signs, we were about to panic when we saw a U.S. Army jeep and decided to follow it. Believe it or not, it led us directly to the PX! Inside we saw all kinds of tempting goodies but bought only cigarettes for Jim and a pair of gloves for me. We ate lunch in the snack bar.

"Can you believe we're really in Europe?" Jim asked, shaking his head. "Frances, it's unbelievable!" I knew exactly how he felt.

We drove around watching and looking. World War II had ended only sixteen years earlier, and we couldn't help wondering what it must have been like. We were thankful our reason for being in Europe was to help preserve peace.

We avoided the Autobahn to try to see countryside. We drove through several small villages, marveled at the architecture, and saw beautiful parks filled with playing children. But more than once as we took a different direction, we found ourselves back in Frankfurt! It was getting late, so we followed signs back to Rhein Mein Air Base where Jim turned in the car, only to learn he had to fill the gas tank at his own expense. His was a sour mood the rest of the day.

We hadn't adjusted to the time change, and when Jim awakened in the middle of the night, I hadn't slept a wink. It was noisy—planes landing and taking off and Volkswagens zooming around. We talked and read until we both fell asleep.

Jim thought he had set the alarm for six-thirty that Tuesday morning so we'd have time to pack and have a good breakfast before checking out at eight o'clock. But the alarm didn't go off, and at a quarter to eight, we both awakened and began to rush frantically trying to get packed and dressed. Jim dressed quickly and went down to secure our plane tickets. It was more difficult for me—oh yes, the maternity girdle—it was not easy if I hurried. We checked out of the hotel, checked in the baggage, checked the time, and glory be! We still had time for juice, coffee, and a sweet roll!

"Have you got the green portfolio?" Jim asked.

"Yep, it's right here with my purse."

"Whew, this morning's been too hectic for me."

We took a bus to the commercial airport and found we had

a two-hour wait for our plane, a Lufthansa Super Constellation. We had coffee and visited with the Renegars.

Finally, we boarded the big plane. It seemed much like the MATS C-118, but more luxurious, and our seats didn't face the rear. The hostesses were gracious, and we lacked nothing in comfort; however, after the take-off in this plane, I'll admit I had a bit more confidence in our U.S. Air Force pilots than in commercial pilots! We mostly saw clouds, though toward the end of the flight, we got to see some of the Swiss Alps. Within one and a half hours and after a nice lunch, we were landing, smoothly enough, at Milan, Italy. There we claimed our luggage, went through Customs, and inquired as to where we could find TWA Airlines to pick up Kelly. We learned TWA was at a different airport and that we should go ahead to the train station and inquire there. We rode *forever* on a bus to downtown Milan and finally stopped at a monstrous building that was the train station. An Italian representative was waiting for us. He knew our names and helped us check our baggage. Jim asked him about TWA and how we could get to Kelly. He told us that she had been shipped on to Verona the day before, explaining that she had come on an airline called Alitalia instead of TWA, and there was an Alitalia strike in Milan, so there was no one to care for her there. He thought it best to send her on to Verona after he called the post, advising them to have someone pick her up. We were somewhat relieved about Kelly, but *then* learned we had a two-and-a-half-hour wait before our train left for Verona. Well, this portion of the trip was a complete let down. It was a helpless feeling to not be able to understand anyone or read anything. All we could do was sit and wait. It wasn't so bad on Jim and me, but we felt sorry for the Renegars and their children whose ages ranged from ten to two-year-old twins. We tried to entertain ourselves while sitting in the uncomfortable, ancient seats. *It even cost 150 lire (twenty-five cents) to use the rest rooms!* Jim exchanged American money for 10,000 lire ($16). We were surprised at how long it lasted.

At train time we rushed madly again, trying to make sure we had all of our personal effects, and soon we were on the train. All baggage was being put on the train when Jim and I realized at the same instant that the red plaid plastic wardrobe was missing. We almost panicked—it held all of Jim's uniforms! My heart sank.

"Damn it," Jim mouthed. I knew he didn't want the children to hear.

"Jim, the last time I remember seeing it was while we were sitting waiting on the train. I've got the green portfolio."

"Okay," he answered. "Make sure you hold on to it." He was able to get to a representative who took him back to the station to try to locate the missing garment bag. By this time, tired and so weary, I was close to tears. I could just see us, with hardly a thing for our baby, having to put out four hundred dollars on new uniforms! I closed my eyes and prayed, "Oh God, thy will be done." I opened my eyes, looked down the side of the train, and saw Jim carrying the garment bag, which I'd now decided was as valuable as the green portfolio!

We were on our way. I knew that inside an hour and a half we would be "home." The countryside was beautiful. Spring had been here longer than in Germany, and we saw many fruit trees in bloom. The rocking motion of the train captured me, lulling me to sleep. I can't remember what I dreamed of, but it seemed it was about something far, far away or long, long ago. When I awakened, outside Verona, I felt sad. Jim smiled and squeezed my hand. There was no time for feelings. The train was stopping.

"We're here, Frances! Hurry, let's get ready."

Still a little groggy, I buttoned my black "chemise style" coat (by then just about out of style), wrapped a pale blue scarf around my hair, and put the long ends over my shoulders. I checked my lipstick, added some more, and asked Jim if I looked okay.

"Come on, Frances," he said impatiently. "It's time to go. You look fine."

My knees felt weak as we gathered our belongings. Jim motioned for me to go ahead, and when I stepped off the train, I saw three American soldiers in fatigue-style uniforms and a woman about my age, all staring at me, unsmiling. *Oh, dear,* I thought, *I must look terrible.* Jim stepped down beside me.

"Lieutenant McGraw?" a tall, dark-haired second lieutenant, asked.

"That's right," Jim answered as he sat a suitcase down and reached out to shake his hand. "I'm Jim, and this is my wife, Frances."

"Welcome to Verona. I'm Trip Tripician, and this is my wife, Beryl." He gestured toward the pretty, young woman standing beside him. "I've been assigned to be your sponsor."

"That's great!" Jim responded. "We're sure glad to be here!"

Trip introduced us to Lieutenants Vic Mitchell, the commanding officer (CO), and Phil Williams, the executive officer (XO) of the 207th Signal Company. Vic, in his forties and balding, was short and a bit heavy. Phil was fair and tall. As soon as he could, Jim asked Trip if he knew where we could find Kelly.

"Not to worry," Trip answered, "we have her at our house. You should have seen her when we took her out of the shipping crate. She jumped up and down—she must have jumped as high as my waist! We thought she was never going to stop."

They assured us that Kelly was okay and that they would get us checked into the hotel before going to their house for dinner.

Beryl was a petite blonde with pretty gray eyes. As the men talked and gathered our luggage, she and I walked to their car.

"When is your baby due?" she asked.

"May eighteenth."

"It's kind of a shock to see you're expecting. No one said anything about it when the company heard you were coming. Trip and I've only been married six months. How long have you been married?"

"Almost four years."

"Oh, that's a long time."

Jim and I went with Trip and Beryl in their little French Simca to Hotel San Pietro, where we would stay until we could find a place to live. There were no military quarters available, so the army's housing office there would help us find a place "on the economy"—a new term to us that would become very familiar. Trip explained that most Americans lived in an area of Verona called Little America, that there were no vacant apartments in their building, but that maybe we could find one close by.

Trip parked at a high-rise apartment building, and then we walked to the heavy, brass-trimmed glass door. He pushed a button alongside of it. After a few seconds, we heard a clicking sound, and the door unlocked. We stepped onto a shiny light-brown marble floor, and at the end of the spacious foyer near the elevator was a small glassed-in office. The woman there had unlocked the door. She spoke cordially in Italian to all of us. Trip and Beryl answered in Italian; Jim and I smiled and nodded. We took the spacious elevator to the fourth floor where we entered a hallway, again with a shiny marble floor, this time with black and white splatter spots. Trip used a key to open the heavy mahogany door. Kelly and their little brown dog were there to greet us!

Our poor little Kelly had lost weight, but was otherwise okay. She was happy to see us, and we were just as happy to see her! We had a delicious American dinner of roast beef, baked potatoes, vegetables, and salad. We visited happily.

Phil Williams, his wife, Joan, and little girl, Debbie, lived two floors below, so they came up after dinner. Joan, a tall, slender, sophisticated blonde, was open and friendly. They answered our questions and made us feel glad to be there.

"You should have seen Phil's face when he came from the train station," Joan said. "I asked him if something was wrong, and he said, 'Jim's wife is pregnant.' I asked him what was so unusual about that, and he said, 'She's really far along, and no one told us.'"

Everyone laughed, and Trip spoke, "It was something of a shock when you stepped off the train, Frances."

"I'm surprised the doctor let you travel," Beryl added.

"Another two weeks and she couldn't have," Jim said.

"That's right. I barely made it," I said. "The doctor at Fort Monmouth was so strict about the weight I gained, that I was afraid I might not get to come."

"Well, we're sure glad you did," Joan assured me.

Phil changed the subject, "Jim, I suggest you sign in at the company tonight so that SETAF headquarters won't scarf you up and send you on to Vicenza or Livorno before morning."

"Could they do that?" Jim asked.

"Sure they could," he answered. "When they learn you're here they might decide they need you somewhere else, but if you sign in tonight, they can't touch you."

"Then let's do it," Jim responded.

I stayed with Beryl and Joan while Jim went with Phil and Trip to Caserma Pasalaqua, the American military post in Verona, which means "fort on the river," and Jim signed in at the 207th Signal Company. When they returned, Trip drove us back to the hotel. We quickly retired, with Kelly at our feet.

The little Westclox alarm clock did its job, and we awakened still high from our recent experiences. Jim dressed to go to work and looked around for the green portfolio. *It wasn't there.*

"Damn it! Damn it! Where is it, Frances? Phil will be here any minute."

"I ... I don't know, Jim," I stammered. "Where did you see it last?"

"I don't remember. I thought you had it," he said impatiently.

"The last I remember it was on the train in Milan when you had to go find the garment bag. I know I had it then."

"Well, hell, that's really great. We get all the way here, and now we've lost it."

"I'm sorry, Jim, I can't believe I didn't think about it." I felt like crying.

"Well, it's not your fault. I should've thought about it too, but what the hell am I going to do for orders?"

"I still have two copies in my purse."

"Oh ... Frances ... oh, thank goodness! I'd forgotten about that!"

I pulled out the two white mimeographed pages and gave them to him.

"Man, I was worried there for a minute," he said as he gave me a quick kiss. "I just hope two copies will be enough. Thanks, sweetie. Get some rest. I'll try to get back as early as I can."

"Bye sweetheart; have a good first day on the job," I said and slid back into bed.

I lay there for a few minutes, and my thoughts returned to the night before when we were preparing to get off the train. I was sure now that my elemental weakness of being so concerned about how I looked had kept me from thinking about the green portfolio. I thought to myself, *You dummy, how could you forget something like that?* But it was not the first time, nor would it be the last, that I'd be late or forget something because I was more concerned about the way I looked rather than presence of mind or passing of time.

I slept until noon.

That evening, Jim told me a warrant officer from the army post at Vicenza, thirty-four miles away, brought the green portfolio to him, fully intact. An Italian man had found it on the train and kindly delivered it to the army post there.

Verona, Italy

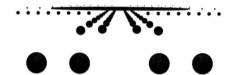

Hotel San Pietro

Upon arriving in Verona for assignment with SETAF, officers and their wives without children stayed in the San Pietro, while officers with families stayed in a high-rise apartment building until they found a place to live. The San Pietro was modern and lovely, but I was bored. I was anxious to get our own place. I wanted to prepare for our baby's arrival; I wanted to cook familiar meals; I wanted to clean until our house sparkled; I wanted to make curtains and baby clothes; I wanted to show my husband I could be a homemaker. And my wants included the things to eat that I thought would make a healthy baby. I was dismayed at the lack of breakfast items on the hotel restaurant menu. One morning, after about a week of having the "continental breakfast" of croissants, orange marmalade, and coffee, I suddenly broke into tears.

"What's wrong, Frances?" Jim asked.

"What … what kind … what kind of baby can I make on this breakfast?" I stammered as I dabbed at my tears with the big cloth napkin. "I need bacon and eggs and toast and … and orange juice, and … and things like that!"

Without saying a word, Jim left the table. He went to the waiter and attempted to explain in English that I was very unhappy and could they please bring some eggs, juice, and toast. The waiter graciously and promptly went to the kitchen. He soon brought a glass of freshly squeezed pulpy orange juice and a plate of scrambled eggs that were as dry as the toast that lay alongside. After making the best effort I could to eat everything, I decided that perhaps the flaky croissants with marmalade weren't so bad after all.

The next morning as we went down for breakfast, I whispered to Jim, "I don't want eggs and toast, but I do want juice with my croissants."

"Okay. I'll just ask for orange juice. Bess 'um heart." Jim smiled and shook his head as he gently pulled me close.

Help Without a Car

While we were without a car for about three weeks, other couples were gracious and very generous with dinner invitations and sightseeing trips around the area. Occasionally, Beryl or Joan would pick me up and take me to Pasalaqua to shop and meet with other wives at the cafeteria, or we would go have coffee at someone's house. I met Polly Mitchell, the CO's wife, and Marge Rita, an air force lieutenant's wife from Portales, New Mexico, where ENMU was located. Marge was a slender blonde with big, green eyes. We learned we had several mutual acquaintances. There was Elli Sanford, an air force major's wife with movie-star beauty and matching singing voice. I met Peg McGinley, a petite brunette who taught kindergarten and was married to a transportation corps lieutenant.

One day over coffee, Joan remarked, "I think you look more like a Fran than a Frances. I'm going to call you Fran."

The other wives agreed, and then and there I became Fran. No one in Italy except Jim called me Frances. I loved it! I finally had something close to a nickname and felt a part of this group of women who were so caring and watchful of me during this special time in my life. They were wonderful surrogates for my mother and three sisters that I missed so much.

I was amazed at the free time they all had, and going to someone's house just to have coffee and talk was new to me. Seems everyone had a maid—I couldn't imagine such luxury.

"I don't think I could ever have a maid," I told Joan one day on our way back to the hotel. "I like to do my own housework, and I don't think we can afford one anyway."

"Of course you can, Fran," she said. "They're paid 160 lire an hour, which is only about twenty-five cents. Everyone here has a maid."

"My goodness," I responded, thinking that it still seemed too luxurious a way to spend our money. But Joan was convincing, and she was about other things, too. At her encouragement, I began having my hair styled each week.

"After all, Fran," my big-city-sophisticated friend said, "it only costs eighteen hundred lire. Everyone here has their hair styled."

Eighteen hundred lire, I thought, *why that's not even three dollars!*

Social Protocol

The SETAF commanding general's wife had a welcoming coffee in her home for recently arrived officers' wives. Elli Sanford was new also and invited me to go with her. A large Italian villa served as the general's quarters, and I was amazed that it was completely furnished by the army with beautiful "quartermaster" furniture. We all stood while chitchatting and getting to know one another all the while balancing china plates topped with special sweets and cups filled with coffee. I was nine months pregnant, and although I felt well enough to wear high heels, I tired quickly and sat down. Elli sat beside me, and we chatted happily. I enjoyed this lovely setting and didn't notice that none of the other ladies sat down. Jim and I learned later that Elli's husband was called in by his commanding officer and "chewed out" because his wife sat down in the presence of the general's wife when she was not sitting. Seems a major's wife should know better! We could not believe such goings on, and nothing was said to Jim. We felt bad for Elli; we realized she was just protecting me. We learned there were many "rules," even minor ones, within military society that we would have to accept if we wanted to be a part of it.

The Blessing of Friends

We found many blessings from these new friends those first few weeks. Beryl and Joan planned a surprise baby shower for us and invited husbands too. We received so many needed items for our baby, and we also played the game "Charades." We had never had so much fun!

Jim had already met the guys, and that evening I met Marge's husband, Joe Rita. Joe was barely as tall as Marge, was Italian-dark, and had a mustache. An instigator of fun and good times, Joe's favorite expression for amazement or dismay was, "Well, pea pick!" I met Elli's tall and handsome Jon who reminded me of my own tall, handsome, air force pilot brother. I met Stan McGinley with the captivating, toothy smile.

I promptly bought thank-you cards. As I folded and re-folded the new baby clothes, I tried to be especially thoughtful when writing words of thanks to these new, special friends.

Via Mario Todeschini Number Sixteen

Post-war Italy was booming, and because of the threat of Soviet Union's flexed muscles in Eastern Europe, American military numbers were increasing. So many were coming to Verona, that the only two-bedroom apartment we could find in our price range was not even completed. We were granted a few extra days stay in the hotel beyond the maximum six weeks. Our apartment was in Little America on a street called Via Mario Todeschini, just one block off Quattro Novembre, a main thoroughfare. The Williams and Tripicians lived just around the corner; in fact, from our rear balconies, we could call to one another.

Our baby was due on May 18, just eight weeks following our arrival. On Friday, May 5, six and a half weeks after we arrived, Jim returned to the hotel about noon.

"What a nice surprise to see you this early," I exclaimed as he gently hugged me. I stepped back and looked at my young lieutenant in his starched green fatigues and shiny black paratrooper boots.

"You look soooo good!" I exclaimed.

He laughed and said, "I got off early because I thought you might like to go see if our apartment is about ready."

"Oh, yes, yes, yes! Is it finished? Do you know when we can move in?"

"Well, it depends on when it's ready, Frances," he said looking around. "I sure hope it's soon. Man, I'm getting tired of this hotel."

By this time, we'd had our car for a couple of weeks. When we arrived at the apartment, much to my surprise, the movers had already left our furniture! The Italian woman, who had been referred to us to help when the baby was born, was unpacking and putting things away! Jim had hired her without telling me;

he didn't want me to want to be there when the movers came. He thought I'd be excited and try to do too much.

"Buon giorno, Signora," Jim managed with the little bit of Italian he'd learned.

"Buon giorno, Teniente," and turning to me she smiled and said, *"E buon giorno, Signora."*

"Buon giorno," I said, spreading my arms in acknowledgement of her work. *"Gracie."*

She smiled and answered, *"Prego, Signora, Prego."* Then patting her stomach and pointing to mine, she raised her eyebrows and asked, *"Subito bambino, eh?"*

"Si, subito, ma possiblé un bambina," I answered nodding my head as if it was needed for her to understand that in my poor Italian I meant yes, soon, but it might be a baby girl.

"Si, signora, possiblé," she said, smiling.

Her name was Elide, pronounced "ä´-le-dee." We communicated the rest of the day mostly with *"si"* and *"nah,"* but we worked well together. An older woman, she had neatly permed, graying hair, big brown eyes behind bifocals, and a warm smile that revealed teeth trimmed with gold. She was married and had a married son and three grandchildren. I would come to know what an angel she was and that God did answer prayers—she was the same age as my mother.

We were home at last. I looked around the apartment and felt so comfortable when I saw our furniture. All of it was there, including the "filter flow" automatic washing machine that we hadn't seen since September. So now, all we had to buy was a refrigerator, stove, kitchen cabinets, and bedroom wardrobes. Apartments in Italy had neither appliances nor built-in cabinets and closets, and we had to buy adapters because the electric current in Europe was different than in America. It wasn't too bad as we were able to buy most of these things at the thrift shop on post where Americans put things to sell when they returned to the States. Our new apartment was on the second floor, and was an "L" shape. It was wonderful! We had only to walk up one flight of nice, wide stairs with one landing. Our door was the same as all the others, tall and wide made of beautiful mahogany and with a brass handle. It locked every time it was closed, and we learned to never leave without our keys—even when we took trash out to put in the trash chute that opened on the stair landing. Our entry was a long, wide hallway. First door to the right was the laundry room with a utility sink. At the end of the hallway was a square area with doors to the right to both bedrooms and bath, the kitchen was straight ahead, and the living room was to the left (at the bottom of the "L"). The floors were of shiny, black and white marble. The bathroom had a strange looking appliance that was similar to a commode but was like a wash basin. We were not accustomed to using a "bidet" and thought it unnecessary, besides we'd learned that most Americans removed it and made use of the plumbing connections to put their washing machines in its place.

There were beautiful balconies off our bedroom on the rear and the living room in front overlooking the street. The kitchen had small ceramic sinks that were lower than we were used to. We bought a stove, refrigerator, and a hutch-style cabinet that sufficed for counter and cabinet space. The back balcony had clotheslines strung from a pole attached to each end of the iron railing. "Quartermaster" furniture on Pasalaqua was able to provide us with a wardrobe for our clothes, a fold-down dining table, a couple of extra chairs, and a large, ugly white chest. The apartment was small and our "Early American" furniture seemed a bit out of place, but we were thankful for everything and so happy to get settled before our baby was born.

Social Discretion

We also learned that sometimes people aren't really who they seem to be. In one particular case, we very painfully became aware of this. About a month after we arrived, Jim went to Livorno, Italy, on the Mediterranean Coast to pick up our car. Livorno was near Volterra, where the famous alabaster mines are located. He brought back some beautiful alabaster statuettes; some for us and some for gifts. We gave a couple to our sponsors, Beryl and Trip, the evening we had them over for dinner, soon after we moved into our apartment. I'd prepared my very best—and our favorite meal—southern fried chicken with all the trimmings.

One afternoon a couple of days later, I was on the rear balcony and heard Beryl calling from her balcony. She said she needed to talk with me. I called back for her to come on over. Well, she proceeded to tell me that there were some things I should know and that alabaster statuettes weren't really a suitable gift for sponsors. I couldn't believe what I was hearing. I was speechless.

"You know Trip went to West Point, and they learn a lot about things like that," she went on. "We also thought you probably need to know that fried chicken isn't really an appropriate meal for entertaining."

My heart began to pound, but as my nature was to be patient and not overreact, I said little. By the time Beryl left a few minutes later, I was fuming! I had no apologies for my upbringing! I remembered the Sunday dinners on the farm when Mother brought out the white damask tablecloth and napkins and saw to it that my sisters and I placed the dishes and flatware, even if they weren't china and silver, exactly as the pictures in the etiquette book she kept close by. I remembered the big platters piled high with golden fried chicken, bowls of mashed potatoes, white gravy, yellow corn, lettuce salad, and green beans or asparagus, the yeast rolls that she always made herself, and the delicious pie, cake, or banana pudding desserts. I remembered my parents' insistence on proper manners not only at the table, but also in all aspects of life. I remembered how they tried to see that we were involved in church, school, and community activities so we could learn proper ways to conduct ourselves. As far as I was concerned, if there was anything wrong with giving alabaster statuettes as gifts and serving fried chicken as a thank-you meal, Beryl's rudeness was much worse! *How dare her!* I was really angry, and now, during this last week of my pregnancy, my emotions were very close to the surface. I had to talk with some-one, but it would be hours before Jim was home. I went to see Joan. By this time I knew that Joan came from a well-to-do New Jersey family, and that she had done, seen, and had things that I could only dream about, but somehow I knew she'd understand.

"Fran, I can't believe she was so rude!" Joan exclaimed. "You know, though, I'm not surprised now that I think about some other things that happened before you got here. Beryl's too impressed that her husband went to West Point."

Joan was sympathetic and understanding. She made me feel so much better. From that day on, we were dear friends.

When I told Jim about Beryl's visit, he was furious! I asked him if I was really that backward. Of course I grew up on a farm and my folks didn't have any money, but we knew what was right and what was wrong.

"Frances, the meal you fixed was beautiful, and absolutely nothing was wrong with it. And if they didn't like it, fine! And if they don't like the alabaster statues, then tough! If that's the way they are, I don't care about being around them!"

Jim responded exactly as I'd expected. He was also keenly aware of my condition and was very understanding. He never mentioned the incident to Trip, and Trip never mentioned it. He didn't seem to have the hang-ups his wife had; nevertheless, our association with them thereafter was rare.

I didn't stop cooking Southern fried chicken, and I gained a reputation for doing it rather well. I did learn, however, that there are easier meals to prepare for guests!

Kevin Martin McGraw

Jim worked on Saturday mornings, as was the custom in those days. When he came home at noon on Saturday, May 20, 1961, I told him I was feeling pains. As we timed them, we rested together. Jim fell asleep, and as I watched this man I loved so dearly, tears surfaced. We wanted a child more than anything, but I realized our lives were changing—it would never be just the two of us again. When he awakened, we decided to take a walk to see if this labor thing was really beginning. We stopped in a stationery store on Quattro Novembre and found some beautiful Italian-style birth announcements—a baby dressed in blue peeking through a door. I told Jim that these were the announcements I wanted if we had a boy, but, now I thought we needed to get to the dispensary.

Jim and Trip were coaches for a little league baseball team, and a game was scheduled that afternoon. He had all the bats, balls, and bases in the trunk of our car. We went to the dispensary at Pasalaqua first where the doctor told us it was time to make the trip to Vicenza to the nearest U.S. Army hospital—thirty-four miles away.

"She's getting ready fast," the doctor told Jim. "You need to get her to Vicenza as soon as possible."

"Aw, gee, Doc," my husband, who had a knack for lightening a heavy situation, asked, "can't we postpone this? I've got a little league baseball game this afternoon."

The captain doctor, who was of a much more serious nature, snapped, "Lieutenant, you started this, now you finish it!"

Sobered by the doctor's manner, Jim responded, "Yes, sir!" and we promptly left, giggling as we got into the car.

At the ballpark, Jim told Trip what was happening. Word drifted throughout the park, and folks came to wish us well. Beryl was bold enough to ask if she could take the trip to the hospital with us. Jim looked at me, and I shrugged my shoulders. "Sure, Beryl, come along if you want to. I have to come back tonight to get Fran's clothes anyway." In our haste, we'd forgotten to bring along my overnight kit.

She came along, leaning big-eyed over the back of the front seat every time we clocked a labor pain. In Vicenza, the doctor said there was plenty of time, so Jim drove Beryl back to Verona. He returned just in time to hear Kevin's first cry. Eight pounds, eight-and-one-half ounces, twenty-and-three-quarter inches long, our big baby boy was born at 10:25 p.m. When Jim came to see me, I said to him, "Well, I got you your boy."

"No, you got us *our* boy." Tears filled his eyes as he smiled and squeezed my hands. "Thank you, Frances. He is so beautiful!"

"He is beautiful, isn't he? Ten fingers, ten toes, and two little bitty balls!"

Jim laughed, and he has never let me live that down. I still insist it was the anesthetic.

We arrived home on Wednesday to find a big blue satin bow on our front door, as was the Italian custom signifying the birth of a son. Signora Elide had put it there.

I was healthy, had a normal delivery, and Kevin was a good, strong baby. I adored this baby boy, who, even at the moment he was born, looked so much like his father. I was content as never before in my life.

"You know, Kevin's a week old today, and you haven't been

out of the house," Jim said. "I thought we'd go to dinner at the club tonight."

"Oh no, Jim," I said quickly, "I can't leave my baby!"

"Hey, remember me?" Jim asked soberly. "Kevin is *our* baby and besides, we can get Elide to babysit. I want to take you to dinner tonight. We won't be gone long."

"Well, okay," I answered meekly, "if we can get Elide to watch him." I realized then that my response must have seemed to Jim that he was now number two in my life, and I certainly didn't feel that way. As we didn't have a phone and wouldn't for several months, Jim drove to Elide's house, and she agreed to come on over. We went to the officers' club at Pasalaqua, had a lovely meal together, and were home within two hours. Kevin slept the entire time.

Elide taught me to speak Italian and assured me that she spoke "high Italian" rather than "low Italian" as did people in the country. I learned quickly and enjoyed the beautiful language. An early learning experience occurred when Elide asked me about Kevin's birth weight. The only Italian measurement I knew was kilo, so I told her "otto kilo." She gave me a sad, serious look and said, "Non possiblé, Signora, non possiblé." I was frustrated because I was very proud of my big baby boy. Later, Joan explained that it took almost two pounds to make a kilo! No wonder Elide had said, "Non possiblé, Signora, non possiblé!"

One of Kevin's first outings was a Sunday afternoon visit to Marge and Joe Rita. The idea was spur of the moment, and when we arrived we saw them together with Phil and Joan on the front porch. Joe came out to greet us.

"Hey, McGraws! Good to see you! Aw, looky here, you've brought that bambino for us to see. Come on in here."

"No, Joe," Jim responded, "we don't want to intrude. You've got company. We'll come another time."

"Get outta that car and come in here. It's great for you to come by. We've wanted to see that big boy!" Kevin, less than a month old, slept the entire time, but we accepted many *ohs* and *ahs*.

We all enjoyed visiting but were flabbergasted when Joe announced they were moving because they'd been evicted from their villa. Joe explained they had to move because of a party they'd had when the guys all got so rowdy. The neighbors called the police because of the noise.

Oh how I remembered that night—the week before Kevin was born. Jim drank too much and tried to play football with a kitchen cabinet! Now he insisted he'd been "just a poor lil' ole innocent second lieutenant" when Phil and Stan started giving him vodka gimlets. He learned a valuable lesson about drinking that night and never again allowed anyone to set him up. At any rate, I needed to get him back to the hotel. Jon Sanford and Dick Hollar, who'd long since learned how to handle their booze, had helped me get him in the car. Even though I didn't have a license to drive in Italy yet and wouldn't until after the baby was born, I was the only one in condition to drive. I concentrated hard on getting to the hotel safely, and luckily there wasn't much traffic. Thankfully, it was late at night and few people were there to see a very pregnant woman helping a very drunk man through the hotel lobby and into the elevator!

As I recalled the party, it dawned on me that the police had come to the house before Jim's outburst, and I was satisfied that he hadn't caused the police visit. But here, now, at Marge and Joe's, I was sad they were going to have to move. By Labor Day they had moved into an apartment building and were ready for another party. To this day Jim has not touched another vodka gimlet—gin martinis, yes; gimlets, no.

The Ski Cabin

In late summer thoughts of the upcoming skiing season permeated the minds of Phil, Stan, Joe, Dick, and Jim. All had skied before except Jim. One of the young soldiers in the 207th Signal Company who loved to ski was married to a beautiful young Italian woman. She had connections with people that had a cabin on Mount Bondoni outside of Trento about sixty miles north of Verona. Phil and Jim knew the location because of the communications site on the mountaintop. As a matter of fact, they used the large basket lift to get some of their equipment to the site when roads were impassable. The soldier approached the guys about renting a cabin for the skiing season. We all discussed it and agreed to pool money to rent the cabin. It seemed like so much money to me when there were things I thought we needed, but it seemed such a fun thing to do; after all, snow skiing in Europe? Wow! Of course, Jim and I would have to buy clothes and ski boots … rent skis … learn to ski … and pay a babysitter.

The deal was made, and one Sunday in September we joined Stan and Peg McGinley to go see what the place was like. From Trento we drove up the winding mountain road, saw the big basket ski lift by the hotel, and then drove up the dirt road the rest of the way to the cabin. We'd packed food to have for the day, and that's when Stan introduced us to London broil. Using a portable charcoal grill, he cooked a marinated flank steak to an incredible level of rare tenderness, topped it with sautéed mushrooms, and we thought it the most wonderful thing we'd ever eaten! We lounged on the mountainside and took in the scenery. In plain sight another thousand feet up, was a huge cement bunker built by Germans during World War II.

"Ski cabin" in America and "ski cabin" in Italy was *not*, I repeat, *not* the same thing. We had visions of quaint log cabins with rock fireplaces, but alas, none were like that here. What we saw were small stucco-type buildings the Italians used mainly for summer getaway. Oh well, we decided later, it's just a place to stay while we ski.

Finally in November, we managed a weekend away for our first skiing adventure. Signora Elide agreed to watch Kevin, who had been on a bottle for some time. We bought ski pants and boots and used the sweaters and parkas we already had. It was cold, and the roads were icy, but we managed fine with Joan and Phil in their little gray Volkswagen Beetle with skis mounted on racks on top. We put on our ski boots and put all of our stuff in the basket lift to begin the long, slow ride to the top. Once there, the only way we could get to the cabin was to ski. All Jim and I could do was attach the skis to our boots and try. I watched as he maneuvered down the trail behind Phil and Stan. He knew how to use his legs; I did not. I don't remember how many times I fell on the one-hundred-yard trek to the cabin, but somehow I managed. The big boots cramped my ankles, but they did support my skiing efforts.

This ski cabin had three rooms and a bathroom. Two rooms were downstairs—a kitchen with wood stove, a table and chairs, and a living room that we had to use for a bedroom. The one room upstairs accommodated six of our twelve cots. Sadly, we learned we could not use the bathroom, as everything was frozen! Oh, how the girls squealed!

The conversation was intense, and we girls didn't like the idea of walking a hundred and fifty yards in the snow to the hotel, or going outside behind the cabin! At least we had flashlights and toilet paper, so we resigned ourselves to the situation. We walked to the hotel before bedtime, but it was difficult in the soft snow. Getting up the next morning was even harder. It was cold! The one fire in the kitchen stove didn't exactly warm up the cabin. I did not want to leave my sleeping bag. Before I knew it, Stan and Phil had each end of my sleeping bag in their hands, took me down the steep stairs, out the door, and threw me into the snow! Jim laughed, and I was angry, but not for long. I got the message. If I was going to ski, I'd better get up and out!

Joe, Marge, and I took lessons, as we were the only ones who'd never skied. We learned how to traverse and snowplow enough that we were able to enjoy the kiddy slope.

The guys wanted to get on the slopes early. They made breakfast quickly, and we soon were on our way—*after* we girls had gone outside to the rear of the cabin while keeping watch for each other.

Phil and Stan told Jim he was doing well enough to accompany them to a higher slope, so he did. Thankfully, he soon realized his limits and didn't try to do anything but get off the mountain! It wasn't a good day for Phil, who, on a run down the steep slope, hit something that broke one of his expensive new skis. We were so grateful he hadn't been hurt; nevertheless, he was not in good humor the rest of the trip.

That evening after dinner, the guys decided to go to the hotel for a drink. Dick Hollar didn't go. When we questioned him, he said, "When I look out at the winter sky and that cloud-shrouded moon, it reminds me of Korea. I expect to see gooks coming over the hill any minute." It had been less than ten years since he'd fought in that war.

The next morning, we gathered our things for the long trip down. The guys managed to get everything in backpacks, and all we girls had to do was ski down the two-mile trail. That's it, just ski down the two-mile trail. *Just ski, just ski!* I was tired, my muscles were sore, my ankles hurt, and my legs were weak. I fell every few yards. *Just ski, just ski!* We finally managed to get to the car. I'd never been so tired. Later that week my right hip was bruised so that it looked like hamburger. Oh well, at least I knew how to fall without breaking a leg.

We enjoyed the time, even with twelve people in the small cabin and without the comforts of home. One after-story came when the guys went up in the spring to bring down the cots and sleeping bags. We laughed as they told about the place out back of the cabin where, upon the snow melting, they could see little piles of yellow toilet paper all in a row. We girls never got over that, but we laughed anyway. That time is one of the most memorable of our lives. Even so, the girls went skiing only twice.

Lago de Garda

Some Sunday afternoons we'd pack up and go to Lago de Garda to enjoy the U.S. Army's special service's recreation area built among grape vineyards alongside the enormous lake. There were brightly colored umbrellas over picnic tables and grills for barbecuing. There were tennis courts, horseshoes, a swimming area, and water skiing behind high-powered boats. Fourth of July fireworks were the most incredible we'd ever seen!

I happily stayed close to the playpen as we watched our baby grow. Kevin was almost three months old, when one Sunday on our way home from the lake, we heard that the Russians had put up a wall that divided the city of Berlin. All American soldiers were immediately on alert, and all of a sudden, our fairy-tale lives were topsy-turvy in a very scary world.

World Turmoil

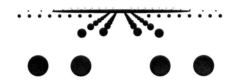

The Military Scene

As the Cold War escalated, alerts were the norm. Our men were gone a lot, so we girls clung to one another and took care of our families. There were wives clubs and unit coffees and luncheons, women's bowling leagues, and volunteer work at the thrift shop and post chapel. In time, Jim's unit returned to a regular schedule—in the field for two weeks, then home for four weeks. The 207th Signal Company had responsibility, in conjunction with the Italian Army, to provide communications for all of northern Italy. The company strung wire, put up antennas, and maintained equipment; all while negotiating the rugged terrain of the Dolomite Mountains.

Though fond of many he worked with, Jim was increasingly dismayed at the lack of leadership, teamwork, and the resulting poor morale throughout the company. For several months he was the junior ranking officer and had many additional-duty responsibilities. As leader of A Platoon, he worked hard and developed a fine rapport with his troops. One of the hardest things he faced was the loss of two fine young soldiers when their jeep went off the road and careened down a mountainside. Another time, a sharp young soldier took leave to go skiing in Germany. An avid and longtime skier, the young man slowed at the end of the trail and hit a small bump. He lost control, fell face-forward, hitting his chin on the ice, and was paralyzed from the neck down. Then my young lieutenant faced another tragedy when his first sergeant was found in the country in a parked car, alone with his teenage daughter. An incestuous relationship was confirmed. Jim was devastated because he'd come to enjoy and respect the amiable veteran of World War II and Korea.

There were also happy and funny times. One funny incident occurred during a field exercise at Site A, a large cave about ten miles north of Verona. The cave was an excellent fortress and served as SETAF headquarters during field exercises. Jim went to the kitchen in the massive cave one morning to bring coffee back to his area. He returned, carrying a large metal can that contained about five gallons of coffee, on which he balanced a couple of cans of evaporated milk. He passed through a first set of double doors when, to his surprise, the second set opened and he was face to face with General Bruce C. Clark, commander in chief of all military forces in Europe! Instinctively, Jim attempted to stand straight, and in doing so, sent the cans of milk rolling down the hall, the sound reverberating loudly in the hollow cave. The general scowled, but passed without comment. Jim said, "I know General Clark doesn't remember me, but I'll never forget my close encounter with him!"

One of Jim's favorite acquaintances at Site A was an Italian major who was a pilot in World War II. The major told that he became so tired of being shot down by Americans that at the first sight of any American fighters, he would jump out of his airplane. He didn't understand why his superiors kept telling him to shoot down his liberators!

A Young Movie Star

During the summer of 1961, several scenes were shot in Verona of the movie *Barabbas*, starring Anthony Quinn. The daughter of one of the American families there was in the movie, so we were eager for the film to be released. One day, my friend Marge and I were shopping at Pasalaqua when she introduced me to a lovely young girl. I remember thinking what an angel child she was, about sixteen, so perfectly put together, and how her sea-green summer dress complimented her fair complexion. Her bouncing, honey-blonde ponytail gave her a sweet innocence as she walked away. I asked, "Who did you say that was?"

"Sharon Tate," Marge answered. "You know, the one in the movie *Barabbas*."

"I don't think I've ever seen such a beautiful teenager."

"She's just as sweet too," Marge said. The tragic events surrounding Sharon Tate's murder a few years later by Charles Manson's minions saddened us unbelievably.

Protestant Chapel

The chapel at Pasalaqua was used for Protestant and Catholic services. Sunday services at 11:00 a.m. were typically Protestant. We attended occasionally, but we found church wasn't the priority it had always been for us. Perhaps one of the reasons was our realization that things in the church aren't always as they seem. We knew the military chapel tried to meet the needs of all protestant denominations, but we were terribly dismayed when we learned we could not have our precious baby boy dedicated in infant baptism during Sunday morning services. Seems the chaplain was of a denomination that did not believe in infant baptism. Well, my, my. Was our baby less than other babies? No, of course not, and the good chaplain said he would ask the chaplain from Vicenza, who happened to be of our Methodist persuasion, to come perform the ritual. That chaplain could not be in Verona on Sunday morning, but he would come on Saturday. We asked the Williams and Ritas to come witness this special event. Phil couldn't be there, but Joan was happy to, as was Joe; however, Marge would not, as she felt she had to be true to her denomination. So Joe and Joan stood with us as we dedicated our child to God and promised to bring him up in the Christian faith. Needless to say, this event sparked several conversations about different denominations and beliefs. Tolerant as we tried to be, we felt cheated that we could not dedicate our child to God before the congregation on Sunday morning.

Christmas in Italy

Christmas presents had to be mailed back home at least six weeks before the big day. We shopped at open markets in downtown Verona while enjoying fried sweetbread sprinkled with sugar that was sold on the street. We bought Italian sweaters, silver, ceramic, and wood gifts for family members.

For Kevin's first Christmas, Santa brought him some wooden blocks with colorful letters, the stuffed toy Quick Draw McGraw, and other toys suitable for a happy seven-month-old!

New Year's Eve

The New Year's Eve ball was our first formal military affair, and alongside Jim in his dress blue uniform, I felt special. Earlier, we joined several couples for cocktails at Jon and Elli Sanford's house. Ladies wore festive gowns, and several had glitter on their eye shadow. I'd never seen anything like it. Elli's tree was decorated with colorful balls and lights that shined faintly through foil icicles—more than I'd ever seen. It was spectacular!

The dinner and dance at the officers' club was a gala affair! All officers were in dress uniforms, civilians in tuxedos, and wives and dates in formal gowns. Glitter was everywhere; in hair, on eyelids and cheeks, and even in the cleavage of some party-minded ladies. Tables were beautifully decorated befitting the season. For dinner, the magnificent prime rib roast was accompanied with a tossed salad, green beans almandine, baked potatoes with all the trimmings, and hot rolls with butter. Dessert was vanilla ice cream covered with crème de menthe liqueur.

Everyone, as far as I could tell, had a grand time dancing to live, big band music. Just before midnight, I was dancing with our friend, Phil, when Jim tapped him on the shoulder.

"Hey, Phil, I wanna dance with my wife."

"Sure, Jim," Phil mumbled, and moved away.

"Hey, beautiful, remember me?"

"Of course I do, my love," I answered, coyly. "How nice of you to remember me!"

"Don't ever worry about me forgetting you, Frances," he murmured. "Havin' a good time?"

"Um hmm, how 'bout you?"

"Better now," he answered, as the band began counting down the last ten seconds of what had been the *most incredible year of our lives.*

The next day, I brushed Jim's dress-blue uniform jacket and pressed the slacks again. He dressed and went to get Elide while I got ready for the Commanding General's New Year's Day reception at the officers' club. In those days, if the reception was before six o'clock in the evening, hats and gloves were required for ladies. I wore a dark green wool-jersey dress softly belted at the waist, rose-beige gloves with matching high-heeled suede pumps, and a large-brimmed, beige felt hat. I knew I looked good, and Jim was proud of me. When we arrived at the club, we joined couples from the 207th Signal Company to go through the receiving line together. Those in line ahead of us were whispering about a piece of paper given to each officer. Shhhh! On it were the "rules" we were to follow for the reception!

I didn't know any better as this was my first military reception, but many were insulted. Husbands felt their wives were not in the military and should not be made to feel as if they were "being inspected." The "rules" were the talk of the post for a long time, and one sign of a future decade of change.

207th Out, 560th In

The 207th Signal Company became Company A of the 560th Signal Battalion in early 1962. Battalion headquarters were at Caserma Ederle in Vicenza, and unit social activities were almost always there. We traveled along the dangerous two-lane highway often following horse-drawn wagons for miles before we could pass. Trucks pulled up behind us and startled us with loud air horns. Motor scooters zipped past as if we were standing still. The only pleasure was seeing the countryside east of Verona, and the castles that Shakespeare made famous in *Romeo and Juliet. How romantic,* we thought, *to see in person the castle-homes of the families Capulet and Montague!* To our great relief, the Autostrada was completed in late 1962, and we no longer had to travel the two-lane highway.

There were many parties—unit, promotion, holiday, private, and parties at the American and Italian officers' clubs, both in Verona and Vicenza. The fun with good friends helped ease the pain of being away from family. And, we always had a baby-sitter—our "Nona," our Senora Elide. She was an angel—the answer I'm sure to our parents' prayers while we were so far away. She adored Kevin, and they were buddies. Having someone so available to babysit, and for so little money, was beyond me. *It seems like we're always on vacation,* I thought.

Changes came. In May, Joan and Phil returned to the States, and Stan and Peg soon followed. It was hard to see them go. Newcomers came, but nothing would ever take the place of the special bond of that first group.

1962 and Kathy Lou

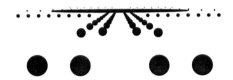

We still observed George Washington's birthday on February 22 then. Jim was home that day, and I was thrilled he could watch Kevin while I went to the beauty shop. When I returned home, I must have looked pretty good because Jim was amorous. We'd planned to try to have another child by the time Kevin was two, but I didn't want to be pregnant again so soon. Too bad. I was soon in the doctor's office hearing him announce a due date of November 15.

I'd adjusted to the idea just about the time I landed in the hospital threatening miscarriage. My blood type was RhA-negative, so I was geared to the possibility of problems. The doctor assured me that was not the problem now, but because I'd lost so much blood, I might lose the pregnancy. He gave me a small white pill and said he'd check with me in thirty minutes.

While I rested, I prayed that even though Jim and I wanted another child, I would leave it in God's hands and accept it as his will if this pregnancy was not to be. Within the hour, the doctor said he thought we might keep a baby. I began feeling better and was able to go home the next morning. The rest of my pregnancy went well.

Summertime in Germany

That summer we took a camping vacation to Austria and Germany. We'd sold the Valiant and now had a Volkswagen Bug. On top was a luggage rack that accommodated our tent. We packed camping supplies under the front hood, and placed suitcases and other items behind the front seats to make a level surface for a bed for Kevin. When he was awake, he sat in his car seat that fit snugly over the back of the back seat. On July 3 we traveled north to Trento, through the Brenner Pass, Innsbruck, Austria, and finally to Bavaria and the town of Garmisch-Partenkirchen where the U.S. Military had a resort. That first evening we stayed in a hotel with a fine babysitting service. Kevin was asleep when we left to go eat and see a show. The band was wonderful, and we loved every minute.

The next morning at breakfast in the hotel, Kevin was at his best. Everyone had to stop by to talk with this cute fourteen-month-old and pamper the unashamedly proud parents.

There was no Independence Day celebration in Germany on the Fourth of July, but there was an "Um Pa Pa" band in the park that we enjoyed immensely.

That afternoon we traveled to Munich. It was raining softly when we arrived at the campground. Kevin was hungry and crying, so we set up his car seat, placing it over the spare tire where the front hood protected him from the rain. This was his "high chair" during our camping adventure, and he loved it. Other campers marveled at how well it worked. Jim set up the tent, we slept in sleeping bags, and the night was uneventful. The next day, we drove around Munich and were saddened at the piles of rubble still left from the war. Much had been rebuilt, but much was left to do. We marveled at so much history and the many beautiful old buildings, parks, and paths.

From Munich we traveled to Augsburg, where one of Jim's friends from college in Oklahoma, also a lieutenant, was stationed. They'd just had a baby boy, and when we arrived, the new mother was having problems. They had no help, and our visit seemed a blessing, as we were able to take care of the baby while she went to the doctor. We were glad to help.

We went on to Ulm and admired the beautiful old churches. We went to Stuttgart, went to the top of the TV tower "needle," and enjoyed looking out over the beautiful countryside. Then on to Karlsruhe, Pirmasens, and to Zweibrucken, where our friends from Fort Monmouth, Ben and Mary Lou lived. They had wonderful quarters, and we couldn't help being envious that all their furniture and appliances were furnished. They quickly reminded us that we received a quarters allowance each month that they did not. We bantered back that, yes, we did, but it all went to pay our rent and utilities. We all agreed that things pretty much balanced out.

Ben and Mary Lou were gracious hosts, and encouraged us to stay with them and take side trips, rather than camping in different towns. That suited us just fine! We visited the rose gardens nearby, saw the huge BX facility at Kaiserslautern, the railroads of Mannheim, the bridges over the Neckar River at Heidelberg, the beautiful medieval castle there, and the pub where the classic, *Student Prince,* was penned by Wilhelm Meyer-Förster.

From Zweibrucken we drove down through the northeast corner of France and entered Switzerland at Basel, then to Zurich, and into Austria. The mountains were incredible, but the driving slow. We camped one night, and then went east through Innsbruck, back into Bavaria, and to Berchtesgaden to another military recreation area. We stayed in the General Walker Hotel, where we could see nearby craters made by bombs from British aircraft during the war. We went up the mountain in a tour bus, and then walked inside a cave to the huge brass elevator to get to Hitler's Eagle's Nest. It felt weird to be in the very place that monster had been. No wonder it was a vacation place because the view of the Bavarian Alps was incredible! From Berchtesgaden, we took a day trip to Salzburg, Austria, and visited the salt mines.

We expected our memories of that vacation to last a lifetime, and they have. The camping experience was good, probably more so because we didn't camp as much as we'd planned, *and* something new contributed much to our pleasant traveling experience—Pampers!

Expecting Babies and More World Turmoil

That summer, Jim had a new company commander, Captain Ray Walsh. Ray's wife, Nora, was expecting their first baby. Lieutenant Byrd's and Lieutenant Tripician's wives were also expecting, so for several months, all four of the officers in Company A were expecting at the same time. Some interesting jokes were made at the expense of those young officers! We gals enjoyed seeing each other at coffees and luncheons and shared our pregnancy joys and tribulations.

Then one day everything changed. Our joy was replaced with fear. World news was grim. American observation planes had discovered missile sites, built with the help of Russians on the island of Cuba. SETAF was on full alert, and all families were to keep supplies of food and medicine on hand, and overnight kits packed. Jim was given the responsibility to get all dependants to an assembly area near the airfield called Boscomontico, in the event of an evacuation of dependants of U.S. Military forces from Italy.

"Frances, I won't be able to be with you and Kevin if there's an evacuation," Jim said. "I've been told that if worse comes to worst, you'll be evacuated with the hospital out of Vicenza, since you're so close to having the baby. The clinic here in Verona will see that you're taken care of."

"That means Nora, Helga, and Beryl, too?"

"Yes, you'll all be together."

The thought of being separated from Jim in any event was almost unbearable, but I kept myself together as nothing indicated there was anything going on *near us*. The problem was those missiles were so close to the *shores of the USA!* The crisis passed; even so, troops were on alert for a long time. After all, Russia was very close.

Kathryn Lourie McGraw

Our baby was due November 15. We'd paid a deposit on a new, three-bedroom apartment we felt we needed with our growing family. It should have been ready by November 1; but to our dismay, it would not be until December 1. That was okay because by then our baby would be two weeks old. But November 15 came, and no baby. Thanksgiving came and no baby, and on top of that, Jim was in the field. On Thanksgiving Day, families joined the men for dinner in the company mess hall. Everyone was concerned about me, but I was fine; Kevin was easy to care for, and Nona came often. Finally, on Sunday morning, November 25, our friend, Dee Hollar, called to check on me. I told her I thought it was time. Dee brought Nona to take care of Kevin, and then took me to the clinic on Pasalaqua where the doctor told me it was time. Jim came in from the field and was able to go to Vicenza with me; however, I was put in an ambulance, and he followed me in our VW. I could see very well out of the back window, so we waved and made faces at each other all the way! The doctor didn't think I was close to delivering, so Jim returned to Verona to let Nona go home and take Kevin to Marge and Joe Rita's for the night. In the meantime, I didn't have the pain I'd remembered with my first delivery, and my water hadn't broken. The doctor went home and Major McClure, a female army nurse, was with me.

"Mrs. McGraw, are you playing possum?" she asked.

"No, I don't think so. I don't feel like I did the other time."

"Well, okay. Your husband's here, would you like to see him?"

"Yes, but, no, wait just a minute ..." I had a terrific pain, my water broke, and our baby was born! I could see the cord appeared to be wrapped around our baby's neck, and I heard Major McClure yell to an aid, "Get the blood kit! This is an Rh baby!" Soon, with the aid's help, Major McClure had our baby taken care of. It was 10:35 p.m. I don't remember how long it was before I got to see Jim, but we were both in shock. The doctor came soon and told us everything was fine—we had a healthy baby girl! Our precious baby that we named Kathryn Lourie, weighed seven pounds, fifteen-and-a-half ounces!

"Thanks for the million dollar family," Jim said as he smiled and squeezed my hand. I was so relieved we had a boy and a girl, and thought to myself, *Maybe I won't have to do this again.*

In those days, when you had a baby in a military hospital, you weren't allowed to have visitors. It didn't bother me too much because I didn't know different, but a friend, Ann Borelli, managed to sneak into the hospital and bring a gift. She found it appalling that no visitors were allowed. I'll never forget her.

The New Apartment

Just two days in the hospital, and we were on our way home. I couldn't wait to see Kevin. Jim assured me he was okay and was with Marge and Joe when Nona wasn't with him.

Jim didn't turn onto the street to our apartment and I asked where were we going.

"Home."

"What's going on?"

"Well, the apartment was ready, so we moved yesterday."

Oh my gosh! A part of me was glad but another was not. I was so tired. I just wanted to get home. We were both quiet the rest of the way. Jim helped me and the baby out of our VW; we entered the wide front door of the four-story apartment building, went into the elevator, and stopped at the third floor. A beautiful pink bow was on our door!

"Here, let me carry her in."

"Okay," I whispered. I was so eager to see Kevin and show him his baby sister! We knocked, and I could hear Nona talking with Kevin. She opened the door, and there he was holding her hand, so clean and so cute.

"Hi, Kevin."

He looked up at Nona, back at me, and then turned away as if he was mad at me. I knelt down before touching him.

"I'm so happy to see you, Kevin. I've missed you so much!" I put my arms out to him. Again, he looked up at Nona, at his daddy holding Kathy, and then came to me to give me a hug! I talked with him a bit, and soon he was showing me his bed and toys in his new room. When it was time to change Kathy, I placed her on our bed and Kevin climbed up. I was a bit uneasy, but as I watched closely, he crawled to her, leaned over, and kissed her on the cheek. My heart flip-flopped! He looked at me and said, "Catee."

"Yes, Kevin, this is your baby sister, Kathy." He smiled sweetly, and then jumped off the bed and ran to his daddy.

The new apartment at Viale Sicilia Number Three was spacious compared to our first one. There was even a built-in closet (almost unheard of in Italy) to the left of the entrance. There was ample room in the slightly L-shaped foyer and the doors of three bedrooms, bath, living room and kitchen all opened to it. The floors here were also of shiny, black and white marble. A long balcony on the west side extended from an outside kitchen door past double doors of the living room, around the corner, and past double doors on the south side. A balcony at the rear extended past the outside doors of both bedrooms. The only drawback (and the reason we could afford this new place) was that it was well outside the main part of Verona. Senora Elide was not happy about having to ride her bicycle so far to work, but she meant so much to us that we gladly raised her salary. One thing I loved about the apartments in Italy were the wooden blinds on doors and windows that when closed, left the room completely dark—wonderful for the children's daytime naps!

Bedtime—Kevin, age two and a half, Kathy, age one

Our Last Year in Italy

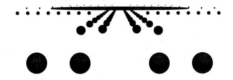

One morning in February 1963, Jim awakened nauseous and couldn't keep balance or focus. I was frightened and asked Nona to stay with the children while I took him to the dispensary. A new doctor was there whose specialty was internal medicine. He diagnosed an inner ear infection and treated Jim accordingly. Soon he was fine, but I was not. I was very tired, my milk was gone, and I couldn't nurse Kathy. Thankfully, she took a bottle well. I learned I was anemic, and my doctor prescribed a thick molasses-type medicine. It worked!

Later that month, several American couples chartered a bus for a weekend skiing trip to Madonna De Campilgio, a beautiful ski resort in the Italian Alps. Now that Kathy was taking a bottle and Nona could watch the children, we decided to go. We skied one trail on Friday, all day Saturday, and one trail on Sunday morning before returning home. It was a good getaway for us after the move, the new baby, and Jim's scary illness.

At home, Kevin greeted us at the door completely covered with chicken pox! We'd not had a clue before we left. Nona told us he'd been a little uncomfortable, but not sick. Three-month-old Kathy had about a half-dozen pox marks and the doctor said if she was exposed again she'd likely have another light case.

Otherwise, they were happy and healthy, and we were so thankfully proud of our family.

But, by the time Kevin turned two in May, we noticed his right eye turning inward. The SETAF optometrist called it a "lazy eye," and prescribed glasses, along with a patch to cover the stronger eye to force use of the weaker eye. If glasses didn't do the trick, he might need eye surgery. Keeping glasses with a patch covering one eye on a two-year-old wasn't easy! One time I found him with his glasses off and instructed him to put them back on. He looked up, smiled sweetly, and said, "No, thank you."

Kevin was delightful, learned quickly, and carried on conversations that amazed our friends. He adored Kathy and loved to sing "You Are My Sunshine" and "Jesus Loves Me." He also spoke Italian very well with Nona but laughed if Jim or I tried to speak it with him. Kathy progressed wonderfully. She had her daddy's big brown eyes and gave us much pleasure with her full-of-life antics!

Officer Efficiency Reports

Nineteen sixty-three was a blur of taking care of babies, saying good-bye to friends, and greeting new folks. We made new friends and had an active social life, but Jim's working conditions improved little. He'd completed all requirements for acceptance to flight school, and now he waited.

In those days, officers were not allowed to see their Officer Efficiency Reports (OER), and thus had no opportunity to dispute undesirable ones. Jim gave Phil Williams permission to look at his personnel records in the Pentagon when he returned to the States. What Phil reported to Jim was not good for either of them. They'd had the misfortune of serving under poor leadership. We were devastated, but Jim reasoned, "Look, I intended to stay in the army for only two years anyway if I didn't get flight school. We've had this opportunity to live in Europe, and it's great. If I do get flight school, then at least I'll learn how to fly."

"But won't you have to stay in the army if you go to flight school?"

"Yes, there's a three-year commitment, but then I'll apply to fly for the airlines."

"So, we're pretty much assured of four more years in the army?"

"Depends on whether or not I finish flight school."

He talked incessantly of learning to fly and during field exercises eagerly joined in tactical operation flights. One such flight was in an H-34 "Choctaw" helicopter that lifted a communications shelter onto a mountain top where his platoon was waiting for it. He also had opportunities to fly in the Army's L-19 "Bird-dog" and the OV-1 "Mohawk," which were fixed wing aircraft that would eventually become very familiar to us. Jim learned soon he'd been accepted for flight training at Fort Rucker, Alabama, and could expect orders by Christmas. We were both ecstatic! He was now a First Lieutenant and the knowledge he'd get additional pay while in flight school lifted our spirits considerably.

Rome, Naples, and Capri

Soon after Kathy was born, Jim traded the VW Beetle for a VW station wagon that was roomy and comfortable. We took day trips to Venice and Bologna, and wanted to see Rome and other points south. Nona agreed to care for our babies, and we took a few days off, traveling first to Livorno where we stayed in a hotel at Camp Darby, the U.S. base there. The next day we saw the Leaning Tower of Pisa, the alabaster mines at Volterra, then went on to Florence and Rome. We visited many places including St. Peter's Basilica, St. John's Cathedral, the Coliseum, the Catacombs, and Trevi Fountain—each competing for most memorable. From Rome, we went to Pompeii below Mount Vesuvius. In hushed awe, we looked at the amazing ruins.

We stayed in a hotel in Naples, looked around the city, boarded a ferryboat, and relished seeing the Isle of Capri. Upon leaving Naples, we realized we had little vacation money left. Thankfully, we had plenty of gas coupons, but we couldn't afford another hotel. The station wagon served us well on the side of the road somewhere north of Rome.

We returned home exhilarated from our memorable vacation to the reality that it would soon be Dick, Dee, Jon, and Elli's time to return to the States. It wasn't long until Joe and Marge left, leaving only us of the original group. We made other lasting friendships—Ray and Nora Walsh, Royce and Ellen Burton, Vince and Robin Reinstein, Tom and Barbara Offerdahl, Jack and Pat Del Buono, Bob and Pat Laramore, Jim and Norma Templeman, and others. When you live overseas, the value of friends is an incredible blessing during good and bad times as we learned that November.

Jim was duty officer periodically, which meant he had to stay overnight at Pasalaqua and be prepared to handle the usual *and* the unusual. Such was the case on November 22, 1963. At about 8:00 p.m. he called to tell me President Kennedy had been shot. I could not believe it! Within the hour, Jim called again to say our president had died. Sadness was everywhere, and the Italians were so sympathetic. A fear reigned among us and our friends that there was more to the assassination than only one man pulling the trigger. Not wanting to venture out much at all, we stayed in touch by telephone. We postponed Kathy's first birthday party because of the president's burial. The twenty-fifth was also the third birthday of John John, the president's little boy. We didn't have a television, so we listened to the Armed Forces Radio broadcast of the funeral and burial services. We hugged each other and cried; it was the saddest thing we'd ever known.

We had Kathy's party the next day. She was precious in her navy blue dress trimmed in red, white, and light blue, and loved opening her presents and eating birthday cake!

Winding Down

Our time in Italy was almost over, and we were antsy to get home. We couldn't wait to show off our children—they were adorable! But time dragged. Christmas Holidays and festivities helped, but fog settled in for six weeks. Each day seemed drearier than the last.

"Frances, guess what! We're going home on the USS Constitution!"

"All right! That's wonderful!" I cheered.

"Oh, I know it. We can drive our car to Genoa, put it on the ship, and it'll be right there when we get to New York, and there's a kennel for Kelly!"

Good news indeed, as we did not want to fly because we'd have to ship our car early, do without it, and hope it would be there when we arrived.

"How long will it take?"

"It's about a ten-day trip. It'll be great because we'll go first class."

"First class? How come?"

"All officers get to travel first class on a ship when you're on military orders."

My, my, I thought, *from no dependents allowed to first class. How things can change in the military…*

For two weeks before leaving Italy, we lived in a motel-like apartment. Nona stayed with the children when we needed her. Ten times we were invited to dinner, and never in the same home twice. We were amazed at the warmth and hospitality of so many friends. Finally, January 31 came and it was time to leave. Nona came with us to Genoa, where we spent the night in her cousin's lovely home. The next day we boarded the USS Constitution, Nona with us. What good fortune to be able to take all our luggage, drive right to the wharf, watch while our car was loaded as we boarded, and take Kelly directly to the kennel at the top of the ship!

It was hard to say good-bye to Nona. We'd all grown to love her. I cannot find words to express how much Senora Elide Cifiello meant to us—would *always* mean to us. This beautiful lady, who stayed with us the entire thirty-four months we'd known her, who could have earned considerably more as a nurse in any Italian home, who came to love and care for our children as if they were her grandchildren—I was sure she was an angel sent from heaven. Why we deserved that, I'll never know. I do know there has always been a special place for her in my heart and in my prayers.

It was time for her to go. She hugged Kevin and Kathy, told them what precious ones they were to her, and then turned to me.

As we hugged and tears came, she said, "Senora McGraw, I would go to America with you if I was not married."

"Cara Nona, maybe someday you can come to America," I managed. She nodded, unable to speak.

Jim escorted her to the ship's entrance, where her cousin was waiting. We never saw her again. We exchanged letters, and for Christmas 1964, I sent a package that contained a framed colored photo of Kevin and Kathy. She wrote back to say she loved the picture and was so happy to see the children were growing beautifully, but to please not send any more gifts because they had to pay customs! After that, I sent small photos inside letters.

Last photo in Italy—Fran, Kevin, Nona, and Kathy

USS Constitution

The first night on the ship was smooth; however, our cabin was not first class as I'd envisioned, but I sure didn't complain! The room was about ten by ten feet with two sets of bunk beds and a crib. The shower and toilet were closed off, the lavatory exposed. We took the children everywhere, as the nursery did not take children under eighteen months. For dinner we *had* to take the children to their 5:00 p.m. sitting, and then at the captain's invitation, we *had* to go to the adult sitting at 7:00 p.m. It was always formal. We would appear together, and then take turns checking on the children every few minutes. Usually by 7:00 p.m., they were asleep, but not always. Ten days of this was difficult, but we managed to enjoy the trip and meet some nice folks. A stop at Cannes, France, was a pleasant diversion. We passed by the Rock of Gibraltar and marveled at its enormity.

As we moved into the Atlantic, the sea became rough. Jim believed that seasickness was all in the head. Well, he's the one who lay face down on his bunk while I dealt with two children with queasy stomachs! My stomach was queasy too, and we realized that when a fourteen-month-old falls prey to it, seasickness is real. The next day, the ship's doctor gave us medicine that kept us on balance. I remember climbing up hill, and then running down hill as the ship met the waves.

Seeing New York Harbor was emotional. We passed under the new Verranos-Narrows Bridge, and there she was, the Lady of the Harbor, holding her torch and welcoming us home!

Marge and Joe, now living near Fort Monmouth, met us. What a joy to see them and then to set foot on American soil!

Jim got Kelly from the ship's kennel just in time to see our VW off-loaded, ready to load, climb in, and drive off. Phenomenal! We were all together and on our way to spend the night with Marge and Joe before heading for Alabama, Texas, and New Mexico. How much more could we have been blessed? I've wondered many times, and simply account our good fortune to our parents' prayers ... and ours ... and Nona's.

Getting Reacquainted with America

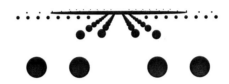

Marge told me she had a coupon for an appointment at a beauty shop. I couldn't wait to have my hair done.

"Gina will watch Kevin and Kathy," she said. "I know you're going to love getting a facial."

"A what?" I asked.

"A facial. That's what the coupon's for."

"Oh dear, I guess I misunderstood. I thought it was to have my hair done."

"No, the coupons are for facials. I don't think there's time to get your hair done."

I was disappointed, but tried to not show it. Marge had been so sweet. The beauty shop was in a mall—a new shopping concept to us, and at the center on a bandstand, a group of young people were making music with guitars and drums. "Why is their hair so long?" I asked.

"They're trying to mimic the Beatles," Marge said. "They just arrived in New York City, and they'll be on the Ed Sullivan show Sunday night."

"Who are the Beatles?" I asked.

"You mean you didn't hear about them in Italy?"

"I guess I didn't."

"Well, they're about the hottest thing going. Their music is a little loud and wild for me, but the kids think they're great. See those pictures of them?" Marge pointed to life-size cutouts of the soon-to-be-very-famous young musicians from England.

"I think they need a haircut," I said.

It was terribly cold as we traveled to Washington D.C., and on to Falls Church, Virginia, where we had no trouble finding Joan and Phil's house. It was good to see them! We'd never seen Troy, who was three months older than Kathy. Debbie was just old enough to want to "mother" the little ones.

While at Joan and Phil's, we called my sister-in-law, Marilou, who, with children Keith and Joanne, was at her parents' home. Marilou invited us to dinner. We looked forward to seeing Joanne for the first time and showing off our Kevin and Kathy. Marilou's parents lived in southeast Washington D.C. in a lovely "row house"—another new experience for us. It was typical of the area with three narrow stories, a front porch, and a nice back-yard. Our visit was nice, but I missed my big brother, Doyle, who was in Tennessee transitioning into the U.S. Air Force's C-130 "Hercules" aircraft. From there, they would go to Okinawa for three years.

We left Virginia, happy to be on our way. For lunch, we found an interesting place called Kentucky Fried Chicken, where we could get fried chicken to take with us. Amazing! A day or so later we found hamburgers in a place called McDonald's. We'd missed out on a lot during our three years in Italy! We traveled through Virginia, the Carolinas, and into Georgia.

"Signing In" at Fort Rucker

Finally in Alabama, we were literally giddy. Arriving at this bustling post was one of the biggest thrills ever! Grounds across the sprawling post were neat and buildings tidy. Streets of new quarters seemed endless, and we wondered if we might get to live there. Jim signed in at flight school headquarters to get on the quarters list, and he was told that within six weeks we'd have a place to live. Our plan was for me and the children to stay with my folks in New Mexico until quarters were available.

The station wagon was a blessing. We'd strapped most of our luggage to racks on top, so with the back seats folded down, the entire back of the wagon was free for the kids to move around. I covered the surface with quilts and blankets, and they were comfortable. Kathy was small enough to stand up and toddle around. I can see her to this day with her little bit of blonde wavy hair and big brown eyes in her pink, bibbed overalls, giggling, and having the time of her life! She and Kevin played and napped when they felt like it. There was rarely an undesirable stop.

We traveled north to Montgomery and then westward through Jackson, Mississippi; Shreveport, Louisiana; and Longview, Texas, where we spent the night. Then, bypassing Dallas, we went through McKinney, Denton, Decatur, Wichita Falls, and on to Amarillo. We arrived on Sunday, February 16, 1964—three years, four months, and sixteen days after we'd left. It was Jim's twenty-ninth birthday.

Grandpa, Grandma, and Texas

For the children's sake, we now called Mom and Pop "Grandma and Grandpa." They had lived in Amarillo over five years, and it seemed like home. Although it was winter, we could tell

Grandma had worked a lot in the yard. Grandpa had suffered more minor strokes and wasn't able to say much, but his eyes teared up when he saw us. He had the most joy at seeing Jim, grinning and patting him on the back. Grandma gave Kevin and Kathy anything they wanted. They had such fun going out back to see her chickens!

Jim's brother and sister-in-law, Ben and Juanita, were now selling furniture alongside carpet and were doing well. We bought several pieces to have shipped to Fort Rucker.

It was cold and windy in Amarillo. We'd forgotten how miserable wind could be, but we rationalized, *it's not as bad as fog!*

Ogden Farm

Arriving at the home place where I grew up was bittersweet. Mother and Daddy (now called Mamaw and Papaw) had traded the farm for a house in Clovis, but they'd stayed there until I came home so I could see it once more. That meant a lot to me, and even though my children would never have any memories of it, at least I'd know they'd been there one time.

The Methodist church family in Fort Sumner gave Mamaw and Papaw a wonderful going-away party while we were visiting. I saw teachers and family friends who had meant so much to me all my life.

We had one last family gathering on the farm. My sister, Christine and her husband, Moreland, who now lived in Clovis, and their two children, Leah and Lyle; another sister, Melva and husband, Shell, from Albuquerque with their two, Barry and Sharon; and the almost grownup eighteen-year-old youngest sister, Cynthia, were there. My younger brother, Royce and his wife, Sammye, who lived in Odessa, Texas, with children Jeff and Terry, were not there, as Terry was only three weeks old.

We had many slide photos from Europe and couldn't wait to show them. It was too much to cram into the short time, though, because after the time it took to set up the projector and screen and begin showing them, everyone fell asleep! The luster of our grand show of all the places we'd seen and people we'd known in Europe was now dimmed, considerably.

Moving was an emotional tug for my folks. They'd moved to the farm in December of 1937 after eight years of marriage and difficult Depression-era times. They'd acquired the farm through a government program that allowed young, qualified families to live on and work the property, and if things went well, it became their own. On this fifty-two acres in the Pecos River Valley, Daddy and Mother (pregnant with me), with Christine, seven, Doyle, five, and Melva almost three, moved into the brand new 1,000-square-foot, two-bedroom, white frame house that had a wide porch in front and a screened-in back porch. Floors were hardwood, inside walls were varnished "knotty pine" wood paneling, and there were large, double-framed windows with screens. There was no bathroom, but there was a porcelain kitchen sink with a drain to a septic tank, and alongside it, an iron hand pump that brought water in from a concrete-lined cistern. Water was trucked in by a family whose prolific well provided drinking water for the entire valley. Behind the house was a small cement-covered adobe "storage house" that provided an even, cool temperature for canned goods, eggs, and fruit. Several yards away was a round corrugated metal outhouse bolted onto a four-inch thick concrete base that could be moved from one place to another. There was a big red barn, a windmill and stock tank, two pigsties, and two chicken houses. Daddy carved a farm out of sand dunes, acres of grass burrs, and red anthills. For twenty-seven years, he agonized over irrigation water allotments, night irrigating, baling hay, weather, and other traumas that go with high-risk farming. Irrigation ditches routed water from the diversion dam north of Fort Sumner and just below Alamogordo Lake (later named Lake Sumner). The land produced glorious alfalfa, sweet potatoes, watermelon, cantaloupe, and garden crops such as tomatoes, cucumbers, beans, peas, okra, and asparagus. There were a few cherry trees and grapevines, and in later years, Daddy planted apple and peach orchards. He established a small nursery, sold trees and shrubs, and landscaped several yards in surrounding communities.

After the war, he remodeled the house by closing in the front porch. This made the living room larger, as well as the kitchen/dining area to accommodate a bed and dresser. In 1955, he enlarged the house to three bedrooms, one and a half baths, and a large, sunny kitchen. The house was always painted white with red-trimmed screens; the elm tree shaded yard kept trimmed and neat. My brother, Royce, was born in 1939 and sister, Cynthia, in 1945.

Now the time had come to move. We watched as Mother and Daddy went into the house together for one last look and walk-around. They lingered for a few moments. Nothing had to be said when they returned to the cars.

Kevin went with Jim in the big truck, Papaw drove their car, and Mamaw, Kathy, and I followed in ours.

The house in Clovis was a small, post-WWII style with three bedrooms, one bath, a modern kitchen with washer hook-up, a living-dining room combination, and a garage. The fenced backyard had sturdy clotheslines, and places for vegetable and flower gardens. It was perfect for Mother and Daddy.

Kevin and Kathy loved it too! They'd never had a yard to play in, and being able to move around outside was quite a contrast from the apartment balconies in Italy. The love story between our children and their grandparents was, and remained, a beautiful one.

Jim had to report for flight school on March 15, so he drove to Alabama alone in the new Chevrolet Chevelle he'd traded the station wagon for. "A two-door car was safer for the children," he rationalized.

He called sooner than expected to say quarters were already available. Mother and Daddy hadn't had enough of Kevin and Kathy, but on March 19, they drove us to Amarillo to see Grandpa, Grandma, Ben, and Juanita before seeing us off at the airport there.

On the reliable Concord 440, we flew from Amarillo, and landed in Oklahoma City, Tulsa, Memphis, Nashville, and *finally* Birmingham. I decided to take that direct flight, even though it landed often, rather than change planes in Dallas. Thankfully, the children were good. Kevin entertained himself, and they both slept some, but on one leg of the flight, Kathy passed the time by singing "la, la, la, la" the entire way! Other passengers might have been annoyed, but they didn't complain; she was much too adorable, *and* she wasn't crying.

Jim was so glad to see us and us him! He talked incessantly, so excited about going to flight school. We arrived late at the Fort Rucker guesthouse—a renovated WWII building set aside for purposes such as ours that night. It was equipped with a kitchenette, a crib, and good clean beds. We were grateful.

Fort Rucker, Alabama

A note inside an Easter card to Mother and Daddy:

March 23, 1964, Monday. Good Morning! Just a line to let you know we had a pleasant flight all the way. Jim was waiting in Birmingham for us at 6:15 p.m. CST.

Our quarters are beautiful and huge! Our household

goods came early Saturday morning, so you can imagine the confusion here. I have a teenage girl helping today. It's beautiful here and peaceful. Kevin is outside playing with some other kids—we're away from any main drags. Our address is 46 Harris Drive, Fort Rucker. There are pine trees everywhere, and we're looking forward to a pleasant stay.

Yesterday we went to the Methodist church in Enterprise, and enjoyed it very much.

I have so much to do. I must get busy. Sure hope you've sent the packages in time for the kids to have their Easter baskets—if not we'll get them some. I forgot to leave you money—tell you what—I'll tear up that check I cashed for Cynthia, okay?

Bye for now. Write soon. Love Ya! Jim, Frances, Kevin, and Kathy

Another note two weeks later on April 4, 1964:

Dear Mother and Daddy, I've been trying hard to get settled as calmly as possible. Caught my washing up today, and now you should see the ironing!

Kevin ran fever on Wednesday so rushed him to the hospital with a good case of tonsillitis. The doctor gave him two penicillin shots—each leg—and fortunately it was soon enough that it took care of him. The poor little guy suffered more from the shots than anything. He's feeling fine today. Kathy got some sunburn—we had such a beautiful day, and we grilled hamburgers.

Just don't know when we've been so content. Having room to move about and a yard makes so much difference. We have a lot of room and lots of closet space—can't get used to it.

Jim starts flying on Monday. He's had classes this past week and is so excited. Our next-door neighbors, Bill and Judy Johnston from Kentucky are very nice. He's in the same class and section as Jim, so we girls have a car everyday. They have a girl, four, and boy, eight months.

There's an ophthalmologist here, so we're waiting on medical records to see him about Kevin's eye.

We have a nice patio in back and a couple of shallow ditches just above our lawn, about eight or ten yards that make a good place for the kids to play. We're doing some yard work and want to plant some flowers. Sure need some gardening tips—we're out of practice.

It's getting late, so I'll close for now. We're looking forward to hearing from you.

We love you so very much! Jim, Frances, Kevin, and Kathy

Our new quarters were magnificent! Three bedrooms, two baths, a study off the huge living room/dining room, and a modern kitchen with a gas range, refrigerator, automatic dishwasher, garbage disposal, *and* there was central air conditioning! I thought I had died and gone to heaven! Kathy, now sixteen months, was comfortable in her crib, and Kevin, almost three, loved his new room all to himself.

One day, a little girl Kevin's age came from across the street on her tricycle and wanted Kevin to play. He got out his new red and white tricycle that Santa brought and off they went. I went back inside, but it wasn't long until I heard him crying. I went to the door and found him, tears streaming, as though his heart was broken. I looked to see if he was hurt.

"What's wrong, Kevin?"

"Mommy … Mommy," he sobbed. "Mommy, it won't go! My tricycle won't go!"

I watched as the little girl scurried down the sidewalk on her tricycle as fast as her little legs could peddle!

"Oh dear, Kevin, come show Mommy what's wrong," I urged. He got back on and tried to peddle as fast as he could.

Half again as big as the little girl's tricycle, it was too big for him. He couldn't make it go fast. My heart sank.

"Oh, Kevin, your tricycle is too big! Mommy's so sorry. We'll see what we can do when Daddy comes home."

The little girl was content to ride up and down the sidewalk while Kevin tried, but he was miserable. When Jim came home, we made a beeline to the PX and bought a smaller tricycle, but the damage was done; the little girl was no longer interested in playing. Fortunately, Kevin and Kathy became fast friends with pretty little Lisa Johnston next door.

In June of that year, Kevin had eye surgery to correct the lazy muscle. Although he still had to wear glasses, it seemed a miracle that his eye was now straight.

The chaplain at the post chapel agreed to baptize Kathy. On Sunday, June 28, our neighbors, Bill and Judy Johnston, stood up with us as we took vows to lead Kathy in the Christian faith and live our lives accordingly. It was our seventh wedding anniversary.

Flight Training

Jim was happier than ever! He came home in the evenings with stories about flying and the people he'd met. The training was in three phases and in A Phase, he learned to fly the O-1 Birddog. Originally designated the L-19 and used as a liaison aircraft, the O now stood for observation. He loved it! One day he came home dripping wet and with a big smile.

"I did it, Frances! I soloed today!"

"Ohhhhh!" I squealed. "Tell me about it!"

"You won't believe this," he began. "I was supposed to make three landings, so I took off and everything went fine on the first landing, and I came back around to land again." He used his hand to show how the aircraft flew and banked. "There was a wire fence that had a board across the top of it that I had to go over right before landing. I thought I had plenty of room, but I hit that board and it broke. *Pow!* Scared me to death, so I didn't land; I went on around, and then tower radioed me to make a full-stop landing. I was afraid I'd be in trouble for breaking the fence. I landed okay, and my instructor came over. We checked the aircraft for damage, and then he got in and told me to make two more landings. I did, and he said, 'Let's go home.' I knew that meant back to Lowe Field. I expected to get a pink slip, but he smiled and said, 'Well, you've soloed.' Frances, I've never been so happy in my life!"

"Why are you all wet?"

"Hey, it's tradition to get thrown in the river when you solo!"

Jim studied hard for the written exams that included weather, weight and balance, navigation, and maintenance. A Phase finished, the "gold hat" class moved on to B Phase with classes on tactics, night flying, and survival.

C Phase was instrument training. Jim loved this and seemed to have a knack for it. Not long before they graduated, every student had to take a cross-country flight.

"Frances, we're going to be gone two nights, and I'll need some money."

"Well, what are you going to do?"

"Hey, you've been taking care of the checkbook. Don't we have any money?"

"Yes, we have some money. I started putting some in a savings account a while back."

"You did? Well, I'm proud of you!"

I'd realized when he was promoted to captain in July that with the extra money *and* flight pay, we had enough money to start a savings account. He didn't have to worry about money and was able to enjoy his cross-country trip flying the U-6 Beaver. The U meant utility aircraft.

"Frances, I have something to tell you," Jim said one day when he came home early. I didn't know what to expect. There wasn't a doubt in my mind that he'd complete flight school, but the tone of his voice was worrisome.

"I was taking my check ride," he began, "when my instructor answered a call from base. He said it was for Captain McGraw, so I took it, and I was told to report to the flight surgeon immediately. I couldn't imagine what was wrong. It kinda shakes you up when you're taking your last check ride and get called to go see the doctor! I went over there, and he told me my physical showed I had a double hernia and that I'll have to have surgery before I can finish flight school."

"You have to have surgery?"

"Yes. It's scheduled for Tuesday."

Jim passed the check ride in spite of the distraction. The surgery went well, and he was able to graduate with his class in December. To get his diploma and wings, he had to climb three very steep steps onto the stage. He did so gingerly, and got a rousing applause from his classmates!

Upon graduation, Jim received orders to the JFK Center for Special Warfare at Fort Bragg, North Carolina. He was told he'd probably be there for three years.

"Fort Bragg's not closer to home," I lamented.

"No, but just think, Frances, Special Forces is *the thing* in the Army right now. That's where all the emphasis is, and I'll be flying for them."

I dreaded another move, but I'd go wherever the Army sent Jim—our family had to be together.

Because of Jim's surgery, we decided to go to home for

Christmas, and then come back and move out of quarters. The doctor agreed that would be okay as long as he didn't drive too much. While all our friends were packing to move, we packed for our trip. We spent the night in Longview, Texas, as we had done in February. We decided to go through Dallas this time to see where President Kennedy had been killed. It was eerie driving down Commerce Street, seeing the schoolbook depository building and grassy knoll. We traveled west through Bridgeport, Lubbock, and on to Clovis. The holidays were wonderful with our families, the first since 1959.

For New Year's Eve, we joined Don Ray and Mary Beth Martin and little son, Jimmy, at her folks' home in Altus, Oklahoma. Don Ray and Jim had grown up together, gone off to college together, and he was best man at our wedding. We'd spent some time with them after they were married in 1959, and I considered Mary Beth one of my best friends, too. Then, back to spend more time with Grandpa, Grandma, and Mamaw and Papaw before we drove back to Alabama. We traveled south to Odessa to visit with Royce and Sammye and little ones, Jeff and Terry. We hadn't yet met Sammye. What a complement she was to my brother, and their children were beautiful!

From Odessa, we traveled southeast to Kerrville, up through Fredericksburg, and over toward Johnson City to drive by the LBJ Ranch. We could see the beautiful setting alongside the Pedernales River. We drove through Austin for a drive-by look at the state capitol. Then on to the Houston suburb, Pasadena, where Jim's sister Nita and her family lived. We'd seen E'laine once, but this was our first time to see Revena. Clois was recently out of the air force and working in the new world of computers. We'd always lived so far apart, and it was good to see them. We spent the night, and arrived home the next day.

We packed again, separating hold baggage from household

goods, so we'd have something when we got to Fort Bragg. The movers came and left in time for us to get to Fort Gordon near Augusta, Georgia, to get gas, cash a check, and spend the night. The next morning as we were leaving the motel, Kevin asked, "Mommy, is that Nona?" I looked to the sidewalk and saw a gray-haired woman about Nona's size, bundled up in coat and hat.

"No, Kevin, that's not Nona. I wish it was, don't you?"

"Where is Nona?" he asked.

"Nona still lives in Italy. Remember when she used to come to the house and say, *'Buon giorno, Kevin, bellisimo! Come sta, bello?'*"

Kevin looked at me with searching eyes and grinned shyly. We'd been gone from Italy almost a year. He never spoke Italian again.

The joys of our lives: Kathy, two, and Kevin, three and a half

JFK Center for Special Warfare, Fort Bragg

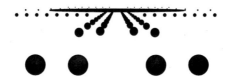

We were weary following Jim's surgery, the long trip out west, the move out of the quarters at Fort Rucker, the trip to North Carolina, and now *it was cold*. We found Fort Bragg easily, and Jim signed in on Smoke Bomb Hill at the JFK Center for Special Warfare. Again, we were able to stay in a guesthouse, this one not quite as nice as Fort Rucker's. It had an odd floor plan, and it was heated by coal that caused a thin coat of soot-like dust everywhere that transferred easily to the children's clothing. The kitchenette was adequate, so we were able to eat there, but it was too cold to go outside, and with no television, the kids and I were miserable when Jim was at work.

The Vietnam War was escalating. Record numbers of troops were at Fort Bragg, and Fayetteville was crowded. No quarters were available and post housing had a list of only a few places for rent. Jim left work early one day so we could find a place to live. We set out looking but were appalled at what was available. Only one place, several miles from town, appealed to us. The rooms were small, and there was no carport, but it was new and clean. We made a deposit to rent it and made our way back to town. Then, just outside of Fort Bragg, we saw a sign offering new houses for sale.

"Let's go take a look to see what they're building," I said.

"Okay," Jim responded and made a quick left turn into the subdivision.

The area was pretty with nice brick houses and spacious land-scaped yards. We passed by several new houses, some recently finished, and a few still taking form. As we got out of the car to go peek inside one, an older gentleman in a pickup truck stopped and asked if we'd like to see it. Well, of course! He proceeded to show the pretty pink brick house with white trim and black shutters that he had built. About 1,800 square feet, it had three bedrooms, bath and a half, living room, and a family/dining room open to the kitchen that had a wide breakfast counter. A refrigerator was furnished that matched the other appliances. There was a carport with an area for laundry and storage. We loved it!

"I think we can make a deal, Captain," Mr. Burford said. Jim's rank and wings were visible.

"I don't know, sir. I don't know if we can manage buying a house. We're looking for something to rent."

"Well, if a captain on flight pay can rent a house like this one, he can probably buy it."

"Well, sir, what does it cost to buy a house like this?"

"This one is $16,400. A down payment of $500 will make it happen. A twenty-year loan with interest on $15,900 will put your payments about $127 a month."

I took a deep breath and thought, yes, $127 *plus* utilities. But, we had the $500 in the bank, and it didn't take long for us to make the deal. Jim and Mr. Burford shook hands, and we left quickly to try to get our rent deposit back on the other house. Fortunately, the owner knew Mr. Burford and was delighted we were buying his house!

In a few days, the mortgage deal was completed. We were ecstatic while we waited, and by February 1, it all came together. We settled into our new house at 7550 Decatur Drive in this charming neighborhood with mostly military neighbors. We attended nearby Cumberland Methodist Church where the children had their first Easter egg hunt experience.

Jim was assigned to the aviation detachment at Simmons Army Airfield, and after initial orientation, was eligible to wear the green beret, which he proudly did. He was checked out in the U-10 Helio Courier, a two-seat aircraft designed for short take-offs and landings, and designed to use floats for water landings.

His work with the Special Forces was mysterious on occasion. I had a call more than once from one of his buddies, letting me know he wouldn't be home that night because he was flying some special mission. He'd call when he could, but sometimes he didn't know himself when he'd be home until the last minute. Such was the nature of Special Forces. He was often pegged to brief General Stilwell, the Commander of the Special Warfare Center, on aviation matters, and the general always made him feel good about it. He was on a first-name basis with the general's aide-de-camp, and when he was reassigned, he asked Jim if he'd like to interview for the position. Jim said, "No thanks, that's just not my bag."

Many of our neighbors were already in Vietnam or had orders to go. Then, the outbreak of violence in the Dominican Republic that summer and the USA's deployment of troops there took many men away from Fort Bragg. Jim had been tapped for a six-week Counter Insurgency Warfare Course so he didn't have to go. Both our neighbors were sent, and for a period of time Jim was the only male on our block!

My brother Doyle now stationed in Okinawa, was flying in and out of Vietnam. When it was reported once that a C-130 had crashed in Southeast Asia, I broke out in hives. Doyle was not involved, *But my goodness,* I thought, *what will I do if Jim has to go to Vietnam?*

Taking care of the household was hard enough with Jim gone so much, and we needed a second car. One day, Jim took me to the local Volkswagen dealer, and we bought a new Beetle. What a relief! I was able to shop without depending on Jim, attend wives functions, and take the kids to Vacation Bible School. Then one day, Jim passed by a car dealership and saw a beautiful white Dodge Coronet convertible. There was no holding him back; he had to have that car. *Oh well,* I thought, *if he has to go away to war, he deserves to enjoy some things...*

A Little Friend Lost

When our little dog, Kelly, became ill, the vet told us she had either an infection or a brain tumor. He treated her for the infection, so we had to wait and see. Then, on the Fourth of July Kevin came down with a high fever. We had no choice but to take him to the emergency room at Womack Army Hospital. It was very hot, so while I was in the hospital with Kevin, Jim drove around with Kathy and Kelly—Kelly in his lap as she had one seizure after another. Kevin was diagnosed with pneumonia and given a shot and pills to take. When we returned to the car, Kelly had died. We returned home quickly then to make Kevin comfortable. As he and Kathy napped, Jim dug a hole on the edge of our lot near huge blackberry bushes, and together we buried Kelly. She was only seven years old. Jim and I cried. To ease our pain, within the week we found another Sheltie puppy. We called her Abbi.

Flying All Over the East Coast

Captain Roger Donlon, the first Medal of Honor winner in Vietnam, was a Green Beret stationed at Fort Bragg. He was in demand to speak at various organization and group meetings. The army accommodated him, and he often asked Jim to fly him around. Jim was impressed with the young captain, and enjoyed the time with him. They made several trips to Washington D.C., and one to New York City where Jim had to land the small aircraft at LaGuardia Airport. The flying was good experience. On one return flight, Jim had to land without any lights or instruments. He managed to land fine and was shocked to learn the aircraft battery had exploded!

We made good friends at Fort Bragg—the Nelsons, Faschings, Walters, Frinks, Urichs, Hoffmans, Novosels, Hughes, Medarises, and others. Jim recalls a story when he became an instructor pilot in the Helio Courier, and it was his job to check out new pilots joining the unit. Mike Novosel was one, but come to find out, Mike had flown the B-29 in World War II, and also had thousands of hours as an airline pilot. Jim was just a few months out of flight school, and it felt strange to be Mike's IP. Mike told him, "Let's get on with it, Jim. We have to go by the army regs."

Orders to Vietnam via New Jersey

Jim learned he was scheduled to attend the Signal Corps Officer's Advanced Course at Fort Monmouth, New Jersey, in January 1966, and then to Vietnam in June. It was a difficult time. I wrote to my folks on December 12:

Jim flew to Monmouth last Friday, and he is weathered in. He found an upstairs apartment—two bedrooms, kitchen, living

room, and bath—furnished for $135, plus electricity. Good-
ness! That's more than we'll get for our house here in rent.
Well, since you asked, guess I'd better go ahead and tell you
that we'll only be in New Jersey until June. Jim graduates from
the advanced course on June 10, and has to be in Saigon, Vietnam, on July 15. We knew it would come sooner or later, and
I'm thankful we have another six months; though, at times
I think I'll go out of my mind thinking about it. The only
consolation I have (if you can call it that) is that he's not the
only one going. He'll be flying a small single-engine plane,
the O1-A Birddog; the kind he learned to fly in flight school.
I would like to spend the year close to you, and it's close to
Amarillo … Jim would like it that way.

At Christmastime, my sister Cynthia, who was working in New-
ark, New Jersey, with Volunteers in Service to America (VISTA),
flew down. We had a fine Christmas celebration, and she joined
us in getting everything ready to be packed and moved two days
after Christmas. All was done in one day, and we watched a
big truck take our furniture away to be stored at Cannon Air
Force Base near Clovis, New Mexico. Another truck took our
hold baggage for shipment to New Jersey for us to have the six
months we'd be there. The VW was sold, and we were on our
way. Cynthia made the trip with us to Virginia where we checked
in at Joan and Phil's. They were always gracious, and we enjoyed
being with them. We also got to see Jon and Elli Sanford, and
Dick and Dee Hollar before we trekked on up to New Jersey.

Living Near New York City at Fort Monmouth, New Jersey

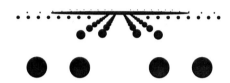

124 Wyckoff Road, Apt 14, Eatontown

We actually enjoyed being in New Jersey again, and enjoyed getting together with Jim's classmates and their wives. We also loved ordering pizza from a nearby restaurant. It was the best we'd had anywhere!

Our apartment was sparsely furnished, but adequate. Two bedrooms separated the kitchen and the living room. A hallway ran alongside the closed-off stairs from the kitchen to the living room, and there were doors connecting all the rooms on the other side so that the children had fun running around the house in a circle. There was a sofa and one chair in the living room; Jim and I had a "wall to wall" double bed in our room, and the children had twin beds in theirs. The kitchen had modern appliances and an eating area. The bathroom was next to the kitchen and was, strangely enough, right at the top of the stairs. It was nice with pink tile trimmed in black that had paint spattered all over it. We didn't much like going up and down stairs, but we knew if that was the biggest of our problems, then we didn't have many little ones.

On my birthday, Jim and I enjoyed dinner in New York City, and afterward seeing Henry Fonda in the play, *Generation*. Then, on Easter Sunday, we attended the beautiful services at the little Methodist church nearby. We all felt so dressed up in the outfits I'd purchased at Macy's in the city.

The Officers' Wives Club sponsored helpful activities. One outing was a tour of the United Nations building in New York City, and the Broadway play, *Skyscraper*.

The time passed quickly, and we planned for the coming year. The army encouraged all soldiers to prepare a will and Jim did so. We talked about how I would take care of the children; manage the finances, car, and household. We were reassured knowing that my dad and two brothers-in-law would be in the same community. One night while visiting about how things would be, we began talking about Kevin and Kathy, and we both cried. It was a rough time, and we knew it was going on in households all over the country.

Trying to control my emotions was hard, and sometimes things got the best of me. After shopping at the commissary one afternoon, I rushed to get Kathy, Kevin, and several bags of groceries upstairs. I was trying to get everything put away and dinner started because Jim had a class that evening. The kids were giggling and carrying on, and they came running through the kitchen.

"Will you two get out of the kitchen and out of my way," I yelled. "Go to the living room and be quiet!"

Kathy ducked out of the way, and as I was about to swat Kevin on the behind, he looked up at me through those thick-lens glasses and huge tears rolled out onto his cheeks. His shoulders drooped, and his hands hung limply.

"Oh, no, not again," he sobbed.

I was startled at his outburst and looked at this precious boy. *What in the world am I doing to these children,* I thought to myself.

I took his hand and said, "Come on Kevin, let's go to the living room." I called for Kathy to join us on the sofa where we cuddled and giggled, made funny faces, and laughed and laughed. I don't remember if dinner was late. It didn't matter.

Springtime in the area was breathtaking! We took side trips, one to Atlantic City where the children enjoyed the amusement park, and one to beautiful Colt's Neck in the country west of Fort Monmouth where some of the best apples in the world are grown. We bought apple juice, and the kids had such fun saying, "This apple juice sure is *good*." We all laughed!

Early the morning of May 10, Ben Jr. called to tell Jim that Grandpa had died. We were heartbroken. While Jim made arrangements for leave, Kathy awakened with high fever. We rushed her to the emergency room because we knew we must leave for Texas soon. The doctor told us she had the mumps, and *under no circumstances* would we put that child on an airplane! We were disappointed; on the other hand, it seemed a blessing in disguise, as the trip was an expense we could not afford when we would be in Texas within the month. Jim flew home for his dad's funeral, and it meant a lot to be with his family; however, his mother didn't understand why the children and I didn't come. She had no concept of why it mattered for a child with mumps to fly. I was hurt by her reaction. I suppose it's always hard for the younger generation to see the perspective of the older one, and vice versa.

When the time came to move I was determined to have the apartment clean so that we'd get our deposit money back. I scrubbed the paint off the bathroom tile walls and floor and had it gleaming. The sinks, refrigerator and stove were spotless, and I vacuumed everywhere, even under the sofa cushions to make sure sneaky cookie crumbs weren't hiding there. The landlady came and we went into the living room where she sat down to visit a bit. She asked if everything was okay; I told her I thought it was, then she picked up the sofa cushions and looked there. She replaced the cushions, handed me our deposit check, thanked me and was gone. I was so relieved, but then I couldn't help but be a bit annoyed that she didn't even look in the kitchen and bathroom to see all the work I had done! Even so, I had the satisfaction of knowing that we were leaving the apartment much cleaner than it was when we had moved in.

The McGraw Brothers: Ben Jr., Jim, and Ghern

On June 9, we left New Jersey. Most of the highways we'd come east on in 1960 were now Interstate, so it was a different trip. The kids loved the convertible top down, and we had to watch to make sure they didn't get sunburned! I actually remember little about the trip. I was too preoccupied with the thought of Jim going to Vietnam.

Vietnam 1966–67

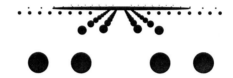

Spending Time with Family

We'd planned to go to Wyoming to see Ghern and Juanita because she'd been diagnosed with breast cancer, but following a double mastectomy, Ghern took her to be with her mother in Midland, Texas, so we went directly to Amarillo. Ghern was still working in Wyoming, and their recently married daughter, Carol, was in college there. Their son, Mike, was in Midland.

We spent several days with Grandma, and visited Llano Cemetery where Grandpa was buried in the veterans' section called Poppy Field. It was peaceful and comforting. Ducks were in a nearby pond, and Grandma opened a partial loaf of bread she'd saved to feed them. When the ducks came close, quacking and flapping their wings, Kevin and Kathy threw bread to them, and then squealed and ran. What fun they had!

We took Mom with us to Midland to see Juanita. We were heartsick to see this precious lady so ill, but we were thankful to get to see her, and she loved seeing the children.

"Jim, I hate it that you have to go to Vietnam," she said.

"Aww, Juanita, don't worry. You know me, I'm tougher'n woodpecker lips!"

We all laughed. We just knew she'd be well soon.

225 Sasser Drive, Clovis

Soon it was time to go to Clovis to look for a place to live. We found the perfect three-bedroom, two-bath house in the perfect neighborhood for the perfect price. We managed the down payment and took on another mortgage similar to the one in North Carolina. We could expect that house to be rented for two more years.

Our house was red brick with white trim, and had a fenced yard, perfect for Abbi and the children. A laundry room was off the fully equipped electric kitchen. There was a family room with a fireplace and a formal living room. The two-car garage had extra storage space and an electric door opener. I soon learned how comforting it was to be able to get the children in the car, push the button on the visor to open the garage door, back the car out, push the button to close the door, and be on our way. Likewise, upon returning home, I could drive up to the garage, push the button, the door opened, I could drive in, close the door, and knowing we were safe inside, get the children into the house. This new-to-me invention, the garage door opener, was a wonderful thing!

Another advantage of living in Clovis was that Cannon Air Force Base was just nine miles west of town. There was a fine medical facility, BX, and Commissary there, and should I need anything else related to Jim's military service, I could go there. These things were a lot of comfort to us.

For our ninth wedding anniversary, Jim and I managed a two-night getaway to Hickman's Guest Ranch at Red River, sharing a sweet, yet melancholy time at our beautiful honeymoon spot. We laughingly recalled our wedding day and how his friends, Don Ray Martin, David Thompson, Don Hay, Mark Clapp and Duane Spellman from his hometown of Borger, Texas, were blamed for our car being "dressed up" pretty bad when we found it after the ceremony. My mother had insisted the Sheriff usher them out of town only to learn that it had been my best friend, Lorena Trujillo, my brother Royce, and my two brothers-in-law, Moreland and Shell who had done the damage! She asked us to apologize to his Borger Buddies, and we did, of course. They got over being run out of my hometown, but it's still a funny memory.

Off to War

Jim had no qualms about going to Vietnam, except for being away from those he loved. He was trained and prepared. He felt strongly about preventing a Communist takeover in Southeast Asia, especially after seeing the threat in Europe with all the "Vota Communista" signs during elections, the Berlin Wall, and the Cuban Missile Crisis. He'd carried a top secret clearance while in Italy, and he used to tease me, "I could tell ya all I know, but then I'd hafta kill ya." Jim loved America and all it stood for. He treasured his dad's stories of World War I, and of course he had seen every movie ever made about World War II! After that war, a fighter plane was placed in the park in his hometown. He used to sit in it for hours and pretend he was the pilot!

July 13 came. Jim had to leave. Mamaw went with us to Amarillo where we picked up Grandma, and then headed for the airport. There were tearful good-byes as Jim boarded the Trans Texas Airline Convair 440. Grandma, Mamaw, Kevin, and Kathy and I watched until the aircraft was no longer visible. My chest was heavy. I loved this man who loved me, who was so good to me and the children. I did not want him to go away, not to war.

We drove back to Amarillo to have lunch, and although Mamaw and Grandma encouraged me to eat, I could not. I was numb.

I knew Jim would land in Lubbock, Midland, and El Paso

where he would change planes, fly to Los Angeles, and spend the night with Don Ray and Mary Beth. He would also see Stan and Peg McGinley in Los Angeles; Marge and Joe Rita at Hamilton Air Force Base, and then leave from Travis Air Force Base near San Francisco.

Back in Clovis, we settled in for our first night with Jim away. The phone rang about seven o'clock. It was Jim. He was calling to say that while in Midland he called to speak with Juanita, and he was told she had died that morning.

"I don't know who answered the phone, Frances," he said, his voice breaking, "but whoever it was didn't know who I was, and they didn't seem to care that I was calling. He said Mike couldn't talk with me either."

"Oh, Jim, I'm so sorry."

"Frances, would you call Mom? I'm not sure any of those people will call her."

"Of course, Jim. Are you okay now?"

"Yes, I'm okay, but I have to go. I asked about getting leave for Juanita's funeral, but I was told it would mess up timing for my departure to Vietnam, and there's no time to change that."

"Okay, sweetheart, I understand. I love you."

"I love you too, Frances. Hug the kids for me."

"Okay..."

"Frances, you're my everything. Don't forget it."

"And you're my everything, Jim. Ohhh, Jim..."

"Bye, sweetheart."

"Bye, bye..."

I knew Jim was heartbroken. He loved his sweet, gentle sister-in-law that he'd known since childhood. He thought it neat that both his brothers' wives were named Juanita, and his sister's name was Anita. Sometimes it was confusing! I didn't know Juanita well, but she was a soft lady with nothing but a positive outlook and precious smile. I was sad for Jim now, traveling alone and grieving. It was a confusing, unreal time.

I met Ben Jr. and Mom in Lubbock, and we traveled to Midland for Juanita's funeral. Heartbroken, Ghern, Mike, and Carol and her new husband, Richard Renner, were there. Carol couldn't understand why her prayers for her mother hadn't been answered. Mike appeared angry and without peace.

Letters from Vietnam

His first letter dated 16 July was written in-flight and the post-mark was from Vietnam: US Army & Air Force Postal Service, Jul 18—96274—1966. He wrote in detail about spending nights with Don Ray and Mary Beth, Peg and Stan, and Marge and Joe. A pleasant coincidence was seeing Doyle and his family at the airport in San Francisco as they were returning from Okinawa.

The next letter was from Vietnam. All mentions of time were now "military time." All I had to do was subtract twelve from any hour later than noon; i.e., 1500 minus 1200 is three o'clock in the afternoon, to know what time of day he was talking about. The return address was:

Capt J. J. McGraw 05409703—221st Aviation Company, APO
San Francisco, California 96296

Jim didn't keep my letters to him. The guys decided to burn all letters once they'd been answered, their reasoning being that, should the enemy overrun their compound, as some had been, they didn't want the enemy to have the letters.

His first few letters set the stage for the year, and there were letters for almost every day, minus the time it took him to get there and back, and time for rest and recuperation (R&R). He described daily activities and events that were critical in understanding his part in the war, his political and spiritual views, and reasons for wanting to do his part. He later divulged that he glossed over many near misses and tragic happenings because he didn't want to worry me. We always dated our letters and recorded the time of day we wrote. All of his letters were full of love and yearning for his family. He began with, "Dearest ones, I hope this finds everyone well and happy" (which he wrote one time that he meant it—it was his prayer), and ended with "give Kevin and Kathy a big hug and kiss," and then some words to the effect "I love you all so very much," and "*Mizpah*." We agreed to end our letters with *Mizpah* that came from the Old Testament, "And Mizpah; for he said, The LORD watch between me and thee, when we are absent one from another" (Genesis 31:49, KJV).

My folks were amazed when his letters came, sometimes three or four at a time, but there might also be three or four days without one. Even if he mailed a letter every day, there wasn't always an aircraft available to take mail out to Saigon.

"That's wonderful, Frances," Mamaw said. "I just never expected old Jimbo to write so often. Do you write him every day?"

"Oh yes, I want him to know what's happening and how the children are doing."

"Well, you just keep it up. It's got to be hard on him to be away from his family."

Much to Jim's dismay, he was assigned as the Avionics Officer for the Avionics Detachment attached to the 121st Aviation Company at Soc Trang in the Mekong Delta south of Saigon. This unit provided radio support for helicopters. It meant he'd be "flying a desk," but he could depend on the 221st located there for proficiency flying time, as they were the only fixed wing unit in the Delta. The problem was that he outranked all but one captain in the 221st, and because of rotation dates and command time assignments, there was no position for him there at the time.

Family portrait before Vietnam

The Mailbox on Sasser Drive

My ears were quickly attuned to the sound of the mail truck, and everything stopped until I'd retrieved the precious papyrus with the red and blue "air mail" markings from the rural-style mailbox in front of our house. I read with wonderment his descriptions of mortar attacks and helicopters going to and from battle areas, and every day I watched the evening news to see if the Mekong Delta was mentioned. And, it seemed my family was as eager to hear from Jim as I was! After my initial read, I'd call Mother and read to her those parts that I *could* share. Kevin and Kathy listened wide-eyed as I read to them. He often mentioned "Charlie" and explained that it was short for the Viet Cong, the black-pajama-clad enemy that the South Vietnamese people who wanted a Democracy instead of Communism, were fighting. In the military world, a phonetic alphabet is used for clear transmission when things need to be spelled out; i.e., "A" is Alpha, "B" is Bravo, and thus "V" is Victor and "C" is Charlie, so the enemy was simply tagged "VC" or "Charlie."

When he received my first letter he described it as a "book" and that he'd read it three times. Getting anything in the mail was the highpoint of his day. I could relate to that as I felt the quicker pace of my heartbeat each time I opened a letter from him.

I had it nice—a lovely house, the children, adequate funds, and family close by. I was thankful for my own strong spiritual foundation, our families' support, and there was comfort in letters and calls from friends. There was an eleven-hour time difference, so each night as I knelt with the children at their bedsides to pray for their daddy, I knew he was up and out, probably flying. Then, when they were in bed I'd write my letter to him. I wouldn't seal it though until the morning in case I'd think of something else to write, which happened just about every morning. Then I'd crawl into our king size bed—on his side while he was away—and think about him until I fell asleep.

Family Happenings

On August 6, Cynthia married John Van Auken. It was a wonderful family gathering, and we all missed Jim. After the wedding, Doyle left for Altus Air Force Base for training in the huge C-141 Starlifter aircraft. Marilou was expecting their baby soon, so she, Keith, and Joanne stayed with Mamaw and Papaw. On August 17 their little girl, Susan Marie, was born. Although not considered premature, her lungs weren't completely developed, and she was kept in the hospital for several days. It was a harrowing time because they'd lost a little boy from the same condition in 1962. But, because of developments in medicine following the loss of President Kennedy's baby in 1963, the doctors knew exactly what to do, and Susan developed normally. Doyle's family then moved to Fairfield, California, near Travis Air Force Base. From there he flew the C-141 around the world several times.

During those first weeks, I settled in and did some yard work. Grandma gave me some iris bulbs, so one day at the front of the house I prepared a flowerbed. I missed Jim so much and even allowed myself the luxury of imagining him doing the work, seeing him without his shirt and watching his muscular arms and massive chest as he'd handle the shovel. My musings were disturbed when Kathy awakened from her nap and came out onto the porch. She saw the mud-filled flowerbed, her eyes opened big as half-dollars and with a squeal, jumped into the mud, her feet slipping two to three inches into it while she ran its length! It was so cute, and I wrote Jim about it. He wrote back, "I laughed about Kathy's experience in the mud. It sounds so much like her—she can find pleasure in so little. She has spirit, and I'm happy for that. Good boy, Kevin, keep up the work of being a boy. I'm glad he gives the girls a fit. Fran, go ahead and buy him a bike. I think he's ready …"

All the while wishing Jim was there to make the decision as to size, what kind, etc., I bought Kevin's first bike training wheels attached, and taught him how to ride it. I so wished Jim could have seen how happy he was when he could ride it without them. He went to kindergarten that fall, riding a little yellow school bus every day. He was so proud, and I knew Jim would have loved seeing it.

Detachment C-4, Fifth Special Forces Group

On August 24, Jim went to the 221st as a pilot in the Second Platoon. His call sign was "Shotgun Two Three." He was with a Special Forces Detachment at Can Tho, and wrote, "I'll be flying in support of Special Forces. There's one other pilot here, and our two aircraft belong to the 221st, with the primary mission of flying border reconnaissance to watch for "Charlie" supplies and equipment coming down from the north. Special Forces has a compound located on the airfield—small, but well laid out. They have a jukebox, and guess what's the number one song played? You're right, "The Ballad of the Green Beret!" Then, on August 25, he wrote, "The C-4 Detachment commander told me tonight that with my experience at Fort Bragg, I should be an A team commander! I just laughed because I want to fly."

I knew Jim had an ego and how he wanted to fly, so I was very happy for him that he was finally in his "Birddog" again. He wrote of flying back and forth to an Island called Phu Quoch in the South China Sea where he supported the Special Forces team there that was trying to help the people keep the Viet Cong at bay. I knew Jim was neither careless nor neglectful about his flying, so I had peace of mind in that regard, and because he was doing something he so wanted to do, I was glad he was in the air rather than with troops that had to slog through jungle and rice paddies. He told me later that he rarely bought a drink in the club because there was always someone there who'd been on the ground when a "Shotgun" came to their rescue by letting them know where the enemy was. He was proud of the work he did.

Flying to Phu Quoch Island

There were thirty letters from Jim in August 1966. Oh! How I loved his letters! His words of love for me and the children were incredible. We cherished them so, and it made all the difference in the world to me. Sometimes Kevin and Kathy would giggle as I read the letters to them, and then tell me exactly how I should answer his questions. They'd sometimes be very serious and ask questions. It was hard to explain to them how long it would be before their Daddy came home, and Kathy would often cry because she missed her Daddy. Kevin would be brave and gently tell her that it was okay because he would be home soon. I thanked God for our precious children!

The Home Front and Family Support

The children and I spent a lot of time with Mamaw, Papaw, and with Christine's family. John and Cynthia moved to Reno, Nevada, where John worked toward a master's degree; Melva's family moved to El Paso in late summer; Doyle's family was in California; and Royce's family now lived in Lubbock.

In Clovis, we joined the Kingswood Methodist Church, where my folks and Christine's family were members. On the Sunday before Jim left for Vietnam, we attended church. I was sitting between Jim and Christine, and as we sang the hymn, "God Will Take Care of You," I began to panic. *I felt like screaming! I wanted out of there!* I moved toward the aisle, but Christine grabbed my arm and held me. The panic left, but I was unable to sing, even though the song was a wonderful one to take with us from that day on.

Kingswood was a wonderful church family. The children enjoyed Sunday school, and during church while I sang with the choir, Mamaw and Papaw took care of them. I participated in the Women's Society of Christian Service (WSCS), and made good friends—most were air force wives whose husbands were also in Southeast Asia. We had good, helpful get-togethers.

Grandma McGraw

At least once a month, I took Kathy and Kevin to Amarillo to see Grandma. Every visit was the same—go by the cemetery where Grandpa was buried in Poppy Field, and then to the pond to feed the ducks, and then go by K-Mart on the way home. Oh how the children loved that! Mom's life story had more sadness than most—she never knew her own mother, her relationship with her father was strained after he married a much younger woman, her first husband died of the flu in WWI, and she lost an eight year-old son because of a tragic accident the year before Jim was born; but, she endured by working harder than most. Following cataract surgery on both eyes in her early forties, she felt no one would hire her outside her home, so she learned to prepare income tax returns. She struggled wearing the heavy, thick-lens glasses and without peripheral vision, but she was thankful *just to be able to see!* Many of her clients returned year after year. I respected the success she had in her work in spite of the obstacles she faced. Even though I would really have preferred to be doing something else, the trips helped pass the time, and the children enjoyed going to see Grandma. I also knew Jim appreciated it.

Tangled Bed Covers and a Garage Door Incident

Two happenings while Jim was away made me realize how blessed I was that I didn't have to take medication in order to sleep. The first, I was awakened one night by muffled crying sounds. I realized quickly they were coming from three and a half-year-old Kathy's room across the hall. I rushed to find her under twisted covers at the foot of the bed, and she couldn't get out! I uncovered her and found she was all right. I stayed until she was ready to crawl back under the straightened covers, and she was soon asleep. I was humbly thankful that I'd heard her cries.

Then, I was awakened one night by the sound of the *garage door opening!* In the middle of the night? Why? Carefully, I tiptoed into the dark hallway and crept through the family room, kitchen, and laundry room, all the while looking and listening. I slowly opened the door leading into the garage and peeked in. The opener light was on and everything seemed intact, so I pushed the button and the door closed. *Hmmm,* I thought, *I wonder how that happened?* I'd just crawled back into bed when there it went—*it opened again!* I felt pretty sure it must be a malfunction of the electronic door opener, so I went bravely back to the garage. I closed the door again then made sure my remote opener was still in the car. My folks lived across town, and they had the only other remote in their car. I knew if they were near they would call before coming, and they would never play games with me. *What in the world is going on?* I wondered. I lay in bed unable to go back to sleep and heard the distant whistle of a train going through town. *The garage door went up again!* Then another whistle and the door closed! Another whistle and up it went again! *Oh my goodness,* I thought, *there must be something about the train whistle and railroad crossings that set off the connection to my garage door!* The next day, Papaw took both remotes to the store where they'd been purchased, and a technician reprogrammed them. Surprised by the story, he said he knew of no similar occurrence. Nevertheless, whatever he did worked, and there were no more unusual garage door openings!

I always wrote to Jim about the things that happened and he would comment in return. He answered my story about the garage door incident saying it must have been an exciting time! One time he wrote that he thought about my day, the time of day I wrote, and he tried to remember what he was doing at the same time. Of course it was the same for me. I read so many of his letters with sadness as he described such things as helicopters putting troops in for an operation and being caught in an ambush. He was so impressed when the famous comedienne Martha Raye, who was a Reserve Army Nurse, worked in the hospital at Soc Trang all night even giving blood for wounded troops.

On October 27 Jim left Can Tho for Vinh Long and related the story of how he learned about his new position. His platoon leader called and asked, "Is this Shotgun Three Six?" and he answered, "No, it's Shotgun Two Three." The platoon leader said, "No, I'm talking to Shotgun Three Six." He went on to explain that three stands for the platoon, and six is the number given to the commander of any unit, so it finally dawned on him that he'd been made a platoon leader! He now was over seven pilots and nine enlisted men. He was so happy to have a command *and to be able to fly.*

I delighted in his happiness and eagerness to do his job, but I longed to know more about it. Everyday I couldn't wait until the mail came. One day when I heard the postman's truck, I ran outside and sure enough there was another letter. I ripped it open and sauntered back through the garage taking my time reading it. I came through the laundry room door to see the kitchen filled with smoke! *Oh, no!* I had put some oil in a heavy, cast aluminum pan to heat so I could sear some meat and now the oil was in flames! I had not turned off the electric burner when I ran outside! I quickly turned it off, then reached into the cabinet to grab some baking soda to throw on the fire. It was immediately extinguished, but I could see I had some mighty black cabinets. Thankfully, the wood had not burned and I was so grateful that all I had to do was clean off the smoke. Interestingly, the heat from the burner had burned rings into the bottom of the aluminum pan. How fortunate I had been! The incident brought me back to the reality that I'd better keep my head on straight and have some presence of mind! The mail could wait.

Regular Army Commission

On November 16, 1966, Jim was sworn into the Regular Army. He'd taken a series of stringent tests at Fort Monmouth and was interviewed by a board of officers that found him qualified. It meant that, ordinarily, he'd be considered ahead of reserve officers for schools and preferred assignments. It also meant he had three more years of obligation to the army and would probably face a second tour in Vietnam. He wrote about his new serial number, "I'll bet you won't believe it—OF109999! The army doesn't hand out RA appointments to just anyone, so I'm really proud. I hope I can live up to it."

He also wrote that some of the guys had met their wives on rest and recuperation (R&R) in Hawaii, and that it cost them about $600. He asked if I'd like to meet him there in February. I wrote back, "Just tell me when and where, and I'll be there!" For the next ninety days we excitedly exchanged letters about spending time together in Hawaii.

The War, Holidays, Scary Things and Prayer…

Jim wrote a lot about the war, but not everything. On November 14, "Something big is happening. There's been more VC activity in the last two weeks than in the four months I've been here. I guess I can tell you now that it's over, but My Tho was hit by mortars and sniper fire while I was there. No one was hurt, but it scared a few people, including me! I don't like being shot at. You know me, I'm like God, I love everyone…" Then on November 18, "There's so much that goes on, and I only tell you about a third of it, mainly because I don't want you to worry, and yet I would like to share it all with you. I wish I could express to you how war is, but everyone has to experience it themselves to know, and I don't want you or the kids to ever know. You keep on being the wonderful family that I have to come home to…"

I *knew* Jim's heart and how hard it was for him to see people die, especially American soldiers. On November 20, "I was flying over an operation in the Kien Hoa Sector, and during heavy contact two Americans were killed…the ARVNs (soldiers of the Army of the Republic of Vietnam) ran into one of the VC battalions. We lost three gunships. I finally made it in about 2200. I went to church this morning, and what a wonderful feeling. I felt so good when I walked into the chapel, like I'd been missing something and found it there. The chaplain talked of Thanksgiving Day and its meaning, especially since we're here ... I'm truly thankful for what I have, and humble, too ..."

Holidays were especially hard, and he revealed his homesickness, "Happy Thanksgiving. Hope your Thanksgiving was as nice as ours. What a great bunch of guys. We decided we didn't want to let being away get us down, so we celebrated by fixing up some h'ors d'oeuvres. Then we played bridge until dinner—had a delicious turkey dinner. We made toasts to our families and to our families being together next year. Yesterday was a sad day. One of the MACV (U.S. Military Advisory Command Vietnam) advisors that I got to know was killed. But we can't live in the past, and we can't think about anything but doing our job and coming out alive. If you start thinking about death, then you're lost. So I try to let it go by, and I live from day to day until the day I'm back with you ... I cherish our life together, and I know it will continue. We have two wonderful children, and we will direct their destiny ..."

He was able to take a two-day rest and recuperation at Vung Tau. Upon returning he wrote, "I have a whole new perspective. Now I know why the army recommends taking R&R ..." Then, his December 8 letter was scary, "We've been alerted that two-hundred VC are located south of the airfield, and we could be hit tonight. I don't want you to worry because we have a bunker right outside our door, and it's well built. 'Charlie' normally goes for the aircraft instead of the billets area. He's definitely not strong enough to overrun this place ..."

Kevin printed a letter to his daddy one time and wrote that he was proud of him for doing his part so we could all be free. Jim's response was, "Bless Kevin's heart. That saying of his touched me deeply. That's the main reason I'm here because I want all of you to be free. Of course, I'm only doing a small part, but when you add them up, it's something big. I hope and pray you'll all be safe and free for a long time to come. I know the system we have is the best. I'm proud to be an American..."

Every day I watched the news for anything about the Vietnam War. Often the news commentators mentioned "guerilla warfare" in South Vietnam. I realized one night during his prayers that Kevin actually believed his father was *fighting gorillas!* I was able to explain, but I can only imagine the visions conjured up in his five-year-old mind!

Then a letter arrived wherein Jim told about a Sunday morning's interesting events. He'd planned to go to church, but at 0800 got a call from the Tactical Operations Command to scramble an O-1 because the U.S. Navy found a company of VC trying to cross the Mekong River and needed reconnaissance. "I grabbed my flight suit and started to put it on, but kicked the crotch out and tore the zipper, so I had to get out my other one. I ran to the jeep when all of a sudden nature called. I finally got airborne and flew to the area, but by the time we got there, they were pulling out..."

Because I so fervently believe in prayer, I was sure our prayers on that Saturday night made a difference. Even though Jim was upset at not getting up and out early, perhaps he was kept from being in the wrong place at the wrong time. I missed Jim, but his words of love kept my heart happy, "I had a dream last night about meeting you in Hawaii at the airport. It was so wonderful. I put my arms around you, and I kissed your sweet lips. Then we walked arm in arm from the airport. I didn't want to let you go. I dreamed I had you so close, and I was ready to kiss you over and over when my alarm clock went off! *Oh, my gosh!* I'm so looking forward to our meeting that I can't stand it..."

As Christmastime approached, Jim's letters were full of longing for home. His loneliness was heart wrenching, as were his words on December 23. "The radio's been playing nothing but Christmas music, and one song really hits home, "I'll Be Home for Christmas." I think they've played it a dozen times today..." Then on Christmas Day, "Merry Christmas. I hope you have as pleasant a Christmas as I did ... all the wonderful gifts I received from everyone. I flew until 1730 yesterday, and then prepared everything for our party. We had our Santa Claus and everyone got a kick out of the sheet. Say, that embarrassed me at first ... I was blushing. That was really something! Who was your model? Man, what a build. It's hanging on my wall where I can see it when I walk into my room ..."

An artist in our waiting wives group drew, on twin-size bed sheets, life-size pictures of good-looking females in bikinis. We sent them to our husbands for Christmas.

We had always made New Year's Eve special, and this year was hard. "December 31. Today is New Year's Eve, and I miss you ... we're so far apart. There's a party tonight at the club, and I don't feel like going because something's missing ... that something is you."

Then there were the things he wrote that made me laugh, "Everything's fine with me ... only one thing wrong, I'm swollen between the legs and I have to walk bowlegged ... the Doc told me it takes two people to handle my problem, and I think you're that other person ..."

He always mentioned the kids and often wrote specifically to them, "Kevin and Kathy, how are you getting along? Time is passing, and I'll be home soon. Kevin, when I get home, we'll go fishing. Kathy, are you being good? Mommy writes and tells me what you're doing. Daddy is so proud of his kids! Now you take care and be nice to Mommy ..."

Then, some scary things, "January 13. I was flying from Soc Trang to Vinh Long, when I got a call from flight following that a

Shotgun had gone down. Well, it happened—it was one of mine. I believe the fifteen minutes it took to get to it was the longest in history. The first report was from a helicopter pilot that the aircraft was on fire with no life around it. Frances, all my life went out of me. The pilot was Dick Calvert. I consider him a close friend, as I do all the pilots in my platoon. All I could think was, *What are we doing in this god-forsaken country fighting a war that no one cares about except us…that we're laying our lives out for a bunch of people that don't care what happens to them…that guys like Dick have to be wasted?* Let me tell you, I had a bitter moment. I don't want to lead you on; I just want you to get the feel of what I experienced. The next report was that the pilot and observer were safe…the pilot was on his way back to Vinh Long for a long, stiff drink! What happened was Dick was making a message drop when the engine quit. He put the aircraft down in a rice paddy, but it caught on fire and was completely destroyed. I was surprised at the bitterness I felt, and of course, I feel different now. I was pleased with the reaction time to get cover over the area. It's one of the worst in the Delta. Thank God, he's safe and well. Had four letters from you…it made my day better after all that happened…"

A description in another letter was an interesting visualization for me. His compound was hit with a mortar attack at about 1:00 a.m. As he was getting out of his bunk he became entangled in mosquito netting. He dragged his bed half way across the room before he got out of it, and fell down some steps. During the next awards and decorations ceremony, he was awarded the Purple Heart. He asked why because he hadn't been injured. He was directed to the medic, who'd treated him for a skinned knee the night of the mortar attack. All such abrasions were treated because of the high infection rate in that climate, and the medic was required to submit the paperwork. Jim could not believe it! He had indeed tripped and fallen trying to get out of the mosquito netting, but thoughts crowded his mind of horrifically wounded soldiers, and he knew he couldn't accept a Purple Heart for a skinned knee! He traced the paperwork to division-level, explained the situation and at his request, it was withdrawn.

Members of Third Platoon: Captains Calvert, McGraw, Freshour, and Gentle, and kneeling, Crew Chiefs Steve Smith and Gale Vinke

Most of his letters by this time had reports the other guys had given him about their R&R time in Hawaii. These R&R trips were usually one right after the other, and they made reservations for the next to go, but sometimes there were complications in getting a definite date. Finally, I received his letter of February 6, "...I have good news! Get your bags packed and reservations made for Hawaii! I'll be seeing you on February 14! I'm so excited I can't stand it. Ron made reservations at the Ilikai Hotel for the twentieth, and it's too late to get them changed, so when you arrive, call from the airport and make reservations before taking a cab. If they don't have space there, call the Reef. There should be no problem...that's about all the news I can give you...I'm afraid any other instructions might arrive too late..."

Five Months to Go

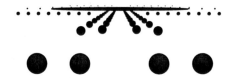

Rest and Recuperation in Hawaii

Mamaw and Papaw said, "Of course we'll take care of Kevin and Kathy while you go to Hawaii." We were so grateful. I spent time in preparation by making a beach cover and a couple of dresses, one with a matching shirt for Jim. A friend loaned me three beautiful muumuus. I was *so ready* to join him.

The flights out of Albuquerque to LA and on to Honolulu were crowded and time dragged, but when flight attendants changed into muumuus and put flowers in their hair, it was exciting!

We landed in late afternoon, and as Jim had instructed, I called the Ilikai Hotel to see if there was a room available. There was not, and there were none at other hotels I called. I watched as others were met at the airport by hotel shuttle attendants who placed flower leis around their necks. Problem was, many people were coming to Hawaii from the unusually cold northeast, and there were many wives coming to meet husbands on rest and recuperation. *There were no rooms available! I was stunned!* I was alone and didn't know what to do; then, I remembered the slip of paper in my purse. I'd jotted down a name and telephone number when Dee Hollar called.

"If you have any trouble at all in Hawaii, call the Lindners,"

Dee said. "They're friends of ours and live at Fort DeRussy. I know they'll help you."

Now, alone in Hawaii, I felt I had no other option. I called the number and heard, "Colonel Lindner here." I had no idea that Dee's friend was a colonel, but I went ahead and explained the situation. He said he understood, and that I wasn't the only one having trouble finding a place.

"Fran, stay right there at the airport. We'll come get you, and don't worry; we'll help you find a place to stay."

I uttered a prayer of thanksgiving for friends.

The colonel and his son took me through Honolulu to their quarters right on Waikiki Beach. *Oh my,* I thought, *what a place to live!* Mrs. Lindner, attired in a muumuu with hibiscus in her hair, made me feel welcome. She showed me to her young daughter's room and bath, and encouraged me to try to get some rest.

Colonel Lindner sat at his desk and made numerous telephone calls to hotels. He also learned that Jim's flight would be in about six o'clock the next morning. The Lindner's generosity was one of the most beautiful things I'd ever known. I fell asleep, but kept waking to the sound of tinkling wind chimes. I was too excited and could not wait to be with my Jim!

Early the next morning, I heard the phone ring. I could tell Colonel Linder was talking with Jim. Mrs. Lindner came to tell me she would take me to the R&R Center where he was waiting. My heart pounded; I could hardly breathe.

I saw Jim before he saw me, but I could tell by the set of his jaw that he was upset. Thinking that it was because I wasn't there to meet him, I decided to surprise him. I walked up behind him and tried to place a lei over his shoulders. It startled him; he jerked around and with upraised arm, hit my arm. He saw me, his face melted, and his strong arms swept me away.

"Oh, Frances, I'm sorry! I didn't mean to hit you. I'm just too jumpy these days."

"It's okay. I shouldn't have startled you."

Then, after a moment, "Hey, who is this Colonel Lindner, and why were you at his house?"

I explained the situation.

"Man, I didn't know what to think. I was worried that something had happened to you, or that I was in trouble or something. He was really nice though, and said his wife would bring you over." We held each other again and his voice cracked with emotion, "Just now while I was waiting for you, there was a chaplain and another officer here to tell a young lady that her husband wasn't here to meet her because he … he was … killed yesterday. That was hard to hear."

Now I understood, and I was saddened too. He'd also learned that we didn't have reservations at the Ilikai, the Reef, the Hilton Hawaiian Village, or at any other hotel in Honolulu! The R&R Center folks were trying desperately to find places for these servicemen who were meeting their wives. They told Jim that a room was available at the bachelor officer quarters (BOQ) there at Fort DeRussy until they found us a place. We quickly got to the BOQ just a few yards away. At about 0700 Jim opened the door to our room. *What a shock! There were seven single army cots! Worse, there was no bathroom! We had to use his and her bathrooms down the hall!* It was a terrible downer for Jim, more than for me, and I could tell it during those precious early hours we'd both longed for. He tried hard to be happy as he took out of his B-4 bag matching tailored pajamas; bright red cotton with white piping trim that he'd had made for us. It was a good thing because I'd brought nothing else fit to walk down the hall in!

We were soon hungry and walked to the officers' club on Waikiki Beach for breakfast. We checked again at the R&R Center, and they suggested we look for a place ourselves, that we might have better luck. We walked up and down the streets along Waikiki Beach trying to find a room in a hotel, but nothing was available. At about 1600, we rented a car, returned to the BOQ, and dressed for dinner. I wore the prettiest muumuu I had because we'd found a flowered shirt for Jim that blended nicely. We walked around the International Marketplace and had dinner at the Cock's Roost, and then went to see the movie, *Dr. Zhivago*. Well … after all … we had been together since 0630 in the morning!

On Wednesday, we drove around then had lunch at the Wai-oli Tea Room. We visited Sea Life Park and had so much fun. About mid-afternoon we checked in with the R&R Center folks. They had a one-bedroom apartment in an apartment hotel for us. We didn't have room service, but it was clean and modern with a bathroom and kitchenette, and two twin beds that we promptly pushed together to make a king-size bed! We soon learned that one of the pilots in Jim's platoon, Lieutenant Gary Varner, his wife, and little boy were next door. What a pleasure to meet them, and we agreed to go out to dinner and spend time at the beach together. That evening, we enjoyed a fabulous dinner and floor-show at the Hilton Hawaiian Village.

Thursday the sixteenth was Jim's thirty-second birthday. He wanted to see the Arizona Memorial at Pearl Harbor and pay respects to those WWII heroes. We drove all the way around the island and had a hot dog at an army recreation area on the North Shore. That evening, we ate lobster at the Fisherman's Wharf.

On Friday after breakfast, we hunted for new swimsuits and dressed for the beach. We learned there was a luau for service-men at the American Legion Hall. We loved the luau—our first! Then, that evening we ate at the Cannon Club, an officers' club at Fort Ruger, right on the side of Diamond Head, with an incredible view of Honolulu! We vowed to return someday.

Rest and recuperation on Waikiki Beach

Saturday, we had corn dogs for lunch on Waikiki Beach. That evening we joined Gary and Peggy Varner and their little boy, Shawn, for a dinner of shrimp curry at the The Willows, a restaurant covered only by the branches of a huge willow tree., It was absolutely delightful!

On Sunday, we went to the beach with Varners, and then made calls home. Later, we took a small gift to Colonel and Mrs. Lindner and visited a while. That evening we had steak again at the Cock's Roost. The time passed so quickly ... so very quickly.

Monday at 0430, the rude sound of the alarm clock awakened us. By 0530 we were at the R&R Center, where we said good-bye and the guys boarded their buses. *It was so hard.*

Peggy, Shawn, and I also boarded an airport bus there. My flight left after theirs, and I was miserable waiting for the flight that I remember little about, except there was turbulence every time I tried to doze off. I hadn't noticed *any* turbulence on the way over.

We'd made prior arrangements with Don Ray and Mary Beth Martin for Don to pick me up at the airport in Los Angeles, so I could spend the night with them. It was good to be with them and see their two little boys, Jim and Jon—both named after Jim.

I flew to Albuquerque the next day and on to Clovis where it was cold and windy—such a contrast to the warm, balmy islands. As wonderful as it was to be home with our precious children, I missed my Jim—I missed him terribly.

Jim wrote wonderful letters about our time together and I was certain that in spite of the cost, it had been the right thing to do. When all the bills came in, we figured the expenses for our week in Hawaii at just under $600 ... and worth every penny!

Tape Recordings

By this time we'd both acquired small tape recorders and made tapes to send back and forth. Sometimes I'd set the recorder up so the kids wouldn't know it was on. Jim wrote in response that he felt as if he was there with us. It made me happy to think that now and then he could have a good, warm feeling about us at home. I could imagine him, probably leaning back on his bunk with his eyes closed, smiling as he listened to the children's voices over ... and ... over ... and ... over.

To have such a "macho" personality, Jim's heart was a gentle as anyone I'd ever known. Nothing bothered him more than to see a woman mistreated. He'd had the sad experience of seeing his Dad hit his mother once, and when he stepped between them, his Dad threw him through a sheetrock wall! Although their marriage survived, and Jim grew to adore his father for many reasons, he knew his folks didn't have the kind of marriage he wanted. We talked long and hard before we were married about that, and decided that should either one of us ever think we had to hit the other, then that was the time that we had to turn and walk away forever. Once when he was still playing college football, he looked out the front door of our apartment to see one of his teammates slap his wife. At the next practice he had the opportunity to play opposite that fellow. After practice he asked Jim what was wrong, that he couldn't understand why Jim was hitting him so hard. Jim proceeded to tell him that if he ever saw him slapping his wife around again, there'd be more of that! And so, it didn't surprise me when I had a letter in which he wrote, "I have to work hard at self-control, especially when I'm flying over an area and a shot goes by my aircraft. You look around and all you see are women and children. You know they probably are VC, and this is what I mean by self-control—it would be so easy to roll in rockets on them, or call in artillery, but it would make me as bad as the VC…" At that time the media made a hey-day of reporting some horrible things done by American soldiers that happened during the war. Some of those things were true of course, as evidenced by photos and court proceedings, but those things were *not* the norm. The values of the man I knew and of the friends we knew who participated in that war did not support that kind of thing. They believed they were there to stop oppression, and they supported that cause with all they'd been trained to do. It was not hard for me to trust them to do the right thing.

TV Star Chuck Conners "The Rifleman" visits with Shotguns:
(left to right) Captain Freshour, Chuck Conners, Captain
McGraw, Specialist Four Vinke, and Captain Poindexter

When Jim called to tell me he had orders to Fort Stewart, Georgia, I couldn't help but be excited, even though disappointed that we wouldn't be closer home. On May 1 he wrote, "I'm up tight and out of sight since I got orders. The more I think about it the happier I am. I must be some kind of a nut because I feel so proud to be doing my part for my country..." My spirit soared upon reading he was happy and proud. So was I!

One time Kevin came home upset that his bicycle tires were flat. He'd ridden over some goatheads, which are dark brown stickers with quarter-inch-long sharp points and strong enough to puncture bike tires. Stepping on one with bare feet is extremely painful! Of course by the time I wrote to Jim about it and received his helpful reply, "I'm glad nothing was wrong with his bike. The best thing for goatheads is Never Leak. Just take the tire off, get it fixed, then buy some Never Leak and put it inside the tire..." the tires had been fixed. I was always able to call on Papaw, who was glad to help. Even so, Jim was involved with our lives as much as possible, and I loved his responses to the various problems we faced. One thing he really missed was being there to celebrate the children's birthdays, and he wrote on Kevin's sixth that he had thought about him all that day. When I read that to Kevin, he looked at me, furrowed his brow a bit, and seemed to go to a far-off place. Then he said, "I'll be glad when Dad gets home."

Jim received the Distinguished Flying Cross for extraordinary achievement while participating in aerial flight in the Republic of Vietnam during the period May 16, 1967 to May 18, 1967. He later explained that while flying over the operation he realized the American troops and the ARVN (Army of the Republic of Vietnam) troops were firing at each other! He immediately radioed, "Ceasefire!" and the firing stopped. Two soldiers were wounded, but it could have been so much worse. "I didn't think anything about it at the time," he said later. "I was just doing my job. Wouldn't you?"

Jim loved Mexican food. What I could find to send him were canned tamales, tortillas, chili con carne, Jalapeno peppers, diced chili peppers and cheddar cheese. At home we often made what I called "Lazy Mom's Enchiladas" where we dipped the tortillas in hot oil just until they were soft, topped each one with a couple of spoonfuls of chili, chopped onions and grated cheese. About three of these stacked were a very good substitute for the real thing. He was able to prepare them using a hot plate and the guys enjoyed them. Fortunately, there were other "Texas boys" there who also loved this delightful fare, and as they all received similar care packages from home, they shared it when they could. He wrote once about such a gathering, "…all the sector pilots were in, and we were sitting around harassing each other when Tommy Smith, who's from Fort Worth, said, 'I'm sure hungry for some Mexican food.' So, I got the food out. Of course there was Boyce Cates, a good 'ole Texan, too. Anyway, we introduced it to Howard Gentle and Earl Williams. It was funny when we opened up the jalapeno peppers. Cates, Smitty, and I were eating them like candy, so Howard and Earl had to try them. I told them to watch out because they're hot, and to let me stuff them with some cheese, but no, they said if we could eat them like we did, they could too. It was so funny when they took that first bite. Earl ran to the water fountain and starting drinking water. Of course, it didn't help and we finally convinced him to eat crackers instead. Howard sat in his place with tears coming down his cheeks and sweat running down his face. We had a good laugh. They both liked the peppers—if they weren't so hot. You're so thoughtful to send the food..." As Jim's time in Vietnam wound down, he talked more about the things he missed at home. He was also sad about our friends, Phil and Joan, breaking up. Joan had written to me that they had decided to divorce and we were terribly saddened. We did remember there were times when we were with them when we thought their discourse between each other seemed unnecessarily rude. We thought at the time that maybe it was just the way they communicated, and surely they would be okay; nevertheless, we were aware that certain words and the tone used could be very hurtful. On June 3 he wrote, "I was hoping it was a nasty rumor. I'm thankful we're so compatible..." I was thankful, too!

While Jim was on R&R in Hong Kong, he called and talked with us all. He told me about his shopping experience there and that I should look for packages that included gifts for all the family, and also two boxes of Noritake china. He was tired of all the shopping and about to go broke on all the bargains!

We decided to sell the house in Clovis because we still had the house in North Carolina. Even though we received a check for rent each month and we could expect it to stay rented, keeping up with two house payments, taxes, and all that goes with property ownership, was just too much. I was certainly capable of handling the finances, balancing the checkbook, paying bills, etc., so it was no biggy for me to attempt to sell the house. When I mentioned to friends at church that we'd be selling it, the organist came to me and said she was interested in buying it. After looking at it she was willing to pay what we wanted, the deal was done and Jim didn't have to worry about it! Fortunately, she was willing to wait until the first of August to move in and that was perfect for us. Jim wrote, "I'm happy the house is sold, *and* that I'll have a home to come to for a couple of weeks. It'll be so nice to be a family again."

Home, Finally Home!

As his homecoming neared, I was a wreck. I was so eager to see him; so anxious for his safe return that I couldn't keep still or quiet. The day before he arrived, I had my hair done in an updo with lots of soft curls. On the morning of July 12, I settled Kathy and Kevin with Mamaw and Papaw then drove the three and a half hours from Clovis to Albuquerque. I checked into the motel I'd reserved, and changed into a new yellow two-piece outfit. The blouse had small white embroidered flowers scattered on it and an embroidered scalloped hem. The skirt was straight and formfitting, and I wore white high-heeled pumps. My earrings were dangling crystal. *Perfect for his homecoming, I knew it!*

At the airport in plenty of time, I waited an eternity that couldn't possibly have been more than an hour. The plane's arrival announcement came, and my heart began to pound. I watched the big aircraft land and race to the end of the runway as it slowed. It reached the far end, stopped, turned around... and... sat there. It seemed so far away, and *I couldn't understand why it didn't move!*

Then, two smaller military aircraft landed and the jetliner began moving *ever so slowly* toward the terminal. I thought my heart would pound right out of my blouse! Finally, the aircraft stopped, and the passengers boarded a bus that brought them closer to the waiting parties. I saw him step off, look for me, and finally our eyes met. We were in each other's arms holding tight, so very tight. Then, arm in arm, we waited until his baggage came off the airplane.

"Come on, let's get out of here."

"I'm ready."

We quickly found our convertible in the parking lot, and we were on our way. *Darn these bucket seats,* I thought, as I leaned over the console to be nearer to him.

He looked at me and smiled. "It's so good to be with you, Frances. You're so beautiful!" He squeezed my hand, and we raced to the motel as fast as the speed limits allowed.

After getting somewhat reacquainted, we relaxed and spent time in the pool. Jim enjoyed the quietness *and* the cleanliness.

"Oh, Frances," he exclaimed, "you have no idea what it means to me to be with you, to be in *America,* and to be on the way *home!*"

The next morning we drove with the top down, enjoying the bright summer day and the incredibly beautiful New Mexico landscape. We passed through my hometown of Fort Sumner and drove past the farm where I'd grown up.

"Oh, dear," I exclaimed. "It looks so strange and seems so small." The people living there had used stucco to cover the white wood frame, and without the edge-lines of the wood, the house seemed to have shrunk. Many of the huge elm trees I'd grown up with were gone. I didn't dwell on the changes; there were other things on my mind.

An hour later, we arrived in Clovis and drove first to our house. It was closest, and he wanted to see it just for a minute. We drove into the driveway, and he pushed the remote to open the garage door. As it went up, a banner unfurled that read, "Welcome Home, Jim!" Christine and Moreland had surprised us!

Upon our arrival at my folk's, Kevin and Kathy came running out the door, across the porch, down the steps and into their daddy's arms. Tears welled in Jim's eyes, my eyes, Mamaw's eyes, Papaw's eyes, and everyone else's eyes as he held his children close.

Family and friends clamored to see Jim and welcome him home. We visited Grandma in Amarillo and then began preparing to move to Georgia. We hated moving out of the house, but Jim assured me he was happy, even if he hadn't had much time in it. He knew we were okay while he was away.

Puppies, Cars, and Travel

In June, Abbi surprised us with five healthy puppies. Kevin and Kathy were ecstatic, but not me when I realized they wouldn't be old enough to give away before leaving for Georgia! It didn't bother Jim at all, but it was tricky managing them as we moved out of the house and traveled to and from Amarillo. Grandma and my folks were good about it; they had garages and fenced yards where they could stay.

Right out of the blue, Jim came home one day with a beautiful new, two-door Plymouth Fury, gold with a black top, a console between the bucket-style seats, and *white leather interior.* My fury matched the car's name!

"Jim, how *dare* you trade cars without talking with *me!*"

"Frances," he said with that set jaw, "I have no desire to take a trip in the middle of summer through the south without air conditioning after being in Vietnam. Besides, the deal was too good to pass up."

I'd already lost the argument. A larger car payment was worth it in his mind.

After we moved out of our house, Grandma McGraw went with us to Casper, Wyoming, to see Ghern and Mike. The time was short and the trip long and hard, but Jim was able to find some closure after losing Juanita. It was also the first time Ghern had seen Kevin and Kathy. The trip was well worth it.

We returned to Clovis to say good-bye to Mamaw and Papaw and get Abbi's family. With lumps in our throats, we headed for Georgia. The five-week-old puppies stayed in a box between the kids in the backseat. Abbi sat on my feet in front. When it was time to nurse the puppies, she jumped over the console into the back, and one of the kids sat with me.

I did not like this situation! The strong air conditioner, powered by the big 380 horsepower engine, *seemed* to have only on and off controls, so when my feet and legs got cold, we turned it off. Well, my, my, the puppies yelped! I managed to find something to cover my feet and legs, and we kept the air on all the time. Sigh...

We stopped in Shallowater, just west of Lubbock, to visit my mother's sister, Aunt Arah and my Uncle Jess Peters, a retired Methodist minister. Our visit was sweet, and then we were on our way to Melva and Shell's, who had recently moved to Dallas. Our timing was perfect for a visit as Kevin, Kathy, Barry, and Sharon enjoyed being cousins and were entertained by the new puppies. The next evening, we four adults went to Cattleman's, a famous steakhouse in downtown Dallas. When we returned home, Barry was awake to tell us that Mamaw called to say that Uncle Jess had been killed in a car accident that afternoon. We were shocked and saddened. Our thankfulness that we'd just seen them was bittersweet.

We reached Americus, Georgia, in the middle of the afternoon and turned left at a stop light onto the street going east toward Fort Stewart. Just then, on the left, we all saw a Dairy Queen.

"Dairy Queen, Dairy Queen!" the kids screamed. Jim instinctively checked his rearview mirror and made a quick left turn. *Crunch!* He had indeed seen a Volkswagen in the left lane behind him, but thought he had enough time to make the turn. Unfortunately, the VW driver sped up, as he thought the lane was clear in front of him. No one was hurt, but the right front fender of the VW was damaged, as was the left rear bumper and taillight of our new Fury. While waiting for a policeman, we put Abbi and the puppies on nearby grass. A small crowd gathered including a boy about thirteen. He wanted one of the puppies!

"Well, son, they're just five weeks old and not quite ready to give away," Jim said.

"I'd really like one, sir. They's fine lookin' pups, and I've raised pups on a bottle. I'd take fine care of it."

"What would your folks say?"

"Oh, it'd be all right with my mom. She likes the pups."

"Okay, I'll tell you what. Do you live close by? Can you go home and get a note from your mother telling me it's okay for you to have the puppy?"

"Oh, yes, sir!" he said. He climbed on his bike and called, "I'll be right back."

The policeman arrived and made out a report. When it was all over some weeks later, both drivers were held "contributory negligent" with both insurance companies picking up the damage expense.

The young lad brought a note from his mother saying he could have a puppy. He took the one of his choice, put it in his handlebar basket, and pedaled away.

When we were on our way, Kevin asked in a quiet voice, "Mommy, is Abbi sad that we gave her puppy away?"

"Well, she might be, Kevin, but I think she's so busy with the other puppies that I think perhaps she doesn't mind."

Kathy began to cry. "I din't want to gif it away."

I reached back and stroked her arm. "I know, honey. The puppies are so cute, but Abbi can't take care of them much longer, and we have to find homes for them. I think that boy will love the puppy and give it a good home."

"Kathy, I know he'll take good care of the puppy," Kevin said, very seriously.

Jim and I looked at each other. We couldn't help being a little choked up ourselves.

Getting Reacquainted with Each Other

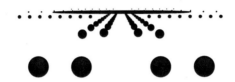

Memorial Drive, Hinesville, Georgia

A guesthouse was available at Fort Stewart; a WWII-vintage cabin located in an open meadow north of the main post. It was comfortable, and we were happy to be there for the short time. Upon signing in, Jim learned his sponsor had a mobile home in downtown Hinesville for rent. This was a blessing because quarters on post wouldn't be available for a couple of months. I'd never dreamed we'd ever have to live in a trailer house, but it was perfect with two bedrooms, one with a king-size bed, and the other with bunk beds.

As soon as the word spread about the puppies, folks took one look at Abbi and wanted one. She was pretty and was often called Little Lassie. We had no trouble finding homes for them.

We enrolled Kevin in first grade and Kathy in kindergarten at the elementary school on Fort Stewart. Luckily, their classes were in the same building. Jim took them to school as he went to work each day, and for the first time since Kevin was born, I had a little time to myself. I actually enjoyed living in the mobile home. It was easy to clean and had all the comforts we were accustomed to, except space. We bought a recliner for Jim and our first color TV—a large Colonial-style console. We soon learned other recently returned "Shotguns" had made similar purchases!

We happily settled in to life at Fort Stewart and were delighted to see so many folks we'd known before. We also got to know the families of several of the guys Jim had spent time with in Vietnam. His position was as School Secretary for the Army's Primary Fixed Wing Training that had moved from Fort Rucker to Fort Stewart. He wasn't very thrilled about it until he learned he'd be able to get off work early enough to play golf often. He could expect only to fly as much as he needed to stay proficient, and for that he'd have to get a check out in the T-41, the single engine aircraft the Army now used for flight training instead of the Birddog. One afternoon he called to tell me he'd be home late because he was getting his check ride. Then about 11:00 p.m. that night he called. He was at Fort Benning on the other side of Georgia.

"Frances, I won't be home tonight."

"I've been worried because it's so late. Are you okay?"

"Yeah, I'm okay, but we had an engine quit and had to land in a stage field way out in the boonies on Fort Benning. I'm so tired and upset because we waited *three hours* for them to come pick us up!"

"Three hours? My goodness, didn't they know you were there?"

"Sure. We called in before we set the aircraft down to tell them we'd lost an engine, and in a few minutes a helicopter flew over and waved at us, then disappeared. We were stuck because we couldn't reach anybody by radio on the ground."

"What in the world took them so long?"

"We don't know, Frances. When they finally got out here they said the guys in the helicopter told them we were standing outside of the aircraft and were fine. I can't believe some people can be such idiots! Anyway, we have to stay here overnight and make out an accident report. The instructor pilot took over the aircraft when the engine quit and banged it in. There's some damage."

"Oh?"

"Yeah, the nose gear is bent up. It's not bad, but we couldn't fly it out, even if we had an engine. Well, I'd better get some sleep. I'll see you tomorrow."

"Okay, sweetheart, see you tomorrow..."

That fall, we attended a parade and awards ceremony where many soldiers were awarded numerous medals, Jim included. That day he was given the Distinguished Flying Cross, his first Bronze Star, the Air Medal with five oak leaf clusters, and the Vietnamese Cross of Gallantry. He'd also completed 1,500 hours of flying and was awarded Senior Aviator wings.

4 Cobb Place

We'd been in the trailer ninety days when we were assigned quarters. *We were ready!* The quarters were similar to what we'd had at Fort Rucker, but smaller and with only one bathroom. There was a huge walk-in pantry that accommodated our freezer; the kitchen had an area for a breakfast table and washer and dryer, and had a huge window over the sink that looked out over the three-duplex court. We were able to purchase the salmon-colored carpet the previous occupants had installed. Best of all, the children's school was only two hundred yards away. What a joy it was for the children to walk out of the house, go down the sidewalk past one duplex, cross the street, and be at school! Kevin and Kathy did well and we were pleased with their progress. One thing we got a kick out of was when Kevin's teacher said he had trouble getting his work done on time—his work was good, but he was just too slow. Well, the next year Kathy had the same teacher, and we got a note from her saying that Kathy "is very efficient in getting her work done; however, if she took a bit more time perhaps she could do better." We laughed because they were such opposites.

Jim and I were involved with unit, post and chapel activities, and bowling leagues. I attended wives' club coffees and luncheons. It was neat to be back into the swing of the military social life we'd grown to love.

During the time we lived there, Ghern came to visit and went on to see Carol and Richard in Macon, where Richard was a professor at a junior college. John and Cynthia moved from Reno to Atlanta and came to see us. We also received a call from Mamaw that Royce and Sammye's twin boys were born prematurely and that one had died. The other little boy, Kipp, was fine. I was sad; both my brothers had lost a baby boy.

Old Friends, New Friends

We renewed our friendship with the Larry Nelsons that we'd known at Fort Bragg and made friends with the Windel Reeds. Other Shotguns there were Hank Collins and his wife, Linda, and Jim Stone and wife, Joyce. When Tommy and Karen Smith came, they put their mobile home in Gary and Peggy Varner's new mobile home park. In time, Howard Gentle, his wife, Laveta, and children arrived. Jim loved these former Shotguns, and we enjoyed getting together.

We had so much in common with Tommy and Karen Smith. I loved Karen's spunk and creativity and became so fond of this German-heritage blonde from Wisconsin. Eventually they sold their mobile home and moved into quarters.

Student Company Commander, Primary Flight Training

When the CO of the flight school student company left, Jim learned he'd been recommended for the position. Then, when he was named CO, he was ecstatic! Since he'd been selected as a Regular Army officer, getting the command was a big step. He'd served eight years on active duty, his career was looking better, *and* his time in the National Guard counted toward pay. It was a nice time in our lives. The student company command was a visible one. Both Jim and I were expected to be present at each class orientation and each graduation. There were four classes in session all the time—red, green, gold, and blue hats—a new class began as each finished. I kept busy attending many student wives' functions. During this time, I was also elected president of the Protestant Women of the Chapel.

Baseball "Bullets"

That spring and summer of 1968, Jim coached the Bullets—a little league baseball team of twelve-year-olds, and Kevin worked as bat boy. Jim soon realized several of his players were exceptional and worked to coach them well. The team performed well and won the post championship. The league also included some area teams, so one afternoon the Bullets found themselves in Ludowici, Georgia, playing the local team for the league championship. The primary pitcher, Scott Fletcher, who was unusually talented, pitched the entire game. When he was at bat in the top of the ninth, bases loaded, and three runs down, Scott hit a grand slam home run to go ahead. Then in the bottom of the ninth, he pitched to shut the other team down to win the game! It was one of the most exciting things that happened during the years Jim coached baseball, football, and basketball.

Our Golf Discussion

Jim also played golf as much as he could. Right away, he was in a golf foursome that included Larry and Windel. He worked hard to improve his game and he was passionate about it. It seemed to me, however, that he spent an inordinate amount of time at the golf course. It didn't cost all that much to play, but when clubs, balls, shoes, gloves, towels, etc., were added up, for me it was an issue.

"Jim, we've got to talk."

"Okay, what do you want to talk about?"

"It's just that I'm not feeling very good about you being at the golf course so much when I'm here alone with the kids, and on top of that, it costs a lot of money."

"Well, Frances, I want to play, and I'd like for you to play too. It's a great game for couples, and I know you'd enjoy playing with the girls."

"Jim, we can't afford for me to play golf and get a babysitter too."

"Frances," he said, looking me squarely in the eye, "I'd really like for you to play, and besides, you pay a babysitter when you go to the bowling alley or to your coffees and teas. Fine thing, if when I retire you're in the bowling alley and I'm on the golf course."

I didn't have a response. I began thinking more and more about what he'd said, and decided that *if he was thinking that far in advance about our relationship, then perhaps I could at least attempt to learn to play golf!*

The Big Promotion

Jim was promoted to Major on April 1, 1968. We were thankful he'd outlived the bad experiences during his tour in Italy. I happily helped his boss pin on the gold oak leaves. The nice pay raise allowed us to buy a VW Bug, and it was nice to have a second car.

His job was not only visible, it was demanding. He worked hard to do well, and I tried to always be by his side. About five months into it, he was tasked to set up the new Warrant Officer Primary Flight Training Program. Just at the right time, Captain Richard LaHue was assigned to his unit, and Jim promptly delegated the job to him. Richard, waiting to begin flight school himself, was extremely professional and did an outstanding job.

But, not all of 1968 was a blessing. Three days after Jim's promotion, Martin Luther King Jr. was killed. We were stunned, and in June when Bobby Kennedy was killed, we were overwhelmed. Then, one of the hardest things Jim ever had to do was tell his secretary that her husband, an infantry lieutenant, had been killed in Vietnam. It was a troubling time. War protests, assassinations, and personal tragedy—we wondered what was happening to our world.

Special Times, Special Friends

We introduced Richard LaHue and his wife, Monica, to Tommy and Karen Smith. They became fast friends, and the guys enjoyed playing golf together.

"Richard, Tommy, and I arranged to take a cross-country training flight," Jim recalled. "Richard hadn't started flight school yet, so we decided he needed some right seat time. Tommy and I had the time of our lives trying to impress Richard with our flying skills.

We were pretty mean to him though because we gave him a flight helmet *without* the insert that would make it fit his head. The helmet kept falling down over his eyes, and when we finally gave him the insert and he realized what we'd done, *he was not happy!*"

Richard began primary flight training and then left for Fort Rucker to complete later phases. As a send-off for the LaHue's, we joined them, Tommy, and Karen for a weekend in Atlanta. We were able to take Kevin and Kathy and stay with John and Cynthia. The guys played golf while we gals shopped all day Saturday. That evening we got a sitter for the kids so we eight adults could see the sights of downtown Atlanta.

We joined the Smiths and LaHues for cocktails at their hotel, and then went for dinner to the prominent restaurant, The Diplomat, where we expected to eat right away. Wrong. The restaurant was crowded, and we waited for over an hour. Jim, Tommy, and Richard, although neither loud nor rowdy, jokingly tried to bribe the maitre d'—to no avail. They told him they were wounded soldiers just returned from Vietnam—to no avail. Jim even faked a limp—to no avail. John and Cynthia didn't know what to think—they'd never seen guys like these! Finally, the good-natured maitre d' who seemed to enjoy the scene, seated us and we enjoyed a fine meal.

OV-1 Mohawk Transition

By April 1969, Jim, Tommy, and Richard had orders to go back to Vietnam. First, Jim was to go to Fort Rucker to learn to fly the OV-1 Mohawk, a twin-engine, turbo-prop reconnaissance aircraft, the most sophisticated the army had. As soon as Richard finished primary flight training, he would also go to Mohawk school, and within a few months, Tommy followed. They all hoped to be assigned together in Vietnam.

It was hard to pick up and move, but such is army life. Our household goods went again to Cannon Air Force Base near Clovis for storage, and "hold baggage" to Fort Rucker to see us through that temporary duty assignment. That included a portable TV, sewing machine, typewriter, pots and pans, waffle iron, linens, extra uniforms, and clothes. By now, I was getting pretty good with this turbulent but necessary part of army life, but I hated seeing the children uprooted. I was determined they would know *home was wherever we were all together,* whether in a car, motel, mobile home, government quarters, or in our own special house. As we sat at the table for each meal, we joined hands and took turns asking the blessing.

Whenever we went on a temporary duty assignment we loaded the car with a few things we didn't want to trust to hold baggage. Priority was given to the cast iron skillet—couldn't cook without that—the Mel Mac plastic dishes, a couple of Revere Ware pots, the iron and ironing board (everything was ironed in those days), a few knickknacks, and the small filing cabinet that held our important papers. Thank goodness for big car trunks, because the golf clubs had to go in, *and* the luggage with our clothes and Jim's essential uniforms!

11 South Catherine, Daleville, Alabama

We rented an unusually nice three-bedroom, two-bath trailer in an especially nice mobile home park, right outside of Fort Rucker in Daleville. We enrolled Kevin and Kathy in the nearby school, where they finished the school year.

Now this mobile home was a split-level design and nice. It had three bedrooms and two baths, *and a washer and dryer!* I had plenty of time on my hands so I bought a lot a fabric and made several outfits for myself and Kathy. Sewing was therapy for me—I kept that machine humming!

We enjoyed Fort Rucker as we had four years earlier—the laid-back rural setting with the constant hum of aircraft engines and *wop-wop* of rotor blades. Jim was excited to be flying the Mohawk. He loved every minute in the powerful, totally acrobatic aircraft. As class leader, he had a lot of responsibility. The men in the class were Captains Ivon Borgen, Ray McBride, John McBroom, Bob Merrill, David O'Hara and Dieter Rietz; Lieutenants Bob Boyd and Bob Larive, and Warrant Officers Cecil "Bud" Davis, Lonnie Bauman, and Dan Michalak. The class bonded well and dubbed themselves McGraw's Marauders.

The time was special. Jim had a fine instructor, a Major Jim Stinebaugh, who'd been on the professional golf tour at one time and was one of those interesting, unforgettable personalities. Occasionally, they played golf together. One day after playing a few holes, Stinebaugh said to Jim, "I'm going to have to file suit against you."

"File suit against me? What for?"

"For calling your game golf," Stinebaugh guffawed!

"You son of a gun!"

There were other stories about Stinebaugh. On his last check ride, Jim said that Stinebaugh appeared to be hung over and asleep during the flight; however, he roused at critical times, and seemed *totally* aware of what was going on.

"I'm always awake," Stinebaugh insisted.

"I'm impressed that you can snore so realistically if you're awake," Jim ribbed.

Jim passed the check ride with flying colors.

When the children were home we all enjoyed the swimming pool. The LaHues lived nearby, and the children played well. Tommy, Karen and Kelli Smith visited at Easter. It was, as Jim would say, "Just like old home week." We spent Easter Sunday together and took pictures that are precious to this day.

While there, Jim bought golf clubs for me. He taught me

how to swing the club, and I tried. We went to the course one day and took the kids along. I tried to hit the ball, but my heart was with my little ones much more than golf. I knew I'd have to wait until they were in school to take up the game.

Fort Huachuca

After Mohawk transition, the class traveled to Fort Huachuca, Arizona, for the six-week OV-1 Mohawk Aviator Combat Surveillance Qualification, 3A-F14 Class 12–69, at the U.S. Army Combat Surveillance School/Training Center.

We traveled to Arizona, via Houston to see Clois and Sis, and Melva and Shell, then to San Antonio to see Dick and Dee Hollar, and on to Amarillo and Clovis. We left Abbi with my folks and continued the trip in our new Chrysler convertible. We'd seen it in a showroom and couldn't resist it. It was roomy, had a big engine, and was *air-conditioned!*

We arrived in Arizona at midday and stopped at a tourist spot that had for several miles advertised a "10,000-year-old secret of the desert." The kids were mesmerized by the mummified body of a small person. At Benson, we turned south onto the highway that would take us to Fort Huachuca (pronounced Wa-choo´-ka). Mountains were in the distance all around, but it was dry and hot. *We thought we had never seen such desolation!*

We stopped at the north gate, where Jim was directed to go several miles past Libby Army Airfield to school headquarters where he'd sign in. There, he was given a list of places to rent.

The main post, established in 1881, was nestled in the foothills of the Huachuca Mountains. For permanently assigned senior officers there were magnificent quarters dating back to the 1880s. The top of the flagpole on the parade field alongside these quarters was a mile high. There were other nineteenth-century buildings, but most were vintage WWII.

We drove through the east gate into the town of Sierra Vista and admired the stunning mountains in the distance. We soon learned the historic town of Tombstone was located there. Sierra Vista had one long main street with streets branching off to make up the entire town. It was a sleepy little two-motel town, and we were lucky to find a room—one of the most interesting rooms we'd ever had—the sofa in the sitting area rested on cement blocks!

El Cortez Apt. #85

Our apartment was close to post and had nice-sized, furnished rooms. We moved in on May 20, Kevin's eighth birthday. Teachers in Alabama assured us Kevin and Kathy were both eligible for promotion, so with only two weeks of school left in Arizona, we didn't enroll them. They were happy kids!

Married guys in the class and their wives were Ike and Kay Borgan, Bob and Paula Boyd, Bob and Jinx Larive, Ray and Sue McBride, John and Raquel McBroom, and Bob and Diane Merrill. We got together often and developed lasting friendships.

Mohawk Class 12–69: (Standing, left to right) Capt. McBride, Lt. Boyd, Cpt. Rietz, Cpt. O'Hara, Cpt. McBroom, Maj. McGraw, (kneeling, left to right) Cpt. Merrill, Cpt. Borgen, CWO Bauman, Lt. Larive, and CWO Davis, (not shown) CWO Michalak

The OV-1 Mohawk

Las Vegas and the Grand Canyon

For Memorial Day weekend we joined the Boyds and Larives in Las Vegas. We took Kevin and Kathy and arrived at our motel on the outskirts of town late Thursday. The motel offered child-sitting services, so we were able to join the two other couples to have a glimpse of the world famous strip. The next day we enjoyed taking the kids to the Circus Circus Casino that offered some things for children.

I called home to see if Cynthia and John had had their baby. Sure enough, Jill Lourie Van Auken was born on Memorial Day. Mamaw was with them in Atlanta, and everything was fine.

We had to leave Las Vegas early Saturday in time to get to the Grand Canyon to stay that night. We traveled in southern Utah through St. George, over to Kanab, and into Arizona at the town of Page. We arrived at the Grand Canyon's north rim at dusk, and stayed there in a cabin. Sunday morning's sun exposed the desert brilliantly, and our view of the magnificent crevice was incredible! By late afternoon, we were back in Sierra Vista.

Jim and I were able to get away once by ourselves to play golf. The Fort Huachuca Golf Course was different from any we'd seen. The magnificent Huachuca Mountains rimmed it on the south and southwest, and looking east we could see the Dragoon and Mule Mountains hosting Tombstone and Bisbee. To the northwest, we could see the Mustang Mountains. There'd been a recent rain shower, revealing beautiful grass and flowers among the cactus and other indigenous plants. The shadows of the clouds and the subtle desert colors were incredible!

"Would you like to live here when I come back from Vietnam?"

"*Oh, yes!* It's so beautiful here, and the quarters look wonderful."

"Then I'll make it first choice. I think I'll have a good chance of coming back here to fly the Mohawk."

"That would be so neat. We'd be closer to our families than we've ever been."

"I know. It'd be great."

After six weeks, we'd fallen in love with this beautiful place that at first had seemed so desolate. "Fort Hoochy Coochy" the guys fondly tagged it.

Vietnam ... Again ...

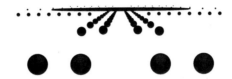

104 Westerfield Place, Clovis, New Mexico

In Clovis we found a big house to lease—a three-bedroom brick with two baths, a formal living room that had a large see-through fireplace to the family room/dining area, a large all-electric kitchen with breakfast counter and laundry closet, a double-car garage with electronic door opener, and a large covered patio looking onto a private backyard. We eagerly signed the lease and moved in.

We'd been in the house a few days when the real estate agent came by to tell us he'd been fired because he'd rented the house to us and was not supposed to. He didn't understand at the time it was for *sale*—not for *lease*, that the owners were divorcing, and the wife wanted the house sold. There was nothing she could do because we had a valid lease, but we might get a visit from her. *Oh dear...*

Off To War

Getting settled this time was harder than three years before. This was old, ugly stuff—Jim having to go away—and I wasn't quite as efficient at getting things ready for him. Relatives came the night before he left and stayed much too long. It was awkward, and when they finally left, we were upset when we realized all we had to do before we could go to bed. I was upset that he had not planned to get his gear together earlier, and he was upset with me because I hadn't planned better! It was not a pretty evening. The next morning as we prepared to leave for the airport, things were cool between us. I was sad and didn't understand his attitude, but I did understand it was harder for him to leave this time. He was going back to a place that smelled, where he would be shot at, and worst of all, to an unpopular war. He was confused and concerned about news accounts of the war. It all seemed so different from the way it was when he'd been there two years earlier. I was with our children in a lovely house and close to family.

Almost all my family joined us at the Clovis Municipal Airport. Jim was cool and hugged only the children. He turned away from me toward the aircraft. I grabbed him by the arm and drew him close. We kissed quickly, and then he was gone. The feeling was the strangest I'd ever had. I was hurting; even so, tears did not come.

Kathy sobbed until the plane was out of sight. As we walked back through the terminal she suddenly stopped crying, looked up at me, and asked, "Mommy, can I have my ice cream now?" We all laughed. It was as if she'd done her good deed, and now should be rewarded! I squeezed her hand, "Of course you can have ice cream, Kathy."

The rest of the day was strange, and I was at loose ends. I wondered if I'd hear from Jim—I'd never faced anything like it before—I'd never seen him act that way.

Having family close helped. My parents, Moreland, and Christine still lived in Clovis, and Melva and Shell came from Houston, Doyle and Marilou from Oklahoma, and Royce and Sammye from Lubbock—all to say good-bye to Jim. They stayed a couple more days and on July 20, the night the astronauts landed on the moon, we all gathered in my living room. There was room for the eleven cousins to play, and we enjoyed visiting, but we waited ... and we waited ... as all of America and the entire world *waited* for those brave souls of Apollo 11 to set foot on the moon in the Sea of Tranquility. At about 9:00 p.m., the phone rang.

"Frances, this is Jim."

"Oh, it's so good to hear your voice. Are you okay?"

"Yeah, I'm okay—I guess. Frances, I'm sorry about the way I acted when I left. I don't know what was wrong with me. I love you."

"It's okay, Jim. I know it wasn't easy for you to leave. I'm sorry, too."

"Well, there's no need for you to be sorry—it wasn't your fault. I love you so much, and I don't want to hurt you. I miss you already so much. Can you forgive me?"

"Of course I forgive you, Jim. You know I love you with all my heart. I just couldn't understand what was wrong."

"I don't know what was wrong either, but I'm sorry. Will you still write to me?"

"Of course I'll write to you!"

"I've got to go. They're calling us to the bus. I'll write as soon as I can."

"Okay. I'll write as soon as I have an address."

"Okay. Give the kids a hug for me."

"Okay."

"Tell them I love them."

"Okay."

"Bye, Frances."

"Bye, sweetheart."

I sighed, and the tears came. I was glad my family was there and the moon landing was their focus. Soon we saw the gray-white boot step onto the moon and heard Neil Armstrong say, "One small step for a man, one giant leap for mankind." It was an incredible time.

The Letters Begin

Jim flew to San Francisco where he met four of his "Marauders," Bob Boyd, Bob Larive, Lonnie Bauman, and Bud Davis, and they traveled together.

His first return address was: Major J. J. McGraw—Nineti-eth Replacement Detachment—San Francisco, California APO 96384. A number appeared after his name—his Social Security number. It had replaced his service number.

It was a lot comfort to get his letter telling about the nice trip over—different from the first time because he traveled with friends. His written words of love for me and the children were so much comfort after all we'd been through.

When he received his assignment he wrote that he was the S-2 (Intelligence/Security Officer) and would be working closely with the S-3 (Operations Officer) of the Twelfth Combat Avia-tion Group (CAG) at Long Bien. This area was north of Saigon and called the Plantation. He was disappointed at not getting a flying assignment, but well knew the worth of a staff posi-tion, especially at group level. In any case, I knew he would do everything he could to get into a flying position as soon as pos-sible! He mentioned that the Seventy-third Surveillance Air-plane Company (SAC), which utilized the Mohawk, was in the Twelfth Group, and he hoped to get checked out and fly some missions with them. I knew I'd be hearing more about the Sev-enty-third! Enclosed in that letter was a typewritten announce-ment on legal size paper that had no official address, nor was it dated. On the back was Jim's handwritten note: "This was issued for information so you'll understand why we got an unpublished telephone number."

SPARE YOUR RELATIVES NEEDLESS GRIEF

Numerous hoax calls to relatives of personnel serving in Vietnam have been reported in recent weeks. These hoax calls have caused considerable anguish and discomfort to the next of kin who are unaware of Department of the Army notification procedures. The hoax calls are malicious and relate primarily to false reports of death, missing, absence without leave, desertion, or other related matters concerning personnel status. The adverse and traumatic impact on the unwary is obvious.

Advise them now that they may be the recipient of such a contemptible call, and that any such telephone call concerning your status should be immediately recognized as a hoax.

If your status requires notification to your loved ones, your army does not use the telephone. Notification is made by a personally delivered message by army representatives, where identity can be immediately verified; or, by a Western Union telegram which can be verified with the Western Union office from which received; or, by correspondence directly from the Department of the Army. The purpose for notifying your next of kin determines the means used.

It was a sign of the times. The anti-war legions were spewing their hatred at the expense of the families of military men and women serving their country. It just made me sick to my stomach! How dare they treat families of soldiers in such a horrible way and how dare them say our soldiers were mean and cruel! I just continued to pray for Jim's safety, and for that matter, the

safety of all our soldiers and their families. It was so heart rend-
ing day-after-day to see news reports of casualties and to hear
that the Paris Peace Talks were not going well. But worst of all
were the protest marchers, many of whom were proved to be
Communist in their belief. I just wanted them all to go to Canada and stay there if they didn't like America! Their actions only
hurt the war effort and damaged the morale of our soldiers, not
to mention what it must be doing to our prisoners of war that
we were reminded about time and again. My family prayed, our
church family prayed, and we knew there were prayers all over
America for our soldiers and POWs and that the war would end
soon. It was good to hear from Jim about reunions with guys he'd
known in Italy, flight school, and other places, as well as with
several of his Marauders. He continued to be apologetic about
his behavior before he left. I was long past that and continued
to write to him with all the love I had. I told him that we were,
in my mind, a very happy family, and that he needn't worry one
minute about me or my devotion to him.

The Rent

The realtor came by one day and told me there had been a mistake and that we should be paying $180 a month rent instead of
$170. I balked at that and wrote Jim. He responded that he felt
the rent was the realtor's problem because we'd signed the lease
in good faith for $170 a month, and that the realtor could be
out the $120 that would be the extra ten dollars for the twelve-
month lease. After all, it was their mistake, and they could take
it off their income tax as a loss. Then one day the realtor came by
with the owner. She saw the house was clean and in order, and
the lawn cared for. I'd already given the realtor a list of things for
the house and yard that we'd paid for amounting to almost $100.
She seemed satisfied, and we didn't hear from her again.

Golf and Rings and Things

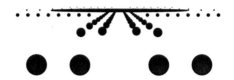

Before Jim left we managed to join the Colonial Country Club, where Moreland and Christine were members. I began taking golf lessons while the children were in day camp. I wrote Jim that the only thing I didn't like about golf was I had to take my wedding ring set off because it was too bulky to wear under the golf glove. I received a quick response from him that warmed my heart, "As soon as I got your letter about your rings I went to the PX and bought you a plain gold band. I hope you like it because it has the same love from me as the rings you have now..."

The first big jolt of reality for Jim that he was back in a war zone came when he learned that Bob Merrill, one of his Marauders, had been wounded in a mortar attack and was in the hospital at Long Bien. Bob was in serious condition with a compound fracture of the leg, and wounds on the head, back, arms and legs. He was eventually evacuated to Japan and then back to the states. My heart broke for Jim when he wrote, "You should have seen the ward Bob was in—the more seriously wounded, and I've never seen so many mangled bodies. Some were unconscious, or in a comma on the verge of death. When I walked out I said a prayer that they would make it, and that we do have a cause here. These boys have laid so much on the line, and a picture went across my mind of the ungrateful in the U.S. that demonstrate and protest for why we're here. I felt so guilty because I'm not doing more in this war. Frances, I became sick to my stomach because of the ungrateful. They should have to experience what the Vietnamese people do to gain freedom. I wish I could do more …"

Back in Clovis …

While Jim was experiencing these horrific tragedies of war, I was back home taking golf lessons. It was a wonderful outlet for me, and I knew Jim wanted me to learn to play, but I was determined it wouldn't interfere with the children's care. I was always home when they came home. I also sang in our church choir, worked in WSCS, and was a "pink lady" volunteer at the hospital.

Kevin and Kathy went to Sandia Elementary, not far from our house. They rode bikes or walked with friends. Kevin's third grade teacher was a soft-spoken grandmotherly type, and he prospered, but I was uneasy about Kathy in second grade. Her teacher, a young wife who was pregnant for the first time, was often ill. Homework assignments were *absolutely unreasonable for her second graders!* I tried to help Kathy and kept talking with her teacher. I mulled the idea of getting tutoring for her because what I tried to do did not help. When a different teacher took the class, Kathy did better, but still had difficulty. I begged this new teacher to keep me posted so I could do what I could to help.

Not long after Jim left, I took K&K to a portrait studio to have pictures made to send to Jim, because we had not managed to get it done before he left. At their ages now they were excited about having their pictures taken. I thought they were pretty good pictures and the response from Jim upon receiving them tickled me, "Your package came today and I got all choked up when I opened the pictures. Frances, those are the best pictures I've ever seen! I can't take my eyes off them ..."

Pictures for Daddy: Kevin, eight, Fran, thirty-one, and Kathy, seven.

Major McGraw, S-2, Twelfth Combat Aviation Group

The My Lai Massacre story constantly on TV and radio was ugly. I hated it and got so tired of hearing it over and over and over. Without my asking Jim, he finally addressed it in a letter, "This Green Beret (My Lai) thing is a mess. I'm afraid the army is going to be embarrassed before it's over." And, of course, the army was embarrassed by the realization that leadership training of young officers and young drafted soldiers was not adequate. Some were so weary of the war and the lack of support from Congress and the media, as well as some of their superior officers, that they broke down when they'd had too much. Much has been said, debated, and written; nevertheless, those responsible for that debacle should have been, and most were brought to justice. It lightened the war news load when the Smiths stopped in Clovis on Tommy's way to Fort Huachuca. He spent a couple of nights, and Karen and Kelli stayed for a few more days before flying back to Wisconsin. Karen and I shopped and "redecorated" the house. While he was there, Tommy changed the heating system filters and helped get the house ready for winter. Mamaw and Papaw thought he was an incredible young man. Their opinion only validated what we'd learned in the past couple of years.

Jim kept writing about another R&R and we decided to meet in Tokyo the first week in December, and the wife of an officer Jim worked with was going, too. We decided to travel together. That was comforting. Jim wrote that I would have to have a passport and a visa to come to Japan, and to check with the lawyers at Cannon Air Force Base to see how to go about getting it all done. That kept me happily going back and forth to the base for awhile.

Jim wrote often about attending chapel services and always mentioned taking communion. I enjoyed hearing about it, and I could imagine him in chapel singing old hymns. He didn't sing much, but he always joined in on hymns like "Onward Christian Soldiers" and "The Old Rugged Cross." *I knew his heart* and that his macho personality was easily penetrated if he saw soldiers die or wounded. As on his first tour, he didn't write much about the horror because he didn't want to worry me. One of the worst incidents he later told about was when a downed helicopter was turned over, and he saw the completely burned bodies of the pilots still strapped in their seats. Forty years later, he still has flashbacks and disturbing dreams of that, and other things. During this time he expected to eventually be assigned to the Seventy-third SAC in Vung Tau; however, the powers that were in the Twelfth CAG convinced him that he would be better off career-wise to have command of a company. That meant he'd stay at the Twelfth CAG until January, when two Birddog units in the Mekong Delta became available.

The time dragged and I missed him so, but plans for our meeting in Tokyo the first week in December helped. Also keeping me busy of course were the children and their activities, and their ups and downs!

One day on a trip out to the base when K&K were with me, I gave them sunflower seeds to munch on. I had no idea that Kevin didn't know to remove the seed hull in order to eat the nut inside. About halfway into the trip he became very sick and threw up in the floor of the back seat. I felt so sorry for him, and certainly very inadequate as a mother to have let that happen. It didn't take long for him to begin feeling okay, but it took him a long time to try eating sunflower seeds again! Fortunately, there were few times they were sick. Oh, there were a few bouts of tonsillitis now and then, but not often enough for the doctor to suggest surgical removal of their tonsils. A dose of antibiotics had them well in no time. I missed Jim all the time, but I didn't give a thought to his not being there when they were ill. I was quite capable of handling things, and my folks helped me; however, I was grateful their problems were never worse than an occasional bout of tonsillitis—or a battle with sunflower seed hulls! Kathy's difficulties in school worried me more.

Jim's letters helped. It was good to hear that he was able to go to Vung Tau on weekends to get flight time in the Mohawk, but one letter after such a weekend in mid-November was chilling. A Seventy-third SAC Mohawk had gone down, and both the pilot and the naval observer ejected, but they were missing and feared captured. He'd helped in covering the area trying to locate them, but by the time he had to go back to the Twelfth CAG, they hadn't found them.

The Downed Mohawk Story

Upon returning to his unit, Jim wrote, "The searchers haven't had any luck in locating the two downed people. I guess they're long gone by now and stowed away in a POW camp somewhere."

It wasn't until 1973 when the POWs were released from Hanoi that stories of these two brave men were told. Captain White, the pilot, was the last American POW released during Operation Homecoming, and it was revealed that Commander John Graf, the naval observer onboard the Mohawk with White, died during captivity. During his debrief, White reported that he was held with Graf in various prison camps until late January 1970, when Graf escaped with another POW. White never saw Graf after that, but his captors told him that Graf had drowned during his escape attempt. Captured documents and post-war reports by former residents of the area supported that information and indicated that Graf's body had been recovered and buried somewhere in Vinh Binh province.

Jim had the opportunity to visit with now-Major White at a reunion years later. He asked White if he knew how hard the 73rd had searched for them. He said yes, he knew, and that at the time it seemed he could almost reach out and touch the searching aircraft, but he was bound and without shoes, and couldn't make a motion at all to let them know where he was.

To me, the stark reality of another Mohawk pilot becoming a prisoner of war was terrifying. Of course, I'd heard stories of what had happened to some POWs, but in my safe little world in the USA, it all seemed unreal. Suddenly I was forced to think about the possibility of my Jim being in that situation. I knew in my heart then that if he was ever captured, he wouldn't last long because his desire to be free, his need to escape and try to survive, would override everything else. My retreat was my own spiritual foundation and faith in prayer—a lot of it! I prayed for Jim to have the strength to do the right thing in whatever situation he found himself in, and that he would feel Jesus' arms wrapped around him.

Then, there was a happier note, "Well, Frances, I do have some good news. I take command of the 221st Reconnaissance Airplane Company (RAC) at Soc Trang on January 17, 1970! That's the best news I've had since I've been here! It'll be exciting to get back down there. I know it won't be the same, but to command the Shotguns! I'm really excited..."

That news was uplifting because I knew how Jim loved being a Shotgun on his first tour. It warmed my heart that the 12th Group folks had supported his request for a command.

Within a few days, I received a letter telling me that we would be staying in the Hilton Hotel in Tokyo, and I happily prepared for the trip. His November 19 letter said, "When you arrive in Tokyo, change some of your money to yen so you can pay taxi fare from the airport to the hotel. According to the USO, it will cost approximately $3, or 1,000 yen. I'm so happy that you and Diana are traveling together. We'll meet you at the Tokyo Hilton, okay?"

Oh, yes! It was okay with me!

Tokyo

Diana Meyers and I shared letters and phone calls and really looked forward to the trip. It helped me relax and enjoy the planning.

My flight took me from Lubbock through El Paso, Tucson, Los Angeles, and on to San Francisco. I was excited and talked to anyone who would listen to me about my trip. On the leg between Tucson and Los Angeles, I sat next to an older lady who listened to me as I told her about my husband and how excited we were about being together in Tokyo. She listened, smiled, and asked a few questions. Finally, I asked her about her trip.

"My husband and I have been living in South America for the last ten years, but he died suddenly last week. I'm bringing him back for burial near our home in California."

"Oh, I'm so sorry," I managed. "Please accept my sympathy, and please do forgive me for blubbering on about my trip."

"Thank you, but you don't need to apologize," she said. "Now more than ever it's a joy to see someone so excited about seeing her husband."

Our eyes were moist as I squeezed her hand. I shall never forget her sweet graciousness during her difficult time.

Diana and I met at the airport in San Francisco. She was tall, vivacious, trendy and interesting. Our flight stopped in Anchorage, Alaska to take on extra fuel for the twelve-hour flight to Tokyo. I could finally say I'd been somewhere that Jim hadn't been!

We landed at dusk, changed some dollars for yen, gathered our bags, and climbed onto the bus that would take us on the hour-long trip to Tokyo. It seemed to me strange that we had to travel so far from Tokyo International Airport to the city, but I was told that because land was so scarce in Japan, the nearest place for an airport with runways long enough to accommodate large transport jets had been on a landfill on the coast of Japan. It was a long way from Tokyo. We transferred everything to a taxi and arrived at the Tokyo Hilton about 10:00 p.m. I was so weary I could hardly keep my eyes open.

At about 1:00 a.m. there was a knock on the door, and then another. I was like a zombie trying to get out of bed. *Knock, knock, knock!* I finally managed to unlatch the door, and Jim was there. I melted in his arms, and soon it was as if we'd never been apart—so much love, expression, fondness, and wonderful completion of our love for each other. Jim was eager to talk, see pictures, and hear about everything at home.

Jim had never looked better. He weighed less than I'd ever seen him; he was tan and workouts on his ExerGenie really showed. He was in good humor, his career was going well, and he was so excited about commanding his old unit.

We toured various places in Tokyo—gardens and temples, and drove by the emperor's home, which of course no tourist could see. Each evening we ate in a different restaurant, and while sitting on cushions on the floor, I enjoyed my first taste of shrimp tempura with chrysanthemum leaves dipped in raw egg. I loved it! I also loved the Kobe Beef Steakhouse—the food was fantastic, and we didn't have to sit on the floor. We visited a museum where moon rocks from the Apollo landing were displayed. Locked in heavily guarded glass cases, they varied in shape, size, and color, but didn't seem much different from earth rocks. We joined the Meyers to see the famous Russian violinist, David Orstrayck, in concert.

One day, Jim and I took the fast train to Camp Drake, a U.S. base that had a golf course. We were studying the signs at the train station when a pleasant young Japanese man asked, in perfect English, if he could help us. Jim responded, yes, please! After assuring us we were on the right train, he said he was studying English at a university and took every opportunity to speak with

Americans. At Camp Drake, we quickly found the golf course. Jim was able to rent clubs, but there were none for me. Because he was so eager for us to play together, he bought a set of ladies clubs right there! The course was crowded, and it took a long time to play, but Jim was proud of me for what I had learned.

The Sanno BOQ Hotel, where many U.S. Military officers stayed, was right next to the Hilton. It hosted many vendors, so we did some Christmas shopping. We'd planned to buy silverware, but instead bought gold-plated flatware—"gold vermeil" that would *never* have to be polished. That was, and is, true. We shipped everything home along with my new golf clubs.

We cherished each moment of our last night together, and had everything ready for Jim to leave at 6:00 a.m.; however, the phone rang at 2:00 a.m. Just as he'd arrived early, now he had to leave early. It didn't make any sense for these guys to have to be disturbed at ungodly hours, but far be it from me to second-guess the U.S. Military! Our farewell was sweetly quiet; no words could express our feelings—and then he was gone. I tried to keep things in perspective and was so humbly thankful for the time we'd had together.

After the guys left and we'd slept awhile longer, Diana and I had breakfast together, and then checked out of our rooms. At mid-day we were quiet as we boarded the bus for the long trip back to the airport, and finally we were on our way to Honolulu. It dawned on me then—this is Sunday, December 7, 1969, exactly twenty-eight years after that morning in 1941 when Japanese pilots made a trip to Hawaii on a *very different* mission. When I was finally able to doze, I dreamed a weird dream in which I saw a huge and noisy open clothes dryer with red mud churning, turning, and falling out of it. I awakened to the sound of the engines right outside my window. I was relieved there was no mud anywhere!

ing up to Christmas. He was more homesick than ever during the holidays and wrote the children a special letter for me to read to them on Christmas Eve. We'd established a cherished tradition for him to read "Twas the Night Before Christmas" to them, and he was sad to hear from me that they'd heard an older cousin *questioning the status* of Santa Claus.

He also wrote about a very hot project he had to work on in a very short period of time. Soon he was finally able to tell me that Vice President Agnew visited Vietnam on very short notice. He later received the Bronze Star and Army Commendation medals for his part in planning and providing security for the Vice President's visit to the aviation units within 12th CAG. An interesting side to the story that Jim recalls, is how lackadaisical the Press Corps was. They'd been briefed about the importance of leaving each area on time, and it was part of Jim's job to make sure they were all onboard the accompanying aircraft. When they lollygagged, he assured them that if they were not there when they were supposed to be, the aircraft would take off anyway. Once he told them to be onboard a Chinook at a certain time. Sure enough, time was getting away while they were sauntering up to the aircraft. He gave the aircrew a "thumbs up" to get the big helicopter airborne. The pilot returned the gesture and the aircraft began moving. "You should have seen them scramble! There was one guy who was hanging on with his feet dangling in the air, but you know what? They weren't late the next time!"

I waited anxiously each day for his letters that described his activities. To others I probably seemed a bore because I talked so much about him. He looked forward to leaving the 12th CAG to assume command of the 221st on January 17, and was excited at the opportunity to have a combat command. He was also very happy that his most recent OER was one of the best he'd ever had. I was proud of him and glad for him.

Combat Command

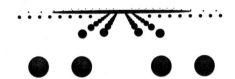

221st Reconnaissance Airplane Company Change of Command

Letters about assuming command from Jim were fun to read. He was bubbly with excitement and comforted to have outstanding officers and First Sergeant on his staff. At first look, the company seemed in fine shape, and they were getting ready for annual inspections. It seemed strange to me that the company would be under the scrutiny of inspectors so soon after he arrived. It didn't make sense to me that he would be found responsible for what had happened during the previous commander's time! He wasn't worried though, and felt that as soon as the inspections were over, he could relax and enjoy it.

His bubble was soon burst as he began to realize the company wasn't in the good shape he'd been led to believe. He wrote, "I can't believe that we're going through such a situation. It's amazing that we have to stop the war to have an inspection!"

When he got his Birddog check ride, he wrote, "I did handle the 'ole bird, and I love flying it … it seems a part of me."

The company did very well on the general inspection (IG) and came out top company in the battalion, but he couldn't relax because they had to get ready for the command material and maintenance inspection (CMMI). I waited anxiously to hear from him, as I remembered the unhappy situations he faced in Italy and the pressure he'd been under due to poor leadership there. He liked his boss, Lieutenant Colonel McRill, whom we'd known at Fort Stewart. They worked well together. Then he wrote that the CMMI was over and they'd passed, but that he'd received a bombshell. He had to give up his outstanding First Sergeant and he'd be getting one that was considered a dud. Now this information put me in a tailspin! As hard as I tried to understand and accept the Army way, it seemed to me Jim was being dumped on. I tried to be calm and encouraging in my letters to him because he certainly didn't need any distress signals from me. He later gladly reported that this Top (as most units fondly refer to the First Sergeant) was as outstanding and perhaps even more so than the first one! I was so glad to hear that.

With another letter he sent an article he'd clipped from the army's newspaper, the *Stars and Stripes*. It was about CW4 Mike Novosel, whom we'd known at Fort Bragg. Mike had received the Medal of Honor for his selfless acts as a Dust Off (medevac) pilot. We weren't surprised at all and were happy for Mike. *Just imagine,* I thought, *we actually know the fellow that's wearing that medal around his neck!*

Jim loved awards ceremonies where his men got promoted and seeing the expressions on their faces, but he also wrote of the disconcerting things—soldiers smoking marijuana, those dealing in money manipulation, and those being caught downtown with girlfriends. It was hard for him to believe the stupid mistakes some of the guys made. He realized that dealing with it was just part of the challenge of being a commander, but it saddened him that the guys wasted themselves. One thing that kept him busy was writing efficiency reports for over forty officers. He lamented that his writing wasn't good enough to do them justice.

Flying the Mohawk for the 244th SAC that was located in Can Tho not far from Soc Trang helped pass the time. When things were quiet at the 221st he'd take late Saturday flights to help out. Once he wrote a letter on a Saturday night before he left to go fly a Mohawk, and I thought his words were especially tender. A fleeting thought passed through my heart, wondering if he was consciously writing those things in case he didn't come back. "I must close for now and go plan my mission. I keep thinking of the wonderful life we have together. It's great when two people like us who've been married for almost thirteen years still have a deep, honest love and devotion for each other. To me, that is the ultimate in happiness..." I rationalized that he always wrote sweet things like that, and he did. I also believed that if anything happened to him, I would know at the very moment...

Even though there was so much negativity, Jim continued to

be optimistic about the war. It was his view in early 1970 that the enemy's capability to fight was not as great as it was in 1966–67. He was afraid, however, that the war might expand to Laos and Thailand.

Although many serving in Vietnam felt like they were winning the war, and some stories like Jim's were reported, the media kept dwelling on the number of casualties, and the anti-war cries burgeoned. The My Lai Massacre didn't help, nor did pictures of civilians caught in napalm rain. All of America was weary of the war. It was brought home to me one day at a ladies' church meeting when a woman I knew quite well started ranting about the war and that we should pull our troops out. I felt personally affronted. She wouldn't look me in the eye when I tried to make the case that our guys *were winning* the war. It was painful and disturbing even though no one else said anything to me, and most within my small acre of life agreed with me. It did bother me that no one seemed to care how the soldiers felt about what they were doing, but they had no qualms about telling the soldiers what they *should* do. It's no wonder many in uniform lost heart and sight of our mission to stem the Red Tide. Every night at bedtime, the children and I knelt at their bedsides with prayers to keep their daddy safe, and I fell into bed lonelier than ever longing for him to be home so we could just get on with our lives. I was so very weary of protesters, the news, the loneliness… only Jim's cards and letters, flowers on special days, and the rare MARS (military telephone system) calls from him helped pass my lonely hours, but there were some light moments. Kevin, Kathy, and I got a kick out of the calls when we'd have to wait until he said "over" before we could talk, then we'd have to say "over" so he could talk. They were so good with it, and liked telling their friends about it. During one such call we talked about our plans for another R&R in Hawaii, and how excited Kevin and Kathy were to be going too!

In the meantime, Jim told about an orphanage that the 221st sponsored. He'd taken a set of crutches that a flight surgeon sent after he'd returned to the states, to a little girl who was Kathy's age. He wrote, "She's very shy, but she crawls to me readily, and I think I have a friend for life. I just wish there was something we could do, but the doctors say she has an incurable spinal problem and nothing can be done. The crutches have been a big help."

Jim inquired about adopting the little crippled girl and bringing her to America, but at every interval it seemed the red tape *and* the cost increased. I responded positively to his query of me about adopting her; however, he began to feel that as an American he was being taken advantage of. It became overwhelming and much too costly. We have thought of the child often and remembered her in our prayers.

On top of everything else, the unit was notified it would be moving to Can Tho about the first of June. The news was disconcerting to Jim because he felt there was no place for a unit that size in Can Tho; furthermore, he didn't have the tents, vehicles, or tractor trucks to make the move! He wrote, "Oh, the wonderful life of a soldier. I'm determined to try to maintain a sense of humor."

Together in Hawaii

The kids were so good on the trip to Honolulu. Marge and Joe met us, dropped me off at the R&R center, and then took the kids to their home while I waited for Jim. Just as we'd hoped, he was soon there. We rented a car and headed for the Diamond Head Holiday Inn. The problems of the world soon seemed far away once we were in each other's arms. We relaxed, shared the time, a little wine, and each other.

It wasn't long, though, before Marge called and said we'd

better come on up because the kids wanted to see their daddy. We used her directions to get out of Honolulu and up to Wahiawa. We chatted happily along the way.

"Do you realize this is my third time to Hawaii in three years?" I asked.

"Wow! Who would've thought that little girl from Fort Sumner would be such a world traveler!"

"It's amazing. I remember when I was a child working in the fields, I'd look up to the east when a train was coming into the valley. I could watch it as it approached the station in town and hear the whistle blow at every crossing... then I could see it climb out of the valley to the west after it crossed the Pecos River. I could see cars and trucks traveling much the same way on Highway 60. And, I'd watch airplanes fly over until I couldn't see them." Jim smiled, and kept his eyes on the highway. "I couldn't wait to grow up. I wanted to go places and see things..."

"Well, you've sure been a few places."

"I guess that's why I married you, huh?"

Our hands clasped, we enjoyed this special time together. Soon we were in Wahiawa.

"Okay, here's the Surf Shop where we turn," I instructed. It was familiar to me after being there in December.

The narrow street wound through the old town, and soon we turned onto the street where Marge and Joe lived and into their driveway.

Kevin and Kathy scampered down the steps, calling, "Daddy! Daddy!" Jim opened the car door, and they flew into his arms.

"My word, look at you two," Jim said as he hugged them. "Look how you've grown! I hardly know you!" He roughed up Kevin's crew cut. "How're you doing, Son?"

"Fine, Dad. Have you been flying much?"

"Sure have, Kev. Golly, it's so good to see you!" They hugged again with Kathy hanging onto her daddy's leg. "Hey, Kathy, my goodness, don't you look pretty!" He lifted her and held her close while she held him as tightly as she possibly could.

"Daddy, I love the dolls you sent me for Christmas."

"Hey, I'm so glad you like them, Kathy. Ohhhhh, aren't you the sweet one!"

Marge and Joe waited on the lanai, and then greeted Jim warmly.

"Hey, you old pea picker, how ya' doin'?" Jim said to Joe as they shook hands.

"Good to see you, Jim. How's our warrior doing? Come in here and let's have a cool one."

We enjoyed Marge's authentic Italian dinner and visited happily while sharing bits of information about others we'd known in Italy. The children were soon tired. I took Kevin's hand and nudged him gently to the car while Jim carried already sleeping Kathy. It seemed a long way back to our hotel in Honolulu.

The next day we took the children to Sea Life Park where they loved watching the trained dolphins and whales perform! We spent time at the Polynesian Cultural Center near Kahuku and Kuilima on the north side of Oahu. We drove on to Waimea Bay made famous by the movie, *From Here to Eternity*, then down through the pineapple fields, through Wahiawa, Schofield Barracks, west through Koli Koli Pass to Waianae, then back to Honolulu. What a beautiful place! The endless view of the turquoise ocean was incredible! That night we enjoyed dinner at The Willows, remembering another evening there in 1967. We talked of the possibility of an assignment in this beautiful place, and dreamed of it happening someday.

On Saturday, we joined the Ritas at Waianae Beach Army Recreation Center, which had cabins and picnic areas right on the beach. We all loved the beach, and it was a nice way to spend the day. The next day was Easter, and we attended services at the military chapel on Fort DeRussy. We felt blessed to be together and to hear the wondrous story again!

The night before we were to leave, Jim and I went to a piano bar in the hotel for one last drink together. The entertainer sang something about leaving on a jet plane. I bit my lip and fought back tears. Jim squeezed my hand, and we sipped our drinks without looking at each other.

The night passed much too quickly. Now it was morning, and we were at the airport saying good-bye... *one... more... time.* Our flights left within an hour of each other, Jim's first. As we hugged, we couldn't keep the tears from coming... it was so hard to see him go back to that crazy war. Then, Kevin, Kathy, and I were on the big jet heading back to the mainland.

Return to Soc Trang

Upon Jim's arrival back in Vietnam, his unit had already moved from Soc Trang to Can Tho. He was very concerned about what a mess everything was in, and on top of that, one of his young pilots, Chief Warrant Officer (CWO) Tom Maehrlein, had been seriously wounded during a mortar attack at his compound over on the Cambodian border. He also told me he finally received the cake I'd sent for his birthday in plenty of time, and paid for the package to go air mail, but wouldn't you know, it went by ship.

So concerned about the pilot that was wounded, Jim went to see him on April 5. He wrote, "He's in a lot of pain, but coming along. He'll soon be on his way home and a long period of recovery. It's a bad way to get an early out of this mess. I have mixed emotions about this war. I want us to win it, yet our country doesn't seem to want to win... all the lives and money seem to be going to waste..."

I could sense his dismay at the lack of support for the war from the country he loved so much, the lack of support for the move to Can Tho, not enough pilot replacements, the loss of aircraft and aircraft engines, and now a very good man badly hurt. He worried about his troops and their poor living conditions following the move, but he was proud of their hard work and tried to do what he could to keep up morale.

In answer to my queries about Mr. Maehrlein, Jim kept me updated. His condition was up and down, and always critical. Finally, just after Jim's last visit to see him, he had improved enough to be evacuated to Japan, and then back to the states.

During the next ninety days, Jim received orders to Fort Huachuca and we fired letters back and forth about how happy we were. The post housing office there sent me all kinds of information about the post, quarters, schools, and facilities. Our folks were happy that we'd be within a day's drive, and Kevin and Kathy were excited about getting to see the 10,000-year-old mummy again! We were also jubilant at being near Don Ray and Mary Beth and resuming our friendship.

Kathy and Ritalin

During that year Jim was away, the children enjoyed school, Sunday school, their friends, cousins, grandparents, Cub Scouts, and Brownies. Kathy took ballet lessons two afternoons a week. I was Cub Scout Den Mother and stayed very busy. I wrote to Jim every day, and we often exchanged a recorded tape. The children loved it and loved making tapes for him. But, even with the stability I thought we had as a family, Kathy struggled. It was hard for her to do all the schoolwork expected. I felt the work, and especially the homework assignments, were much too advanced for second graders. Kevin's third grade work wasn't nearly as severe. Homework time became a struggle between Kathy and me, and sadly, there were unpleasant times. When I made suggestions, she would say, "No, that's not what my teacher wants!" The problem was compounded by Kevin's good behavior, and most of the time, good grades. Kathy couldn't understand why I could compliment him and be upset with her.

Eventually, Kathy's teacher was replaced by another young U.S. Air Force wife with a more sensible approach to teaching. Kathy loved her, but still struggled. This teacher suggested we have Kathy tested to see if we could find the root of her inability to handle the work and some classroom situations. It was her opinion that Kathy was easily distracted and seemed unable to focus on the work. I agreed, and the school district provided the academic testing while the Cannon AFB Hospital system provided physical testing. It took several weeks for the tests to be completed, and they revealed that Kathy was neither mentally retarded nor incapable in any way of doing the work. Quite the contrary, she was healthy and precocious, and as one test administrator said, she was quite the manipulator!

A young medical doctor captain at the Cannon AFB hospital (and recent graduate of one of the Ivy League medical schools), did tests that revealed Kathy was "hyperactive." His diagnosis was that this condition was causing her to be distracted in the classroom, resulting in her inability to do the work. He suggested treatment with a medication called Ritalin. I'd never heard of it and asked him how long children had been taking it. Only recently, he told me, but went on to say there had been startling results in children who had taken the medicine. He said that it was only in recent years that the medical community had been able to focus on behavior problems, that prior to the vaccination era, they were busy just trying to keep children from dying of childhood illnesses. He assured me he'd monitor her carefully.

He also admonished me to pay a lot of attention to Kathy, to try to keep her on a strict schedule, and return to him quickly if problems developed.

Of course I wrote to Jim about all these things, but he responded adamantly that he did not want me to give Kathy pills! I was very torn between what the doctor was saying and what Jim was writing about. He'd read articles about so many kids of all ages and circumstance becoming drug addicts, and he saw no reason to give her pills when she didn't appear to be physically ill. I was so torn, but I also could see the turmoil in Kathy's life. I finally wrote to him saying I thought we should at least give it a try, that we could certainly control things at her age now. He reluctantly agreed and the doctor prescribed the medication.

School was out for the year by the time Kathy began taking Ritalin, but I could immediately see the difference. Rather than running and playing with other children at a picnic that first day, she wouldn't leave my side. I called the doctor and he surmised the dosage was too strong. A lesser amount did the trick. Kathy seemed herself but calmer, was able to sit still, her handwriting improved, and she was much less disruptive. It was a blessing to see her happier with herself.

We had watched as Kathy's personality developed through the years, and saw what a special little girl she was—what spirit she had! But, along with that spirit came a stubbornness—an "I'm gonna try this world on…in my own way…in my own time" attitude. She was constantly into things she shouldn't be, and constantly trying things she'd been told not to. One time when she was about two and a half, she and Kevin were along-side Jim as he worked in the yard. Some larger children were across the street, and Kathy kept trying to cross the street to get to them. Finally, after about the third time of telling her to not go into the street, Jim brought her to the front porch, paddled her, explained to me why, and put her in the house. She was screaming at the top of her lungs and I said to her, "Kathy, you are hurting my ears. You may cry all you want in your own room, but I don't want to hear it." I closed the door and turned away. She immediately opened the door, stopped crying, and marched right back outside!

I'll admit there were a couple of scary incidents, regretfully, because of my negligence. At age three, she ate an entire bottle of baby aspirin that I'd carelessly left out on the bathroom counter. I called a pediatrician who lived down the street. He came immediately, gave her medicine, she threw up, and there were no ill effects, much to my prayerful thankfulness. Another time, a friend borrowed some bleach. She returned it in a jelly glass, placed in on the kitchen counter, and before I remembered to put it where it belonged, Kathy, age seven, drank some of it! I heard her call, "Mommy, what's this? I don't like it!" A call to a doctor resulted in her drinking a large glass of milk, and all was well.

Jim and I weren't perfect parents; we know none who are, but we tried. We wanted our children, they were planned, and we loved them with all our hearts. If something happened while Jim was away, I didn't wait for him to get home to discipline them—I didn't want him to be the "bad guy" that they were afraid of when he got home. I knew I was strong enough to take care of whatever situation there was at the time, give the appropriate punishment, and move on.

One time Jim was playing the game Chutes and Ladders with Kevin and Kathy on the floor of the living room. He became increasingly frustrated when five-year-old Kathy refused to, or could not understand the organization of the game, and insisted on placing her game piece wherever she wanted. He gave up, came into the kitchen where I was cleaning up, puckered his lips, shook his head and went, "*Bleeewww,* I don't know what to do with her! She reminds me of me when I was little because I was always in trouble. Doggone it, she's supposed to be like you, not like me!" I didn't know what to say, but we both knew to keep loving and taking care of our children. Sometimes in groups Kathy would get frustrated because she couldn't always be the star, and there were resulting problems. Strangely enough, she always had friends. A big problem was that Kathy had always wet the bed. I talked with doctors and read all I could about it. I did know that if I punished her for wetting the bed, we would always have problems manifested in one way or another. It was not hard for me to change her bed everyday, although I sure didn't like it. I limited her liquids in the evening, and when she was old enough I tried to explain to her what was going on. She willingly helped take off the sheets in the morning and took them to the washer. And then, *well, glory be!* Ritalin helped in this area considerably!

Kathy took Ritalin only on school days and did *very* well in third grade. Just before her fourth grade year, a different doctor at Fort Huachuca suggested we have her start school without the medicine. But, just about four weeks into the year, Mr. Williams, her incredibly talented teacher whom she adored, called me in for consultation. It was the same story—Kathy's disruptive behavior, her inattention, and inability to adjust to classroom situations. He described her handwriting as "chicken-scratching" and he wondered if something was wrong at home. So, Mr. Williams got the story, as did then her fifth and sixth grade teachers because we were hopeful at the beginning of each year she'd do okay without the pills. Each time when she was put back on Ritalin, she was able to absorb without demanding attention and disrupting the class.

Kathy was on Ritalin for five years. As she grew the dosage

was decreased, and when she had doubled her weight and the dosage was half the original, the doctor felt Ritalin had done all it was going to do for her. Although still hyper, she was able to manage very well. I believe in Ritalin, *properly monitored by parents and doctors.* In the meantime she had an older brother that deserved some attention too!

As the year wound down and baseball was in the air, Jim and I were happy that Kevin wanted to play little league baseball. He was selected by the "Phillies" and loved it. Sadly, the team didn't do very well and I had to write Jim about the sad situation. He always wrote back with wonderful words of encouragement, and when Kevin earned a starting position and the team began to win, he was so excited! I think I missed Jim during that time more than any the entire year because, I knew how much he loved the game and working with the boys. Mamaw and Papaw came to almost every game and that was a very nice thing for us all.

One night not long before Jim came home, I was kissing Kathy goodnight after she'd said her prayers. I said to her, "Just think, Kathy, only six weeks until Daddy's home!" She looked up at me and said, "You mean my Daddy's not dead?" I was shocked! Where in the world did she get that idea? But I just said to her, calmly, "No, Kathy. Just wait. I'll bet we have another letter from Daddy tomorrow!" She seemed content, but in my own room I prayed, "Dear Lord, please let these next six weeks pass quickly…"

Tucson

We'd agreed to meet in Tucson this time so we could drive down to Fort Huachuca and Jim could sign in to get his name on the quarters list. I flew from Clovis and landed a short while after he arrived. From the aircraft window I saw him standing there waiting, looking, and I waved, even knowing he couldn't see me. I have no conscious recollection of getting off the aircraft or walking onto the tarmac where he was waiting. He came to me, and I was in his arms.

He'd already rented a car and motel room, so we were soon on our way. After a couple of frustrating missed turns, we found the way to Interstate 10, downtown Tucson, and the plantation-style motel that seemed a little out of place in the desert. It didn't matter.

The next day we drove to Fort Huachuca, where Jim signed in at the U.S. Army Combat Surveillance and Electronic Warfare School. The post and surrounding desert and mountains were familiar, the air fresh and clear, and we realized we were already lost in the beauty of that special place. We were so glad we were going to live there! We drove out the main gate into Sierra Vista, where the Martins had moved from California just a few weeks before.

What a joy to see them and their two little boys! The happiness we felt about being assigned there and being near these good friends was incredible. We spent one night before driving back to Tucson to take the flight that took us to Silver City, Albuquerque, and on to Clovis. There was one scary moment in Silver City when the ticket agent told Jim he might not make the flight because he was flying military stand-by. It was hard for him to keep his cool, but he did, and fortunately a seat was available.

Everyone met us at the airport. Christine and her family joined us for dinner at Mamaw and Papaw's. We listened to Papaw's beautiful table grace that he always began, "We thank you, dear Lord, for these and all other blessings ..."

We had to be out of our house by August 1, and the days passed quickly. We spent several days with Grandma and then took the children for a stay at Hickman's Guest Ranch at Red

River. The time there with the children was sweet. Jim helped them fish, and we watched as Kathy caught her first fish! The mountains echoed her enchanting squeals and the moment stood still on the banks of that beautiful lake.

It wasn't so hard to leave our folks this time. We knew we'd be just one day's drive away.

Amarillo, Summer 1970:
(back row, left to right) Grandma McGraw, Jim, Fran, Nita, and Ghern, (front row, left to right) Revena, Kevin, Kathy, and E'Laine.

Family Life in the Arizona Desert

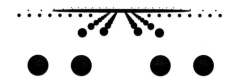

120 Crandal

At Fort Huachuca, we learned we'd have quarters in about a week. For now we'd stay in a guesthouse apartment on main post near the museum, theater, and parade field. Built in the 1880s, the guesthouse had large, charming screened-in porches. Several other families were there, and the children enjoyed getting to know and playing with one another.

Jim's sponsor was Major Jerry Collamore. Jerry and his wife, Merle, and their four children welcomed our family for dinner in their huge turn-of-the-century quarters. We wondered if we'd be eligible for something similar; however, these quarters had four bedrooms and were assigned only to families with four or more children of both sexes. We wouldn't get these older quarters, but we were grateful that we were eligible for the newer flat-roof-southwestern-style that had three bedrooms, two baths, and a carport.

Our quarters were at the corner of Wilcox and Crandal streets. We moved the third week in August, only to learn that our house would be painted just after Labor Day. We couldn't unpack everything until that was done. What a bummer! But heck, what's a few more days after the year just past? We were together.

However, we couldn't understand why the quarters needed to be painted. We could see no problems and I loved the pale pink walls in our bedroom. The bouquet of daisies in the miniature water-bowl-pitcher on the dresser appeared quite perky. When the room was painted an off white, you could hardly see them! However, we had no choice as to whether or not to paint, when to paint, nor were we given a choice of colors. Oh well, considering everything else, that was small potatoes. The quarters were roomy and all the rooms had wall-to-wall windows on at least one wall that were covered with venetian blinds. We walked from the carport through a nicely fenced-in patio and then into the kitchen/dining area. The kitchen was small but adequate—although we had to purchase our own dishwasher. I had certainly become used to that! There were big windows where I could have used more cabinets, but hey, there was a nice area for our dining table and a long, wide living room with wall-to-wall-ceiling-to-floor windows and the currently-popular sliding glass door on the west side. That entire wall had ready-made insulated drapes that hung from ceiling to floor with pull rods to move them back and forth. We were so thankful the drapes shaded the west-side windows in the afternoon. There was a nice nine foot patio that ran the length of the living room, and two shade trees. All three bedrooms were nice sizes, and a small room just off the seldom-used front door was wonderful for a desk and filing cabinet. From the driveway in front of the carport, the sidewalk angled in an L-shape around a storage area that opened onto the patio. What a blessing that was without a garage! There was honeysuckle on the south side of the carport, and Oleander bushes, prickly pear cactus, and other bushes that rounded out the landscaping. We thought we were in heaven!

Our next-door neighbors were Cliff and Rose Walker with children Connie and Clifford. Cliff had flown the Huey helicopter in Vietnam. Rose grew up in Germany. She and I were the same age, and I couldn't help but compare my childhood on the farm, where we were safe and had plenty of food, with hers in war-torn Germany. They were wonderful neighbors.

Kathy and Connie were good friends and walked to school together every day. When the Walkers moved to Okinawa, Kathy missed her little friend and cried so that my heart ached too.

We were close to everything on the post, except Jim's work at Libby Army Airfield about three miles away. We had to have two cars, so Jim bought a little Toyota Corolla. It was great for his commute to work, the golf course, and little league games. We so enjoyed time with Don Ray's family, and joined them on Labor Day weekend for a trip to the Chiricahua Mountains. They had a pop-up camper, and we were able to rent one from U.S. Army Special Services.

We camped near Rucker Lake where it was cool and comfortable, but on Saturday night we were awakened by clanging noises in our campsite. Jim and Don sprang to action with their flashlights and beamed them out toward the noise. There were bears in the trashcans! They shooed the bears away, secured the trashcans, and finally after the children had calmed down, we were able to settle down again. The children loved talking about the bears at our campsite!

Kevin began fourth grade at General Myer Elementary while Kathy began third grade at Captain Whitside School. They walked to school with friends; they were happy and did very well. The theater was close enough for them to join their friends on Saturdays for the movie matinee. They rode bikes, went mountain climbing and fishing, and had about the best time kids could have anywhere. Most of the days were bright and sunny. We continued to love this quiet place in southeastern Arizona. Life was perfect...

Hopes and Dreams

At Fort Bragg, Fort Stewart, and in Vietnam, Jim had received outstanding efficiency reports. The reports had boosted his morale and whetted his appetite for a military career. We thought that his appointment as a Regular Army officer following grueling tests and interviews, along with the outstanding reports, would most certainly overshadow the marginal OERs from Italy. He'd been awarded the Distinguished Flying Cross, three Bronze Stars, twenty-six air medals, the Army Commendation medal, the Vietnamese Cross of Gallantry (2), and others. He would soon be eligible for consideration for selection to attend Command and General Staff College (C&GSC) at Fort Leavenworth, Kansas. We really hoped to be at Fort Huachuca at least two years before another move; nevertheless, we were looking forward to it all.

We participated in chapel, unit, and community social activities. Jim and I were leaders for Boy Scouts and Camp Fire Girls. We were busy. We eventually joined the little Methodist Church in Sierra Vista, where the Martins were members.

We established a friendly relationship with Bob and Joyce Stachel whose son, Bobby, was Kevin's age. Bob and Jim had worked together in Vietnam and had a deep respect for each other. Joyce and I enjoyed golfing and bowling together, and she seemed to delight in Kevin and Kathy. Upon learning that she couldn't have more children, she needed more to keep busy and became a real estate agent. They bought a house in Sierra Vista and moved, but Bobby stayed with us often. He was one of our favorites of Kevin's friends.

Combat Surveillance and Electronic Warfare School

Jim was assigned as Chief, Maintenance Branch, in the Combat Surveillance School's Airborne Sensors Department, where pilots and enlisted observers trained in the surveillance qualification classes—just as he had done the year before. He supervised civilian instructors who taught maintenance of the sophisticated equipment. Fortunately, he was able to fly a lot. As always, he formed friendships among his peers, and we enjoyed the company of several couples. His boss was Lieutenant Colonel Cecil O. Carlisle. Friends and associates dubbed him Good Old Cecil O, and it stuck like glue. We had good times with Cecil and his wife, Betty, but Good Old Cecil O was a hunter and fisherman, not a golfer.

Some of the men who worked for Jim were Masons, and they invited him to attend lodge—King Solomon Lodge number five, the oldest in Arizona, in Tombstone about twenty miles away. Jim enjoyed being part of this benevolent fraternal order and moved his membership there from his lodge in Georgia.

Even though we were so busy we played golf every chance we had. I played with ladies on Thursdays and any other time I could manage. Jim generally played on Saturdays—and any other time he could manage, and we played with couples on Sunday afternoon if the children were with friends. Sometimes they went along with us. I loved the game, but I could not give it priority. There was simply too much going on with children's activities, and besides, I really enjoyed just being home.

One difficulty we did face was that Sierra Vista was a small town and shopping was limited. At least once a month we drove the eighty miles to Tucson for major shopping concerns and for any attention our car might need. In late spring 1971, we took our big blue convertible to Tucson for some warranty work. Well, there *just happened* to be a beautiful blue Chrysler Fifth Avenue with white vinyl top, loaded, and with cruise control and cassette player on the lot. It *just happened* to be a demonstrator with a well-discounted price that made this car-of-our dreams affordable. We traded for it that day, and what a fun trip we had going home! That new cruise control was something else; as was the cassette player with a complimentary tape of the best music we'd ever heard—Glenn Campbell, Tom Jones, Englebert Humperdinck, and others. Life was perfect … almost …

Jim was not selected for C&GSC in 1971. He was not that upset because he felt his time would be later anyway, and we were glad we didn't have to move. Then, in May, Good Old Cecil O was reassigned, and the unit had a farewell party for him and Betty. Jim was in charge of the arrangements, so I sat next to Cecil. We chatted happily during the meal.

"I can't say enough about the outstanding job Jim's done this year," Cecil told me. "He's a fine officer, and I'm proud to have served with him."

"Thank you so much," I answered. "I think he's pretty special too."

"I'd like to serve with him again one of these days."

"I'm sure Jim would like that too," I responded.

So, it was a *terrible* shock when Good Old Cecil O gave Jim his OER.

"You're kidding, aren't you, sir? Come on, sir, where's the real one?"

"That's it, Jim."

"Sir, you know this is a killer," Jim said as his stomach began to churn. He hadn't been upset about an OER since Italy.

"I wanted to give you a higher rating, Jim, because I think you deserve it, but General Albright has made it clear that we have to go by the book. He's said in no uncertain terms that he will not let OERs go out of his command if he feels they're inflated. I rated you at over ninety percent, and yours is the best of the bunch."

When Jim told me about his OER we both sat, stunned. The next day we drove to Tucson and talked all the way.

"That son of a gun! I can't believe he did that to me! Well, I'm just going to have to overcome it," Jim said. "The only problem is I probably won't get selected for C&GS, and my chances for promotion to RA major may not be good."

"I can't believe he did that either, Jim, especially after what he told me at the party."

"It's just the way the system's working now that everything's being cut back. Man, I sure hate that we have to deal with this."

Since Jim had received the Regular Army commission, he was hopeful of being selected to special schools. He was now an RA captain, and it would be a couple more years before he'd be eligible for RA major. The rank was so important because, as an RA Major, even if you were not selected for promotion to the rank of Lieutenant Colonel, you could stay twenty years and retire. We'd seen officers caught in reduction-in-force periods, commonly called "the RIF." Many no-longer-indispensable army aviators were caught in this situation as the Vietnam War wound down.

"What would it mean if you were caught in the RIF?" I asked.

"It means I'd have to leave the army, but they do give you a certain amount of cash when you leave. I think it's about $10,000."

"That would help."

"Yeah, but that's not much these days. If you're a major and get RIFfed, you can come back in as a warrant officer *if* the army needs you, and then when you retire after twenty years, you retire as a Major. It's not so bad, except for the stigma of being RIFfed."

Three other officers in Jim's unit were hurt seriously by the OERs Good Old Cecil O gave them. One Major chose to resign, one reverted to Warrant Officer, and a Captain reverted to a previously held enlisted rank to be able to retire.

New boss, Lieutenant Colonel Ted Wright, arrived that fall. The atmosphere was upbeat, but unit social activities increased. Jim and I were asked to attend once-a-month dinner parties for VIP students. It was obvious that he had the respect of his peers and bosses, and he always seemed proud to have me by his side.

When General William Westmoreland visited Fort Huachuca just before he retired, Jim was one of only two majors from the Combat Surveillance School selected to be invited to the general's reception. A firestorm arose, however, and we were relieved when *all* field grade officers were invited! What a reception it was! I remember shaking the general's hand and thinking, *Oh my, this man is one of the most gorgeous I have ever seen!*

Jim was not on the selection list for Command and General Staff College in 1972. We were disappointed this time.

"I'll just keep on working like I have been, Frances. It's all I know to do."

"You'll be all right, Jim," I told him. "You're a fine officer, and I'm so proud of you."

Subsequent OERs at Fort Huachuca pleased Jim; however, the war was grinding to a close. Many officers left the service, and Jim learned his ranking among Signal Corps Officers was now in the top of the bottom third, rather than the bottom of the top third.

"I just can't outlive those early OERs," he told me.

I watched my proud warrior continue working, contributing, and looking good. He deserved better.

Visits Home

That summer, we took a couple of weeks off and drove to Clovis and Amarillo. Then we joined Don Ray's family at Creede, Colorado. The first day out on I-10, just west of Las Cruces, New Mexico, our new car's performance indicated it was running out of gas.

"Shoot, I hoped we'd make it to Las Cruces," Jim said, as the car began jumping along. "I didn't have a feel for when this new car would get empty. *Dadgummit!*"

We were on the downhill slope of the west side of the Rio Grande River Valley, and we must have coasted for two miles before we were able to turn right into a gas station! *Another prayer answered*—I was sure of it! Another car was there, and a man was looking under the hood. The station operator came out, and Jim noticed he had a pistol strapped to his belt. He looked us over and said, "I'm sure glad you came along. I was getting ready to close up," he nodded toward the man and said quietly, "but I'm worried about that guy over there. I should've already closed, but he just keeps hangin' around. Sure would appreciate it if you'd stick around for a few minutes."

We'd heard recent stories about stations being robbed just at closing time. Soon the other fellow closed the hood of his car and drove off. Jim filled the car with gas, and we were on our way. *Maybe we were an answer to the station operator's prayers,* I thought.

We spent the night with Aunt Winnie and Uncle EJ in El Paso, and the next morning drove to Carlsbad Caverns. Jim and I enjoyed seeing the famous fissure again, and the kids had a ball! We drove on to Lubbock where Moreland and Christine now lived. We had a great family gathering as all six of the Ogden kids and our families were together with Mamaw and Papaw.

Papaw had a mustache and goatee—we thought he looked like Colonel Sanders of KFC fame!

Then, we were off to see Grandma. Sis and her family came also, and we helped celebrate Grandma's seventy-third year. She was happy and seemed as strong as ever. We visited Jim's hometown, Borger, and joined several of his high school friends at the country club in a scramble golf tournament. Jim looked especially good in slightly-belled light blue slacks, matching golf shirt, white shoes, and wide white belt—the look of the early seventies. I overheard the teenage daughter of one of Jim's high school friends tell her mother that she thought Jim was cute. I saw him a bit differently after that…

At Creede, the guys did some fly fishing while the gals and kids hiked, picked flowers, and collected rocks. The last night we were there, Abbi became acquainted with a friendly, yet fragrant skunk. What a mess! Jim bathed her as best he could, but the trip to Albuquerque the next day was miserable. We bought tomato juice, sneaked her into our motel room, and bathed her in it. It helped some. At least tomato juice smells better than skunk!

Survivor Assistance Officer

In summer 1972, Jim was appointed as a survivor assistance officer for a couple living near Phoenix whose son was missing following a helicopter crash in Southeast Asia. Jim made periodic trips to see Retired Army Colonel and Mrs. Toomey to give them the most recent Department of the Army information.

These sad parents were gracious to Jim, but the trips were physically and emotionally draining. The U.S. Army provided a military sedan and credit card for gas, but the sedan was not air-conditioned. Traveling three to four hours to and from Phoenix in an un-air-conditioned car, sometimes in over one-hundred-degree temperatures was unbearable. Jim chose to drive his own car and pay for the gas—without reimbursement. He did not want his "tan-worsted" uniform, or TWs that had to be dry cleaned, to look bad when he arrived at the Toomeys.' I agreed with him—it was worth every penny.

Then, on one of those trips to Phoenix, there was the time he stopped in Tucson for gas. A young woman carrying a child in her arms stopped, looked at him, spat at him, and yelled, "Baby killer!" Jim was shocked beyond belief, and the scene has never left him. His love of his country and the uniform he wore meant everything. But news accounts persisted of the My Lai story four years earlier where women and children were killed, and those who were so against the war tried to diminish the American soldier by making him the "bad guy" instead of the Communist enemy. The sight of the uniform added fuel to their fire. It was little comfort to learn others had experienced similar treatment—it only added fuel to our feeling of contempt for the protesters.

It didn't help Jim's spirit either to see news broadcasts after the Vietnam War that showed equipment including helicopters and other aircraft being dumped from U.S. Navy vessels into the ocean. I listened as he shouted curse words at the TV directed at Congress, and asking how they could let that happen. He wondered why they didn't know *how hard* he had worked to take care of his troops and aircraft; *how hard* he had worked to get replacement aircraft and parts; *how hard* it was to see his men wounded; and now, *how hard* it was to realize that the people of South Vietnam that he'd worked so hard to keep from being oppressed, were taken over by Communists! I tried to console him saying it wasn't his fault that the war had been lost. In fact, it was my feeling that it had not been lost; yes, maybe for South Vietnam it was, but after all, there had not been a total Red covering of Asia as some had expected when America pulled out. Jim just couldn't find too much comfort in that after all he'd been through.

That war has never, will never leave us. He didn't get a welcome home from anybody but friends and family. It hurt him so that there were those who treated the military with disgust. We talked about the children of the orphanage and the little girl without use of her legs that he'd taken crutches to. We wondered what became of them all under an oppressive government that had no regard for the individual—only the "state."

Just before the POWs returned to America in February 1973, and before all the names were released, Jim was directed to tell the Toomeys that their son was not in that group. Jim asked me if I'd go with him, and I did. He called in advance so they knew we were coming, and they were very gracious when we arrived. Jim and the Colonel visited a while, and Mrs. Toomey took me to their backyard to show me their orange and lemon trees. She told me about their daughter-in-law who was so torn because she was lonely and wanted to get on with her life; on the other hand, it was hard to give up the idea that her husband might be alive somewhere. It was a tragic and sad time. As we drove home, neither of us had much to say. Then, when the POWs' return was televised, we cheered, but we also cried.

In 1990, Major Samuel Toomey III was laid to rest at Arlington Cemetery in a group burial. The Vietnamese government had finally allowed the U.S. to search for remains of missing military personnel. Major Toomey's remains were not positively identified, but the remains of others on his team aboard the helicopter were.

Surgery, Again . . .

In the spring of 1973, Jim complained about lower abdomen pain. The flight surgeon's examination revealed a hernia on his left side.

"Doc, I've already had a hernia fixed on the right side."

"When was that, Jim?"

"In sixty-four."

"You have one on the left side now, and it'll have to be fixed, or you'll be grounded. If you ever had to punch out of that Mohawk, the jolt of the ejection would rip your insides out."

"Whoa! I don't want that to happen. Schedule me for surgery quick!"

Jim made it through the surgery fine and recuperated well. He was a good patient and took good care of himself because he wanted to get back to flying and to the golf course!

Having medical care through the military was a big deal for us. We also tried to not take the system for granted by taking care of ourselves and our children. More than once the thought crossed my mind as to how in the world did people manage health problems if they couldn't afford medical care. To me, it was a matter of how you wanted to live your life. You must decide what you want, set goals, plan, and work to that end.

As for us, Jim wanted to fly and I respected his dream, but we'd had to work hard during college years to figure out how to accomplish that. We also had to postpone having children we dearly wanted. After serving some time as an enlisted man in the New Mexico National Guard and learning about the military's flying programs, medical care and other benefits, Jim thought about how he would have received a commission as a second lieutenant if he'd completed ROTC at Oklahoma A&M. So, we set a goal and planned to that end. With me in total agreement,

Jim transferred from ENMU to West Texas State University and re-entered ROTC. For a part of that time, we lived with his parents until we could manage an apartment of our own. Overall, it took six years for Jim to finish college because some of his college credits didn't transfer, but he was working toward his dream—our dream.

The army gave Jim the opportunity to fly, and he repaid his commitment by serving another three years following flight school. He could have easily resigned and applied to the airlines to fly, but we knew of several who'd made that choice and were soon furloughed. Some had to restructure their lives completely which left them and their families in turmoil. We certainly wanted to avoid that; furthermore, if Jim stayed twenty years and retired from the Army, he was promised medical benefits for life. It all seemed worth it to us.

Chiefs, Chiefs, Chiefs!

In 1970, Kevin had his first football experience. We supported his team, the Chiefs, and went to all five games, but saw him get to play only one down the entire season. We couldn't help but be disappointed.

That next fall, the Army Dependant Youth Activities (ADYA) office announced that teams for a post league would soon be selected, and made a call for coaches. Kevin said he wanted to play football again.

Overall, Jim had played football for twelve years and he loved the game. So did I. I had watched my two brothers and two brothers-in-law play, and had learned so much about the game from them that Jim had been impressed when we met.

"Jim, why don't you coach the Chiefs this year, since none of the coaches returned?" I asked.

"Frances, I just don't think it's a good idea for a man to coach his own son. If I did, I'd always be accused of playing favorites."

"Do you want him to sit on the bench again? I don't think he learned anything last year. Who's going to teach him to play?"

"You think I can do it?"

"Of course you can!"

"Well, if I can coach the Chiefs I'll do it, but I'm not going to show Kevin any favoritism."

"I know you won't, Jim. You're just not made that way. But you can teach him things that no one else can because he'll respond to you. I'm sure of it, and you'll have other guys to help."

"Okay, I'll check it out."

The teams that year in Kevin's nine-to-twelve age group were the Chiefs, Cardinals, Rams, and Raiders. They played each other twice. Jim was thrilled with the coaching experience and loved his players! Coaches Rice and Chadwick helped, and they were a credit to the team. Jim sent a letter to the boys' parents about his coaching credentials, philosophy, his care of the boys, and how he'd manage the games. He explained what officials were supposed to do, and appealed to the parents to support the team while respecting coaches and officials. Not a negative incident occurred that year. He and Coach Rice worked with Kevin at linebacker and fullback. With Jim's attention and insistence *that he pay attention,* Kevin did very well. He captured the concept of blocking and loved it! The time for Kevin and Jim was priceless.

Football Family

ADYA also wanted a cheerleader program coordinator, so Jim asked if I'd be interested. I said yes because I'd been a cheerleader five years in junior high and high school. It was also an opportunity for me to be close to Kathy in a different environment. Each football team had a set of cheerleaders; sisters had to cheer for their brother's team, and each group had an adult leader.

Games were on Saturday at Brock Field. Built of native rock in the 1920s, the charming stadium was not far from all quarters. Those autumn Saturdays were almost always cool, brisk, and sunny. I made memories of that time and place that would never leave me. It was a beautiful, special time in our lives.

Parents were all complimentary of Jim and his coaching

staff, despite the team's losing record. Following the last game, Jim hugged all the boys, tears streaming down. He and Kevin couldn't wait for next year!

The 1972 season brought more boys and more coaches. Major Rob Robinson was an incredible offense coach, and CW2 Chadwick again coached the line. Good, new players joined the team. Kevin improved playing linebacker and fullback. He scored a couple of touchdowns, and his blocking talents increased. What fun to see him block an opposing player as his teammate scampered into the end zone! This season was successful, as the Chiefs lost only one game. Jim loved the boys and seeing them work and improve. Kathy was a happy cheerleader, and very proud of her dad and brother.

The 1973 season was bigger and better. There were more teams, more boys, more coaches, and ten games to play. Captains Barzscz and Olson, who worked for Jim, joined the coaching staff. For me, there were more cheerleaders to organize, more mothers to work with, and more uniforms to make. I loved it all.

At mid-season, Jim had to leave, as our three years at Fort Huachuca were over. He had received orders to helicopter school at Fort Rucker en route to an assignment at Fort Benning. Jim was granted permission for the children and me to stay behind so we could move during the holidays. Jim flew home for the final game, and what a happy former coach he was. The boys still called him Coach! He was proud of all the boys who had improved and had played with such spirit. There weren't many dry eyes among players, coaches, cheerleaders, or parents. This season was the best yet; the Chiefs did not lose a game!

Happy as the time was for our family, it turned out to be not so great for Jim's career. With the winding down of the Vietnam War, U.S. Army Aviation took some hits—there were simply too many aviators. Jim was told he needed a ground assignment to "punch his ticket," and he received permanent change of station (PCS) orders to Fort Benning, Georgia. There he'd be assigned as the signal officer for the 197th Infantry Brigade, and would not be on flying status.

"Why do they want you to go to helicopter school if they want you to take a three-year ground assignment?" I asked.

"That's just the way the system works, Frances. You know ours is not to wonder why; ours is to function and comply," he said. *Well, I'd heard that phrase more than once!* "Besides," he continued, "it sure won't hurt to be dual-rated."

The Ford "Pinto" station wagon that had served Jim so well as a coach was packed, we said our goodbyes, and he was gone . . . again. It was never easy to see him go because I just flat-out enjoyed being with him. I missed his talks with the kids at mealtime, his appreciation of meals and my housework, our end-of-day conversations, and always his touch. Now with him gone I had to get the children to school, to Boy Scouts, Camp-fire Girls, football and cheerleading practice, Sunday School and church. I dealt with their cuts and bruises and fusses with each other. But, I was pretty accustomed to Jim's being away, and managed okay. I'd also been elected president of the Ladies Golf Association in the spring, so I stayed busy and the time passed. Thankfully the children did well in school, and Jim called often which helped a lot.

We didn't like being separated, though, and when Jim called after his visit home, we couldn't stand it.

"I don't like being apart," I said, almost crying.

"I don't either, Frances. Do you want to come on down?"

Without even considering all the complications, I said, "Yes!"

"Okay, I'll find us a place to live if you really want to come. You know you'll have to clear quarters and drive all the way by yourself."

"Yes, I want to; I can do it," I sobbed. "I think the kids want to, and they'll be all right. They're both doing well in school."

"Okay. I'll call transportation and get things started. I'll call you tomorrow night. I'm glad, Frances. I miss you all so much."

Kevin and Kathy were okay about moving. It seemed harder for Kathy because she had some dear little friends that she enjoyed so much; but they missed their daddy, and had so many questions about helicopter school. It was exciting that he was going to be a helicopter pilot!

Jim made the necessary arrangements, and as I prepared to clear quarters myself, I got appointments for us to have physicals. The children were fine, but I was not. I didn't feel bad, but the doctor said I had fast-growing fibroid tumors in my uterus and I should have a hysterectomy immediately. I explained to him that I needed time to get to Fort Rucker and on to Fort Benning.

"That will probably be okay," he said, "but see the doctors at Fort Benning as soon you can. We just don't know how fast the tumors will grow, and if you notice any bleeding, get to a doctor as fast as you can. In fact, I know the head of the OB-GYN Clinic at Benning, and I'll call him and tell him about you."

I felt fine, had plenty of energy for the move, and cleared quarters by myself on Friday, November 30. The car was loaded with six weeks of necessities. Abbi, the kids, and I were ready to be on our way to Fort Rucker. But, wait! Almost at the last minute we remembered that Saturday, December 1 was the day of the little league all-star football game in Tucson! Kevin was starting fullback, and Kathy was an all-star cheerleader! Oh, okay, we had to do what we had to do. So, we spent that Friday night with the Martins, and the next day did a detour through Tucson. The Fort Huachuca All-Stars won the game; we said our good-byes, found ourselves on I-10 going east, and made it to Aunt Winnie's house in El Paso around 9:00 p.m. We were exhausted!

The next day, we drove to Clovis. I loved driving through the New Mexico desert and mountains. We all sang along with the radio, those especially good songs of the 1970s. One we loved singing was Eddy Arnold's "It's Such a Pretty World Today."

My folks were puzzled that I wanted to undertake this trip across the Southern USA by myself with the children.

"It's not good being apart," I said. "We all need to be together." I knew they understood.

"Be careful, Frances," Mother admonished as we left for Amarillo.

"Oh, I will. You don't have to worry about that. There's too much at stake," I said as we hugged. "The best thing for me on this trip is cruise control!" The federally mandated fifty-five-mile-per-hour speed limit was especially painful on southwest highways.

We spent time with Grandma in Amarillo, and at Jim's prodding, I had some routine warranty work done on the Chrysler while there. The mechanic said there was a problem, and that if I had driven the car just a few more miles it could have been very serious. The warranty took care of it, and we were soon on our way. "Thank you, Lord," I prayed with humble heart. We stopped at Altus Air Force Base to see Doyle. Preparing to retire in January, he'd already relocated his family to Granbury, Texas.

"Where has the time gone, Doyle?"

"I don't know, Frances," he said, shaking his head, "seems just like yesterday I was an Aviation Cadet in San Antonio."

"Oh, I know. It's hard for me to believe Jim's been in the Army thirteen years!"

We drove on to Keesler Air Force Base, Mississippi, where Marge and Joe Rita lived. Jim flew from Dothan, Alabama, to Biloxi, and Joe picked him up there. Things seemed strained in the Rita household, and we were heartbroken to learn their marriage was ending. From Mississippi to Alabama we reflected on what had happened to the friends we'd known in Italy. Joan and Phil already divorced, Dick Hollar died from cancer, and now Marge and Joe were splitting. We listened to Charlie Pride's "Kiss an Angel Good Morning" and squeezed each other's hands. We had talked often about what broke up Joan and Phil. We'd decided they were two very strong personalities that just didn't mesh. That was sad because they looked so good together. We remember them saying things to each other that we thought hurtful—and in front of us, no less. I'd remembered Joan mentioning that Jim and I seemed to get along so well. I told her that I still remembered the reasons I married him in the first place! Once, when she asked me if I was going to spend the summers with my parents, I answered no, that as much as I cared for my parents and all my family, I never wanted to be with them more than I wanted to be with Jim. She seemed amused at my answer and stated that she would always spend as much time with her family as she could. I just couldn't see a marriage working well that way, especially when you're military. As for Marge and Joe, their backgrounds were so different in the first place; Joe was the son of Italian immigrants who lived in Pennsylvania, and Marge was a farm girl from New Mexico. Joe was Catholic and Marge was Protestant, so they raised one child Catholic and one Protestant. It seemed an odd way to us to meld a marriage and raise children, but we certainly never voiced our opinions. That was theirs to work out, and there were probably dynamics we knew nothing about, and never will, even though they both remain our dear friends.

Deer Park Mobile Home Park, Daleville, Alabama

Jim found a mobile home for us in an unusually nice area and park outside of town. It was fine for the next six weeks; although, we did get pretty weary of only two bedrooms. The larger bedroom had twin beds for the kids, and Jim and I slept on a double bed in the small middle room. The kitchen had modern appliances and there was also a washer/dryer combination. It wasn't the nice, roomy mobile home we'd had during Mohawk training, but we had to take what we could get for such a short period of time. Another problem was that K&K had to go to a school several miles away rather than in the town of Daleville, so they caught a bus to school each day. They didn't like riding the bus at all, but settled into it and we were pleased at how well they did for the six weeks they were in that school. Once daily chores were accomplished, I headed to the golf course with the wife of one of Jim's instructors. On Christmas Day after opening our presents, we drove to Atlanta to be with John and Cynthia. Now with two little girls, Jill and Andrea, they lived in the upscale Dunwoody neighborhood. What joy to be with family at Christmas in that lovely setting!

In mid-January 1974, helicopter training was over. "It'll probably be a long time before I get to fly a helicopter again," Jim said. "With a three-year ground assignment, I'll probably forget how to fly it."

We cleaned the mobile home, packed the car, got the kids and their school records, said good-bye to friends, and headed for Fort Benning, the "Home of the Infantry." We checked into guest housing just outside the main gate.

Life With the Combat-Ready Infantry

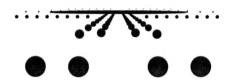

213 Blessing Street

A blessing on Blessing Street is what our quarters were. They were red brick with some white wood siding and white trim. We could have had quarters up in the main post area that were much older, two-story and so very charming in that tree-lined area; however, with my surgery looming we felt the one-story set was best. We also had a carport that many other quarters did not have. Besides that, our furniture fit perfectly. The entry way accommodated the small antique chest that I'd refinished the first time Jim was in Vietnam; our round breakfast table and chairs fit beautifully in the window-lined breakfast area of the large modern kitchen; there was a huge walk-in pantry and an area for the washer and dryer. From the kitchen we passed into the dining area perfectly suited to our prized hard-rock maple hutch buffet and oval table and chairs. There was no separation between this area and the living room except a door to the patio outside. From the living room we went down the hall to three bedrooms on the left. On the right was one bathroom, a large linen closet and the air conditioning system closet. Our large bedroom was at the end on the right which also had a full bath.

Decorating each time we moved was always a challenge and there never seemed to be enough money to do what I wanted to do. Fortunately, the curtains I had made for the bedroom windows in Arizona fit very well with minor alterations, and the children were content with these familiar things. We did have to purchase drapes and panels for the living room and dining room windows—thank goodness for the Sears charge card! Kevin and Kathy rode their bikes to Don C. Faith Middle School. They signed up for band, as they had at Fort Huachuca. Kevin played trombone, and Kathy the clarinet. They had good friends at school and in the neighborhood. We settled in at Fort Benning.

As Brigade Signal Officer for the 197th Infantry Brigade, Jim was responsible for communications for this combat-ready unit that spent a lot of time in field exercises. Late that spring, Jim's friend, Paul Burke, who was at Signal Corps Branch in the Pentagon, called to tell Jim that he was eligible for promotion to Regular Army Major, and he'd let us know as soon as he could whether or not Jim was on the list. We knew that if he was not, the possibility of being caught in a RIF was real. Jim, now resigned to the fact that he wouldn't be selected for the yearlong C&GSC course, enrolled in the non-resident course there at Fort Benning. He attended night classes and two summer camps at Camp Shelby near Hattiesburg, Mississippi. Completing the course would not assure promotion, but Jim knew he certainly would *never* be promoted if he didn't.

Surgery For Me

The doctors at Martin Army Hospital agreed that a hysterectomy was necessary. I did not want to hear that; I was thirty-six—much too young for that sort of thing—and even though we didn't plan to have more children, the reality saddened me that we never would.

The surgery went well, but I was in the hospital over a week which turned out to be unnecessarily long because a nurse didn't pay enough attention to detail. Seems my doctor left on vacation and there just happened to be a change of nurses on the floor at the same time. The new nurse didn't check my record thoroughly and saw only the report about an optional mole removal at the same time as the surgery. She treated me accordingly. When I began to run a fever and was very uncomfortable, Jim made some noise. Well, when that nurse learned I was in there because of major surgery, she began to get a little nervous! She immediately called a doctor to come who found that my stitches should have been taken out the day before! Needless to say, Jim let it be known that we weren't happy. I was treated with kid gloves thereafter, and was able to leave the hospital very soon. Thankfully, that was the worst of our military hospital experiences.

By now Kevin was thirteen and Kathy almost twelve, so they knew what they had to do while I was recuperating. They were very well tuned-in to Jim's expectations of them, and they knew I would always agree with him, so they had no chance to play us against each other. I tried hard to not treat them any differently while he was away than I did when he was home. As a result, they were never confused about where Jim and I stood in their regard. That was one reason I respected Jim so much—if the children fussed at me, he'd say, "Listen to your mother; do what she says."

For the past several months, our money situation had been critical. We still had debt because of an ill-fated airplane purchase in Arizona, and we felt the best opportunity to recover was for me to go to work for a couple of years. I passed the Federal Service Entrance Exam on the first try, applied for a position on Fort Benning, and by mid-July was on the job as a clerk-typist. The extra money, amazingly, made an immediate difference. I also felt very well, and realized what a joy it was to not have to worry with monthly female issues. Our prayers had been answered!

The Social Climate

We enjoyed getting to know others who were a part of the 197th. Jim's boss in the S-3 Shop was Major John Campbell. John had been seriously wounded in Vietnam and had a plastic jaw, although we couldn't tell by looking at him. John and his wife, Jan, didn't get to have a week's R&R in Hawaii as we did—they had several months there while John recuperated at Tripler Army Hospital.

Other friends were the Paynes, Sodanos, Spencers, Kornehans, Hills, Calverts, Woods, Jones, and Barnes. One of our favorite couples was Charley Barnes and his wife, Fran, who lived a couple of doors down the street. We really liked each other. Fran and I both worked at Fort Benning, and we could share working-gal stories. There was a *plethora* of social activities at this bustling post, and we enjoyed most of them as long as we were comfortable with K&K's situation while we were gone. They were too old for baby sitters, but we were content with the activities they kept themselves busy with. There was good family entertainment on TV, and Kevin had his head in a book most of the time.

There were enjoyable couples' golf tournaments on weekends. Kevin and Kathy joined us on some Sunday afternoons playing golf, and both did well, but Kathy just wanted to be with her friends. By now they were both strong swimmers, and enjoyed more swimming lessons and fun in the nearby Officers' Club Pool. We felt safe on post where there were playgrounds and lots of kids. Kevin continued Boy Scout work. Camp Fire was not offered, but Kathy fared well and always had friends whether from school, church, or swimming. It did sadden me occasionally that our children's lives were uprooted so often, they were constantly saying farewell to friends, and had to adjust to different school situations. However, the fortunate thing was that most of the kids they knew were in the very same boat, so it was just the way it was. Also, much that had to do with military life was similar from post-to-post—Saturday matinees, swimming classes, bowling alleys, good schools, and Sunday services at the Post Chapel. We saw to it that there was constancy in their lives with a stable home life. There were often telephone calls and letters from grandparents, aunts and uncles, and friends. Their world revolved around family and things familiar to them regardless of where we lived.

Jitterbugging in 1974

Storage Section, Supply Division

The clerical work I did wasn't very glamorous; nevertheless, I enjoyed it. I worked in the storage section of Supply Division in an office in the middle of a warehouse. There were about eighty people employed there, mostly blue collar. My boss was Ronald G. Short, one of the finest men I've ever known, and the best boss I ever had. Mister Short, I always called him, was more patient with me than I deserved and taught me so much. I prospered, and after one year, I was promoted one grade. Mr. Short told me my people skills were invaluable in that warehouse environment.

Although I missed being home, especially when the kids came in from school, they didn't seem to miss me, and took care of themselves very well. The hardest thing for me was having to do the grocery shopping after work. The big, new mall-type commissary and PX were clear across Post and just getting there seemed to take an inordinate amount of time. One day I came home with a car load of groceries just as Jim came in. I was really strung out because of time, money, and whatever else, and I began crying. In a high, squeaky voice I complained to him that this was just too much; I couldn't handle it all myself! He looked at me and calmly said, "I'll help, Frances. From now on just make me a list and I'll do the grocery shopping. The commissary is much closer to my work than yours." Well, glory be! Why hadn't we figured out this little bit of convenience and efficiency before? Probably because I was afraid of losing some of my control over the grocery budget. I needn't have worried because Jim was good to help, especially after that outburst. However, there were those inconvenient field exercises that kept him away for days at a time. I had to plan very well to get around that *and* football season!

The ADYA football season began with the Rams selecting Kevin. Kathy was a cheerleader, so once again I found myself working with cheerleaders and making uniforms. Jim volunteered to help coach, but he couldn't always be there, as the 197th was in the field so much. He missed much of the season, and the team was left wanting by the rest of the coaching staff. Even so, Kevin did not lose his desire to play football.

Hearts in Our Throats

One Saturday morning, I found Jim on the golf course to tell him Paul Burke had called and wanted to talk with him. We returned home with hearts in our throats, expecting the worst. Jim returned the call and Paul congratulated him, saying he was on the RA Major list! We knew then that even if Jim was not promoted to Lieutenant Colonel, when he'd become eligible in 1976, he could stay for twenty years and retire. What an incredible relief!

Windsor Park

We had brunch one Saturday morning in the home of friends who lived in a beautiful area in northeast Columbus called Windsor Park. Their home was a southern-style two-story and had a wood-burning fireplace. It made our mouths water! Later, we drove around Windsor Park and drooled over nearby houses—a mixture of large ones with spacious lawns, and smaller ones not quite so grandiose, nevertheless appealing.

The next Sunday afternoon we were out looking at new houses in Windsor Park. We talked with a realtor.

"Jim, do you have your VA loan eligibility certificate?" he asked.

"As a matter of fact, I do," Jim responded. He'd gotten it before he went to Vietnam the first time, but had never used it.

"That's great. You can get into a house without a down payment. All we have to do is run a credit check."

This realtor took care of the paperwork, and in spite of the money problems we'd had, our credit was fine and our income adequate. We looked at several houses, but none appealed to us.

"Have you thought about building?" the realtor asked.

"Not really," Jim said. "How long would it take?"

"About four months if all goes well."

He took us to see vacant lots, and then to his house that he'd recently built. It was the perfect size and had many appealing features.

"The builder can change the plans to your specifications," he said, "and he'll fix the elevation so you can't tell we have similar plans."

So that was it. We found plenty of reasons to justify moving off post, and had plans drawn for a 2,000-square-foot house— three bedrooms, two and a half baths, a game room, kitchen with breakfast area, formal dining room, and a two-step-down great room with wood-burning fireplace. A large carport was at the rear with adjoining storage area. I *loved* the building process and poured over the plans until the pages were frayed! Then, what fun to be able to pick out my own cabinet styles, light fixtures, wallpaper, and carpet! I was in heaven!

Built with new, old-look brick, the house was ranch-style with barn red siding and white trim. Jim was nervous; the building took almost six months, and then with the house completely ready, rain delayed the pouring of the driveway. Finally, August 15 was moving day.

My fondness was for things Colonial style, so I chose dining room wall paper with a gold and green eagle design, the breakfast area (with a bay window) was a soft green and off-white plaid-check; the front bath had a somewhat muted red, white, blue and black design, and in our bathroom that did not require much paper, was a small flower design. The kitchen and master bath cabinets were a maple finish, while the front bath had white cabinets. Both the kid's rooms and bath in between had window seats. Talk about charming!

There was quite a to-do about our master bath. We chose a design that had both a shower and a tub; problem was, the builder had to find a special size tub for the space we had. We also insisted on two lavatories. Getting ready for work in the morning with just one lavatory could get interesting, and this idea we loved! Room for his stuff and room for my stuff—oh my, this was heaven! We also had a huge walk-in closet, an idea whose time had finally come.

Water Everywhere!

On our second day in the house, I was using the washer, which was between the kitchen and game room. As I walked through the game room to put things away, I noticed the carpet was wet. I put old towels down to soak up the water while Jim tried to figure out where it was coming from. As the towels soaked up more water, I put them in the washer on the spin cycle to spin dry. Jim turned the water main off, and Kevin and Kathy pitched in to help. We used the towels over and over, but we could see the water still coming and getting dirtier. We finally realized it was coming from under the base of the commode in the bathroom at the back of the game room! Jim called the builder who promptly sent out a plumber. A blockage was found in the pipe between the laundry area and the drain to the sewer, so all the water from the washer backed up to the commode each time I spin-dried the towels! The builder, one of the finest in Columbus, was extremely upset. The plumbers had the flaw fixed in short order, and of course any problems such as this were taken care of with a first-year warranty by the builder, so there was no cost to us.

Disney World

One day, Jim noticed a "for rent" sign on a large RV in a neighbor's yard. His mind was working where mine wasn't—he wanted to rent the RV and take a trip to the new Disney World in Orlando, Florida. What I wanted was to nest and get things settled in our new house. We had things to do and a vacation didn't seem important to me. He finally convinced me, as he had a way of doing through firm, but gentle persuasion, and maybe this time a slight bit of disgust with my objection, that we needed a break over Labor Day weekend. The kids were ecstatic, but I was tired when we got on the road that Friday afternoon. I slept all the way through Georgia and into Florida. It was late when we pulled into the space Jim had reserved in the rustic Wilderness Camp Ground. When we awakened the next morning, what a sight! We loved it! Right on a pond, the kids were able to paddleboat and swim. We saw as many sights of the amusement park as we possibly could, and the trip was priceless for all of us. Jim knew what he was doing.

Church and Other Activities

While on Fort Benning, we attended Protestant Chapel Services. I sang in the choir, and the fellowship was wonderful in that military environment. When we moved to Windsor Park, we joined the close-by Wynnton Methodist Church that had wonderful youth group activities.

Getting settled in the house was a happy time. Jim worked hard getting the lawn in shape, and he put up a charming split-rail type fence along the sidewalk to the front door.

Kevin signed up to play in the Columbus Municipal Football League. Jim volunteered to coach, and they were assigned to the Packers. Kathy wanted to be a cheerleader, and so for the fifth year in a row, I helped. We all spent a lot of happy time at the football field.

The 1975 Lieutenant Colonel List

In the summer of 1975, the Lieutenant Colonel's List came out. Many eligible were passed over. Some folks who had not made the RA Major's List were now facing a RIF and probable release from the Army. The news came soon that some of these passed-over majors—many women, minorities, and some from previous years—were suing the Department of Defense for civil rights violations. It would be interesting to watch this scene play out. It seemed to us that merit mattered less and less—your gender or color, or who you knew seemed to override everything else.

Christmas in Our New Ho-me

The great room had a vaulted, beamed ceiling with a large brass chandelier. Coming through the front door you stepped onto shiny black tile in the foyer, down onto another wide black tile step, and then down into the gold shag-carpeted great room. We placed large pots of red and white poinsettias on the steps. Garlands hung beautifully on the wood mantle of the floor-to-ceiling brick fireplace. Jim found a huge tree, the largest we'd ever had, that fit perfectly to the left of the fireplace. It was exciting to decorate the tree and the house! As we did so, we reflected on the different trees we'd had through the years; the tiny one we bought for our apartment our first Christmas with the last three dollars we had before payday even though we'd be spending Christmas with our folks, the one in New Jersey that we decorated with only blue ornaments and lights, and spun-glass angel hair; the one in the mobile home in Alabama that we decorated with popcorn and cranberries because we already had so many ornaments in storage; and we laughed about the tree in Arizona that a new puppy had knocked over. We'd had to use string to anchor that one to the wall! What a time we'd had through the years, and now here we were in this beautiful house with such beautiful decorations. It might have been easy to forget the reason for the season, but we did not. We rejoiced and were humbly thankful.

1976 - To Move or Not to Move

We began the new year busy as ever, and I flourished in my job at the warehouse. Mr. Short was an eager mentor, and I worked as hard as I could so that I might move up in federal service. Even so, I longed to be home. *If Jim gets promoted to lieutenant colonel this summer,* I thought, *I'll just quit all of this and be a stay-at-home mom!*

Jim was in Mississippi for his C&GSC summer camp when the promotion list came out. His name was not on it. It was a blow, but not entirely unexpected, as we'd seen so many others passed over the year before. I'd planned to attend an Ogden Family Reunion in New Mexico while he was away, but I stayed home to be there when he came home. Kevin was on a Boy Scout encampment, and Kathy was with the church's youth group in the Appalachian Mountains. When Jim arrived, I met him at the door.

"I'm sorry, Frances," he said. We hugged tightly.

"I'm sorry, too, Jim, but mostly for you. You're a good man, and a good officer, and you deserve to be promoted."

"Well, it's good that you think that, but obviously the U.S. Army doesn't."

I could hear the dismay and even bitterness in his voice, and watched as he mixed a drink. He sat in his recliner, and I sat on the end of the sofa. He looked at me, quickly looked away, closed his eyes, and frowned. "Jim," I said as I took his hands in mine, "let's pray together."

We'd not done this often as we each prayed our own prayers in our own way in our own time and place, but I knew this time was unusual. I voiced the words, asking our heavenly Father to be with us at this crucial time, to help us get through it, to be strong for each other, and for our children. As we squeezed each other's hands, I thanked God for all our blessings, our children, our families and our new home, and then in Jesus' name, amen. I was thankful for the strong spiritual foundation that we'd established our marriage on, and I knew that this, too, would pass. We'd been through an awful lot during and since his two combat tours, and we surely would get through this. In a soft voice, Jim managed, "Thank you, Frances."

It was harder for Jim than for me because he had to face all the questions at work. His peers and cohorts were dismayed, and the Brigade Commander offered to help him any way he could. Jim contacted his former boss, Cecil Carlisle, and Colonel Mayfield who had been the endorsing officer in Arizona. Both now retired, they sent letters to the Pentagon, stating that Jim was certainly the victim of the system and should not be punished because of it. That was all well and good; nevertheless, it was hard for us to get through that time, and it was especially hard to attend social gatherings. We did anyway, and we tried to live above the unfair situation. Our good friends remained our friends, but I watched Jim closely. He seemed to be drinking more. My prayers continued, and I was grateful that he had always been a hearty eater. Fortunately, he continued eating well, and there was nothing the children noticed, at least that they talked with me about, and I was sure they would if they were concerned. After a time the drinking evened out.

Adding insult to injury was seeing on this promotion list the names of previously passed over females and minorities, *and* two officers we'd known personally who had *not* been promoted to Regular Army Major when Jim *was!* What injustice! They'd won their lawsuit at the expense of many like Jim. There were only so many slots available for promotions. How unfair indeed, and it was very hard to take.

Jim continued to work hard and remained valuable to the 197th. He was made Brigade Operations Officer—he didn't ask for it, but his boss told him he needed him to do the job and, furthermore, he had full confidence that he could. Jim found he not only had responsibility for all communications, but everything else in brigade operations! He was gone for briefings and planning meetings for field exercises in conjunction with the U.S. Air Force.

Family Matters

Our children, although dismayed that their father had been passed over, did not let it affect them. Kevin was a sophomore, and Kathy was a freshman at Columbus High School. Kevin played football on the Varsity B team that fall, and all in all had a good experience. Kathy, now off Ritalin, was still a lively, free spirit, but did well. She loved her room and spent a lot of time there. She chose yellow shag carpet, a multi-colored pastel bed comforter with matching curtains, and fluffy pillows and stuffed animals for her window seat. Kevin chose red, white, and blue shag carpet for his room, a red bedspread and drapes, and red, white, and blue pillows for his window seat. They both had friends they shared time with, but they enjoyed being home.

By late 1976, we'd been at Fort Benning for two and a half years. Jim knew he could expect change of station orders soon. We didn't want to disrupt the family with another move, so he talked with Signal Corps Branch at the Pentagon about a one-year unaccompanied tour in Korea. If he took such a tour, he'd likely have his choice of assignments, and then he could be reassigned to Fort Benning. His OERs from the 197th had all been outstanding, and we were hopeful he'd be promoted in 1977.

"Have you got a flying job for me in Korea?" Jim asked the Assignment Officer. "I'm offering to go to Korea for a year so I don't have to disrupt my family again."

"Nothing in Korea right now, Jim. In fact, the only flying assignment I can offer because of your rank is as Commander of a Cavalry Troop with the Twenty-fifth Infantry Division in Hawaii. Can you go to Hawaii?"

"Whoa, there! Did you say Hawaii?"

"Sure did, Jim. You'd need to be in Hawaii the first of April."

"Man, I sure didn't expect that. You mean I'd be flying helicopters?"

"That's right. We have a cavalry troop that needs a commander, and you're available."

"Can you give me a few hours to check it out with my family?"

"Sure, Jim. Get back with me as soon as you can."

Jim drove the nineteen miles home, his head spinning. He asked us that evening. The kids were ecstatic, and I was excited too! We'd longed for an assignment in Hawaii. We talked a long time about it and decided that, yes, it would be worth it, as we might never have the opportunity again. Jim would go ahead; the kids and I would stay in Columbus until school was out, and then join him when the house sold. I was capable of handling things without Jim for two or three months. Sure, I'd done that before, and then I began to think about it. Sure, all I had to do was see the kids were off to school each morning, get to work every day by 7:30 a.m., come home and see that the children are okay, their homework done, their clothes ready for the next day, prepare dinner, keep the house in order to show in case someone wanted to see it the next day; write a letter to Jim, fall into bed, sleep if I could, and get up at 6:00 a.m. the next day and start all over again...until the house sells. Then we'd move into an apartment nearby until school was out. But, my fear was if the house didn't sell, then the kids and I would have to stay until it did. Having to stay there without Jim if the house didn't sell was the dreariest thought of all. But even if it did sell, I'd be the one dealing with the Transportation folks to set a moving day, begin preparations for moving by separating hold baggage from household goods, keeping the house in order—all this while Jim would be in Hawaii of all places! All of these things going through my mind were giving me a headache!

We waited on official notice and finally the PCS orders came stating the reporting day to the Twenty-fifth Infantry Division was April 1, 1977. We'd planned a trip to Texas and New Mexico for the summer of 1977, but we'd be in Hawaii by then, so we decided to go for Christmas. In the meantime, we traded our big Chrysler for a more gas-efficient Fiat Sedan and our VW for a Fiat X-19, a snazzy little yellow and black sports car. The money we'd save on gas, especially in Hawaii, should make the difference, shouldn't it?

Off we went, crowded into the Fiat sedan. Oh! How we missed the big Chrysler! Jim drove, and Kevin, now six feet tall, sat in front; Kathy and I sat in the back. It was a long way from Georgia to New Mexico, but spending the holidays with family and friends would be worth it. Tommy and Karen Smith would be in Azle, not far from Fort Worth, for the holidays and Richard and Monica LaHue planned to be there for New Year's Eve. We'd be there too!

Time with our families was short, and Grandma was sad to see us leave on Thursday, December 30, but we were eager to get to Fort Worth to see the Smiths and LaHues. It had been almost eight years since we'd been together for Easter at Fort Rucker. We met at a restaurant in north Fort Worth for dinner and made plans to meet the next evening at the home of a friend of Tommy's in Weatherford, near Fort Worth.

We spent that night with Royce and Sammye in Burleson, just south of Fort Worth. Royce and I had seen little of each other since we graduated from high school, and we enjoyed being with him, Sammye, and children, Jeff, Terry, Kipp, and Tammy. Jeff and Terry were close in age and size to Kevin and Kathy.

Tommy's friends were gracious, and we enjoyed being in their home for New Year's Eve. We knew we'd be in Hawaii for three years; LaHues were going to Germany for three years; and Tommy was facing a one-year unaccompanied tour in Turkey while Karen would stay in Wisconsin to be near her mother who was dealing with life-threatening cancer. As is always the case when we leave friends or family at anytime, there's no way to know when we'll see them again. Tommy's death just over a year later while he was in Turkey would reveal how very special this time was with our dear friends.

We spent New Year's Day and night with Doyle and Marilou in Granbury. Kevin and Kathy had fun with cousins, Keith, Joanne, and Susan.

The next morning was cold and wet. Ice began to accumulate, so we left earlier than we'd planned, hoping to outrun the treacherous weather. As the trees began to capture the cold, humid air, the landscape turned into a winter wonderland. Most of Louisiana was covered with snow, and ice was heavy on trees. We'd planned to travel all the way to Columbus on this first Sunday of the year, but travel was slow, and we made it only to Vicksburg, Mississippi. We spent the night and traveled home the next day.

Preparations for another Move

Back home, we settled into life as usual, but faced the move to Hawaii. When we built our house, we thought we'd be in Columbus until the kids graduated, but who could turn down the opportunity to live in Hawaii? Not us. Even though the thought of selling our beautiful house was heart wrenching. When I thought about leaving the house we loved so much, I prompted myself to think of palm trees, beaches, pineapple fields, volcanoes, and a host of other things that would open an entire new world for K&K. By this time they each had a special girl friend and boy friend, but they couldn't keep from thinking about palm trees, beaches, pineapples and volcanoes either! It's harder for teenagers to pick up and move, but they didn't seem very upset about moving to Hawaii.

In the meantime, Jim learned from Signal Corps Branch that he would not be a cavalry troop commander in Hawaii. Seems the XO of the 125th Signal Battalion there had been promoted to Lieutenant Colonel early, and that battalion needed an XO worse than the cavalry troop needed a commander. Jim was disappointed—he didn't want another ground assignment, but there was nothing he could do. He called the commander of the 125th, Lieutenant Colonel Gordon. He seemed skeptical and concerned because Jim had been passed over.

"Sir, I'm not a dud, and I'll do a good job for you," Jim told him. "Sure, I'm an aviator, and I'd rather fly, but when the Army gives me a job, I'll do it, and I'll do it to the best of my ability." That seemed to be what Lieutenant Colonel Gordon needed to hear.

We put the house up for sale, hoping the kids and I could stay until school was out; but we knew we should prepare to move in the event it sold quickly. I looked at several places, but could not stomach the thought of moving into a strange place without Jim. I became increasingly uncomfortable with the situation. One evening at dinner, it was Kevin's turn to ask the blessing. He also prayed that his dad's trip to Hawaii would be safe and that we would be safe while he was away. I burst into tears.

"What's wrong, Frances?"

"I don't want you to go to Hawaii by yourself," I sobbed.

"Then we'll go all together."

And that was that. We needed to sell the house quickly, so our realtor set up an open house on a cold Sunday afternoon. When the first couple set foot in the foyer and looked across the great room at the fire in the fireplace, they looked at each other and said, "This is it!" We were amazed, but not really surprised; we understood the feeling.

By March 1 the deal was done, but the new owners wanted our refrigerator that matched the other kitchen appliances. When the realtor asked about this, we barely had time to buy another one, and it was put on the truck in its original packing, sight unseen.

"I think they said it was harvest gold," Jim said.

Driving Across the USA

We left Fort Benning early and planned to be at Nita's in San Leon, Texas, that evening. Jim had Kevin and Pandy (the Sheltie puppy we'd gotten to give Abbi some company) in the X-19; Kathy and Abbi were with me in the sedan. Both cars were packed with our needs for the trip across the Southern USA, plus what we'd need once we got to Hawaii while we looked for a place to live.

Interstate 10 was complete and made the trip bearable, but we didn't make the good time we'd hoped. It was dusk when we arrived in Houston. A cold wind blew dust and debris everywhere, which made reading signs difficult. We soon realized we'd gone much too far, and Jim was exhausted. I called to tell Nita we'd spend the night in a motel and come by for breakfast.

Nita and Clois had divorced, and she was now married to Bill Seymour, a childhood friend. Jim was fond of Bill, and we were glad to see Nita, E'Laine, and Revena so happy. Nita had completed her degree, was teaching high school math, *and* working on her master's degree. We were so proud of the progress she'd made after a difficult divorce.

We traveled northwest on 290, then north on Highway 6 to Bryan-College Station, where Texas A&M is located. We showed the kids the campus, and stopped for coffee.

"It sure is a lot different than it was in 1954," Jim said. "I was offered a football scholarship by one of the assistant coaches at A&M. He told me they had a new football coach and his name was Bear Bryant. I asked, 'Bear who?'"

"Dad, you mean you could've played football for Bear Bryant?" Kevin asked.

"I'm not sure I could've made his team, Kevin. I've heard he was rough on those guys that year."

"Aw, Dad, I'm sure you would've made it."

"Well, I came down to visit the coaches and see the campus, but it was cold and windy. Sand was blowing everywhere just like it was last night, and all the buildings were old WWII buildings. It wasn't appealing after I'd seen the campus at Oklahoma A&M, so I just turned around and went home."

"I think that's the way it was meant to be," I said, putting my slant on the story. "You see, your dad had football scholarship offers to several colleges, but he had to get to ENMU sooner or later because that's where I was!"

"Sure, Mom, sure," Kevin said. "Why did you leave Oklahoma A&M, Dad?"

"It's a long story, Kev. My freshman year was great playing football, but the second year there was a new line coach that for some reason didn't like me. I was playing second team behind Buddy Ryan who was our first team right guard. I don't know why the coach didn't like me, but one day we were practicing blocking, and one of the guys on defense was having a hard time beating me. I blocked him every time. This coach told that guy to watch and he'd show him how to beat me. He put his cap on backwards, got down in a stance, and told me to come on and try to block him. I said, 'No, coach, I don't want to do that. You don't have pads on.' He said 'come on, come on,' and even started taunting me, so I got down in my stance. He told me to come on again, so I fired off and knocked him on his hind end. He got up and told me to try that again. I said, 'No, coach, I don't think it's right,' but he kept egging me on. So, I fired off and blocked him better than the first time. He got up kind of stunned and didn't say anything. Practice ended about that time, and the next day I was on the fourth team! I tried the rest of the season, but I couldn't make it back. Then, when spring practice came around, I went out and played my heart out, but that coach was still on me, so I thought it would probably be my last game. Coach Armstrong, you know, the Chicago Bears coach now? Well, he tried to get me to play center so he could coach me, but I'd already made my mind up to leave."

"That's when you went to ENMU?"

"Yeah, well, the ENMU coaches had recruited me out of

high school, and Grandma liked them best of all. I gave them a call, and they told me to come out and talk about it. So that's how that all happened, and how I got to meet your mother. Hey, we've got to get going. We'll be late for lunch!"

We traveled to Killeen, Texas, near Fort Hood to see friends, Cliff and Rose Walker. We hadn't seen them since Fort Huachuca in 1972. We enjoyed our visit there, and then went up on I-35 to Burleson to Royce and Sammye's house to spend the night. It was March 11, my thirty-ninth birthday.

The next day we went by Doyle's, then to Lubbock to see Christine and Moreland, and up to Amarillo to see Grandma. Almost seventy-nine years old, she couldn't understand why we wanted to live so far away again. I'm sure to her it seemed selfish of us, but we were in the prime of our lives and wanted to live and see and do all we could. To have the opportunity to live in Hawaii—well, wouldn't anyone?

"Mom, I'll buy you an airplane ticket so you can come see us," Jim told her.

"No thanks. I'll come when they build a bridge to Hawaii," she responded. Saying good-bye was hard.

It was equally hard to say good-bye to Mamaw and Papaw. Papaw proudly showed us his first-ever Visa credit card and quickly assured us he used it only when necessary. I admired my daddy so much. He was a proud man, standing tall and doing what he thought was right along the way, and he was proud of his family. Now, he was a janitor, but he was okay with that because he brought home a paycheck and had good health benefits.

"Maybe we'll come to see you in Hawaii," he said.

"I hope so, Daddy," I said, hugging him tightly. "That would be wonderful!"

We stopped in Fort Sumner to see Melva, Shell, and Sharon. Barry was in college and wasn't home, but we met Sharon's future husband, Bobby Lopez. What a change there would soon be in the quality of life for this family; Shell, age forty-one, had recently answered the call to go into the ministry!

We left Fort Sumner traveling south through Alamogordo and west across the White Sands. A sandstorm there was so strong it took paint off the front license plates. We drove through Las Cruces, Deming, Lordsburg, Benson, and to Sierra Vista where we spent the night with Don Ray and Mary Beth. We loved this part of the world. The desert and mountains were so familiar, and we were glad to be there again.

"You know, we're lucky to have friends and family all over the U.S. so we can spend the night and not have to stay in motels," I said.

"Yes, we are lucky, and they're all so wonderful."

At Don and Mary's, Jim told them, "I'll try to get assigned to Fort Huachuca again when we leave Hawaii."

"That'd be great, Jim," Don Ray said. "I'll start working on my golf game since I know you don't like to go hunting anymore."

"Good! I'd like to get you out on the course and show you a thing or two!"

These lifelong friends ribbed and loved each other as if they were brothers. When Jim stopped hunting, Don had been disappointed, but Jim told him, "Don, since Vietnam, I just don't like holding a gun anymore."

On to California on I-10 through Blythe and Palm Springs, Jim let Kevin drive the X-19 on these wide-open highways. He was excited!

We stopped in Palm Springs that Saturday, March 19, and I told Jim the sedan wasn't handling right. He drove it on to Los Angeles where we found a Fiat dealer. Mechanics determined the balance bar was broken, but it was very close to quitting time, and no one who could work on it was still there. Jim was told the car was safe to drive, but to be careful. There we were in Los Angeles with a broken balance bar, and we had to get to San Francisco by Monday, the day Abbi and Pandy were to be shipped to Hawaii.

The next morning, we traveled Highway 101 up the coast to Highway 1. Jim drove the sedan along the winding scenic ocean drive, and I got to drive the X-19! It was dusk when we got to Monterey, and because of construction in the area we saw little. Driving was a nightmare, and our travel slowed. We finally found our way to the center of San Francisco and checked into the hotel where transportation folks had made reservations for us. They had scheduled our pets to be shipped on Monday, the cars on Wednesday, and us to fly out on Thursday.

Early on Monday, Jim and Kevin took Abbi and Pandy to the kennel where they were prepared for their trip, and then they took the sedan to have the balance bar repaired. An attempt was made under warranty, but on Tuesday morning we realized it was *not* fixed as we drove down Lombard Street—the "crookedest street in the world!" We dared to drive over the Golden Gate Bridge to Sausalito for lunch anyway.

On Wednesday, Jim drove the sedan and I followed in the X-19 over the Oakland Bridge to the Oakland Shipyard. We took a taxi back to the hotel, and the rest of our time walked around San Francisco. We rode the cable cars and had lunch in a famous Chinese restaurant. We visited the shops on the waterfront and stopped at a nice seafood restaurant for dinner.

On Thursday morning, we took a bus to the airport where we boarded Northwest Orient Flight Number Thirty-four for Honolulu. What a time we were having!

Aloha, Hawaii!

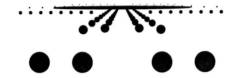

Even on this, my fourth time to Hawaii, the sight of the magnificent mountains sprawling to white beaches and turquoise water was breathtaking! My stomach was atwitter as the aircraft taxied to the terminal. The airport was much bigger than in 1970, and we walked a long way down an open-air walkway to the main terminal. A uniformed officer with nametag Gordon and a pretty lady came up to us. Jim saluted; it was returned, and they shook hands.

"You must be the McGraws."

"Yes, sir. I'm Jim, and this is my wife Fran, our son Kevin, and daughter, Kathy."

"I'm Larry Gordon, and this is my wife, Julia. Welcome to Hawaii!" Julia placed Plumeria leis on us all.

"It's nice of you to meet us here, sir. I was expecting Major Reilly," Jim said.

"Well, the Major is working, and his wife had a commitment. Julia and I were available, so we came to meet you."

We chatted as we waited on our bags. Jim rented a car and soon had it loaded. The Gordons offered to help us anyway they could, and assured Jim that his sponsor, Major Iain Reilly, the Battalion XO who had been promoted early, would be in touch.

Soon we were on H-1, which rivaled the interstate highways

on the mainland. It was so different from the street we remembered on our first trip. Now two levels; the lower level went into Honolulu, the upper level went out. We turned onto Kalakaua Avenue and wound our way through the Waikiki Beach area to the Outrigger Reef Hotel—not the nearby ritzy Reef, but it was on the beach and paid for by the Army for up to two weeks while we found a place to live. Our suite, with no "ritz" about it at all, had minimal decoration and was rather bare; nevertheless, we had no need to complain—we were in Hawaii in a hotel on Waikiki Beach! It had a kitchenette, two bedrooms, two baths and a sitting area with a TV. A sofa bed in the sitting area pleased Kevin, and Kathy took the second bedroom. Our two balconies overlooked the interior patio, and we thought it interesting that so many people we saw day after day appeared to live in the hotel. They were not typical tourists or other military families. We were also near Fort DeRussy and the International Market Place with shops and restaurants galore.

The next morning we visited Abbi and Pandy and were happy they'd been placed together in a large kennel. We put them on leash and walked around. They were so happy and we hated to leave them, but we had no choice; all animals that came to Hawaii had a *six-month quarantine!*

We drove to Schofield Barracks where Jim signed in with the Twenty-fifth Infantry Division. He checked the post housing office, learned it could be sixty to ninety days before quarters became available, and was given a list of rentals. We then drove by the high school in Wahiawa where Schofield Barracks kids attended. We found the football stadium, and there it was—a logo that was a caricature of a mule. The sign on the stadium read, "Leilehua Mules."

"Mules! Oh no!" Kevin exclaimed. "I don't want to be a mule!"

"Hey, Kev," Jim said, "the West Point mascot is the mule, and you're thinking about going to West Point, aren't you?"

"West Point's mascot is the mule? I didn't know that."

"Sure is, and Schofield Barracks is a big part of the Army. Most of the officers back in the 1920s went to West Point, and they had a lot of input when this school was established."

"That doesn't sound so bad," Kevin responded.

"How do you pronounce the name of the school?" Kathy asked.

"Okay, you always pronounce each consonant, but the vowels sound different," I told them. The *a* is pronounced "ah," the *e* is "aye," the *i* is "ee," the *o* is "o" and the *u* is a double "o" sound. So the school's name is pronounced *Lay-le-hoo-a*."

"When did you learn that?" Kevin asked.

"Hey, I've been to Hawaii before."

We decided to wait until Monday to enroll the kids in school. This weekend would be our little vacation before the living as usual began. We checked out some of the rentals near Schofield, but none were to our liking, so we decided to look at a townhouse on the North Shore that was listed.

From Schofield Barracks we traveled through pineapple plantations and into the little town of Haleiwa where shaved ice was invented. There began the incredible North Shore of Oahu. Not only are there beautiful ragged and rocky shorelines, glorious beaches, and surfer-heaven waves, but the North Shore had its own Hollywood history. Many movies had been made there; one of the most famous was *From Here to Eternity*, in which the beach scene with Burt Lancaster and Deborah Kerr has its own indelible eternity.

We passed Waimea Bay, Pupukea Beach, the famous Sunset Beach, and finally saw the sign to the Kuilima Hotel. Alongside was a golf course, the fairways lined with townhouses. We couldn't believe this rental was a townhouse on a golf course! A split-level design, it was perfect—two bedrooms and a bath upstairs, a master bedroom and bath off the kitchen on the mid-level where the entrance was also, and a living room on the lower level with sliding glass doors that opened to a large patio. It had all the modern appliances and a washer-dryer combination. It was also on the number three fairway. Jim was grinning.

"What do you think, Frances?"

"What do *you* think?" I asked.

"I never dreamed we'd have the opportunity to live on the North Shore. Let's do it!"

And I agreed. We actually got to live on the North Shore of Oahu at 97 Kuilima Loop, Kahuku, Hawaii 96731. We'd been married almost twenty years; it was address number twenty-four.

Leilehua High School

On Monday, we took the kids to enroll in school. Kathy was a freshman, and Kevin a sophomore. We were directed to the office of Mr. Koga, who would be their counselor. He was very pleasant and seemed genuinely interested in these joys of our lives.

"Kevin, do you play any sports?" Mr. Koga asked.

"Yes, sir. I wrestle, and I play football."

Mr. Koga picked up the telephone and immediately called the football coach. Soon, Coach Yoshida came. Mr. Koga introduced him to us, and as Jim and Kevin stood up, he was obviously struck by Kevin's size.

"What position do you play, Kevin?" the coach asked.

"Fullback."

"Uuhmmm," he responded in a brisk, Oriental way. "We're beginning spring practice next Monday, so you come on out to practice."

"Thank you, sir. I'll be there."

Mr. Koga asked Kathy what her interests were.

"Oh, everything, I guess," she said. "I'd like to be a cheerleader."

"All right, we'll get you into classes and go from there, okay?"

"Yes, sir," Kathy replied, smiling shyly.

Kevin made friends in football and wrestling programs. Kathy adapted well and before long had many friends. They were eager to move onto Schofield Barracks.

Twenty-fifth Division and 125th Signal Battalion

Jim's sponsor, Iain Reilly, a sharp West Point graduate, went with him to introduce him to the Division G-1, where all new officers were interviewed. After the interview, the G-1 said to Jim, " I want to make sure you understand why you weren't given the cavalry troop commander position."

"I was told the Signal Battalion needed an executive officer, sir," Jim responded.

"Well, not exactly. The cavalry commander felt your lack of experience flying helicopters, and the fact that you'd been passed over would be two strikes against you, and he didn't want to put you in that position."

"I don't understand why, sir. I've already been passed over. What difference would it make?" Jim felt he'd been kicked in the gut unnecessarily.

"That's a good point, Major, but that's the way he felt."

"Thanks for your concern, sir. Tell the commander I would've done him a helluva good job."

"Thank you, Major. I'll tell him."

After they left the division, Iain said to Jim, "You really like to fly, don't you?" "You bet. After spending three years in an infantry outfit and still being passed over—hey, that's all I want to do until I retire."

The Division Deputy Commander, General Brown, also interviewed Jim and assured him he'd have an aviation assignment after serving as XO for eighteen months.

Iain was a helpful sponsor for Jim, and he and his lovely wife Barbara invited our family to dinner in their home. They both had lived in Hawaii as children of military, and shared some things with us that you don't see or hear about as tourists—such as making sure you wash that beautiful, delicious Mango before peeling it, because you might be allergic to it. Sure enough, I forgot the rule once and my hands itched for hours.

Social activities associated with the unit were usually held at the Officers' Club on Schofield Barracks, but sometimes they were at close-by Wheeler Field, Pearl Harbor, or Hickam Air Force Base Officers' Clubs. It was a part of military life, and we always enjoyed attending. But, sometimes the best get-togethers were in private homes. Larry and Julia Gordon were capable and talented hosts. One evening, they had a dinner party for other battalion commanders, executive officers, and division "brass" and their wives. The Division Commander was unable to attend, but the new Deputy, General Fry, who'd replaced General Brown, and his wife were there. Most of the guys wore white slacks and colorful Hawaiian shirts; the ladies wore muumuus.

Most guests did not know each other, so to get these folks acquainted Larry and Julia pinned the name of a famous male on the back of each male guest and the name of a famous female associated with that male on the back of a female. The idea was to question other guests to try to figure out who you were and who your dinner partner would be. It was a wonderful icebreaker. I've never been as complimented as I was that night when I learned my dinner partner was General Fry—he was Spencer Tracey; I was Katharine Hepburn!

General Fry endorsed the fine OERs that Larry gave Jim,

and when Jim's time was up at the Signal Battalion, he honored General Brown's promise to give Jim a flying assignment.

Working in Hawaii

The second week there I took my application to the Civilian Personnel Office located on Fort Shafter. I was soon interviewed and selected for a clerk-typist position with the U.S. Air Force Audit Agency at Hickam Air Force Base. It was a nineteen-mile drive one-way from Schofield Barracks, and more from Kuilima. The drive was incredible along the North Shore and more than once I could see whales playing in the ocean! *Oh my, this is something* I thought, and I couldn't wait to tell K&K! At Wahiawa I turned south, down through the pineapple and cane fields framed by mountains on each side. Then through Wahiawa, across the old, narrow bridge and past Schofield Barracks, and on down the winding highway overlooking the South Pacific. The turquoise water always amazed me, but even more amazing were the tankers, ships, and boats on the water that looked as if they were as high as I was on land. Every day I saw the *USS Arizona* Memorial. I was humbled. All the while, I longed to be closer home; especially after being there a few months and discovering the office dynamics to be stiff and unfriendly. I actually enjoyed the work, but some attitudes and methods were quite foreign to me.

Fiat Trouble

For his sixteenth birthday, Kevin wanted to have dinner at the Cannon Club, halfway up the side of Diamond Head. We traveled from the North Shore and were in the middle of Honolulu on Friday night, May 20, when the Fiat suddenly stopped running. Jim managed to coast it to the side of the freeway, hitch a ride, and go for help. He returned with a tow truck and rental car so we could be on our way. We had a delightful dinner, although late, and Kevin was happy.

Jim had the Fiat towed to the dealership and learned the trouble was the transmission. It was a very costly repair, and of course, no longer under warranty.

Soon after that, I was driving the X-19 to work when it stalled. This time it was the timing chain—another expensive repair. These two car repair bills and rental car expenses depleted our reserves. Sadly, the X-19 timing chain quit on more than one occasion and was not under warranty. Every month we watched huge sums of money go for car payments and repair bills. Our financial situation tightened so that it became a source of tension at home. Kevin and Kathy wanted brand name clothes, rather than going to Sears and JC Penney, where we had charge accounts. Jim and I were dismayed that at this time in our kids' lives, we were unable to do more. We rationalized that, well, maybe they'll be unspoiled and appreciate the value of money. The situation was hard on Jim and me, too. More than once I found myself at work without the checkbook, very little money, and it was too far to go home. Unbeknownst to Jim, I sometimes made do with M&M chocolate covered peanuts for lunch. I could do without, but I would not have him do without. I would not have him embarrassed in front of other officers because of our financial situation! The interesting thing about living in Hawaii is that you finally realize you're not on vacation—you have to live there just like you do anywhere else. But I don't think we made a mistake in that regard; we were just unfortunate that the two cars cost us so very much more than they should have.

427 Funston Road, Schofield Barracks

We moved into huge U-shaped quarters on Funston Road that had three bedrooms, two baths, a screened-in lanai that accommodated our pool table, and with maid quarters alongside the laundry area behind the kitchen that Kevin grabbed for himself. With two teenagers, it was perfect and was the most incredible place we'd ever lived. From that lanai at the entrance, we turned right through French doors to the living room that had a fireplace at the opposite end. Parallel to the living room, and almost as large, was the dining room. Both had triple windows opposite each other. Entering the hallway from the dining room, Kathy's room was to the right. It had triple windows also. Another bedroom that accommodated guests very well, was between hers and the bathroom. Our room was at the end of the hallway alongside the bathroom. The hallways were on the inside of the U and were screened in. Most of the windows could be closed, but that was a rare occurrence in Hawaii. Another single door from the lanai opened to the dining room and immediately to the left, a door opened into the former butler's pantry that we made into an office. It was open to the breakfast area and kitchen. There was a window over the kitchen sink and double windows at the breakfast area overlooked the back patio. Our furniture fit well, and even the unseen harvest-gold refrigerator we'd bought in Georgia matched the sinks, stove, and dishwasher! Unbelievable! I was even pleased that our Colonial-style furniture fit just fine in this tropical setting.

A plumeria tree was outside our kitchen window. Kathy and I often made leis from the sweet-smelling pink and white flowers. There were avocado trees, palm trees, a banana tree, and a poinsettia bush. We felt incredibly blessed to live in such a beautiful place!

But, it would be another three months before we could pick up our poor little dogs in the kennel, and we visited them often. When the time came to get them, the required blood tests revealed that Abbi had heartworm disease. The kennel wouldn't release her until we had her treated. A nearby vet gave her a very expensive shock treatment to rid her of the disease. We'd never even heard of heartworm and were shocked at spending $400 for treatment. It was incomprehensible!

January 21, 1978

Jim was home on that Saturday morning, and we were listening to the radio in the kitchen when we heard a news bulletin that a U.S. Army U-21 aircraft had crashed in Turkey. No details were given, except that there were no survivors. Jim and I looked at each other in horror. *Our friend Tommy Smith was in Turkey and flying a U-21!*

"I'm going to call Karen."

"Okay," Jim said quietly. "Oh, I hope it's not Tommy."

"I hope not too."

I dialed Karen's number in Wisconsin. She recognized my voice.

"Karen, we just heard there'd been a U-21 crash in Turkey. It's not Tommy, is it?"

"Well," she said hesitantly, "what do you know?"

Thinking she might not have been told there were no survivors, I lied, saying that we'd heard they didn't know if there were any survivors.

"Well, I've had a call from some folks that are coming to see me. They also said my phone would be cut off temporarily, so I was surprised when you called."

"I'm glad we got through to you. Will you call as soon as you hear anything?"

"Yes, I'll call, but I don't know when it will be. I'm glad you called. Love you."

"We love you too, Karen. Bye, bye."

Jim and I were zombies the rest of the weekend. We did not want to believe for a moment that it was Tommy. Then, on Sunday evening, Karen called. Jim took the phone in the kitchen; I took one in the bedroom. She told us, yes, it was Tommy's airplane that had crashed into a mountainside, and that he was gone. We both sobbed and listened as Karen told us that Tommy had been to Ankara to pick up some fellows who'd been on leave, and they were returning to their base at Sinop. The weather was fine to fly over the mountains, and there had been no mayday calls. An investigation was underway. Jim and I were inconsolable.

"Now, I want you both to listen to me," Karen said. "You know my heart is breaking, but I want you to know this. Tommy and I always said to each other what we wanted to say, and we always gave to each other what we wanted to give; so for me there are no regrets, only sadness, but I hurt so for Kelli and for Tom's parents because he's all they had."

"Oh, Karen, it's going to be so hard for them," I managed. I could hear Jim sobbing.

"Fran, Jim, I've got more calls to make, so I've got to go. I'll call you again when I can."

I hung up the phone and moved into the kitchen where Jim and I fell into each other's arms. Our hearts were broken. We both loved this dear young man who had such happy eyes, special personality, and good heart. It would not be easy to let him go. Jim told me that on Monday morning when he went into work he found, still laying on his desk, the yellow legal-size pad on which he'd written, "Friday, January 20, 1978. Dear

Tommy,"—something took him away from finishing a letter, but he remembered thinking about Tommy and the strong tug he'd felt to write to his buddy. Monica LaHue called to say Tommy's funeral would be at Carswell Air Force Base in Fort Worth. The time was so short that Jim could not get a seat on a flight out to the mainland with connections to Fort Worth, nor could he get on a military space-available flight. I couldn't have gotten off work anyway, but he really wanted to go. It was hard not to have that closure. We grieved for a very long time, but I have never forgotten Karen's words about hers and Tommy's relationship. If only that were true in all marriages.

Jogging at Forty

Turning forty wasn't terribly traumatic, except that I knew I wasn't in very good shape. I was not overweight; in fact I was only five pounds above my wedding weight, but I didn't have much stamina. I'd watched our neighbor go running three times a week, and decided if she could do it, so could I. About my third time out, Jim drove in from work and saw me struggling.

"Do you really want to do this?"

"Yes, I need to get in shape."

"Okay, I'll help you. We'll get up in the morning and go together." He was up early three days a week to run, and he was in fine shape.

"Okay," I responded, surprised that he'd have me join him.

It was hard, and I struggled, but Jim encouraged me. It was also hard for me to get up and out in the morning, but he gently nudged me letting me know he was proud of me. My heart swelled. Soon I was jogging alongside him for two miles, three times a week. Then when the children joined us on occasion which they often did, we were both proud!

Friends and Family Visit

We'd been in Hawaii about a year when Papaw called to say they were coming to see us. We were excited! They were to arrive on a Thursday afternoon, and it would be so simple for me to go from my job at Hickam Air Force Base to the airport to pick them up, but I *couldn't get off work!* Thankfully, Jim was able to meet them and take them home. I was never so glad to get home as I was that day! I had to go back to work on Friday, but that was okay because Mother and Daddy needed to rest. I took leave the next week. I also vowed to look for another job.

What fun we had showing Mamaw and Papaw the island! We took them to the famous Sunday brunch at Tripler Hospital; they were in awe at the *USS Arizona* Memorial, and intrigued by Koli Koli Pass. We saw Waimea Bay, showed them where we'd lived on the North Shore, and took them to the Polynesian Cultural Center. We all smiled as they slipped off their shoes and dipped their toes in the water on Waikiki Beach. Larry and Julia Gordon had us bring them to their home for dinner one evening. We were joined by Dave and Becky Medaris, whom we'd known at Fort Bragg, and were now the Gordons' neighbors. Becky's parents were also visiting from the mainland.

While there, Mamaw and Papaw asked if we'd be able to come for their fiftieth anniversary celebration in November of 1979. We told them we'd try to manage, but after all, it was over eighteen months away. But, I knew once back at home, they would sit at their breakfast table, pray as they always did, and they'd ask the Lord if there was some way our family could come for their special occasion. We had no idea what strange events would unfold that would allow us to be there.

After their visit, we had a clearer idea of how to plan an itinerary to see and do as much as we could in the shortest time possible if visitors came, and we encouraged friends and relatives to come. Then, just before Christmas 1978, we had a call from Ray and Ann Borelli, a couple we'd known in Italy. Earlier that year, one of their twin daughters was killed in an automobile accident, and they could not bear to spend the holidays at home. They asked if they could spend Christmas with us.

So on that Christmas Day, we met Ray and Ann with son, Michael, and daughter, Pat, at the airport and brought them to our home for Christmas dinner. It was a special time for all of us and gave the Borellis a chance to enjoy the day without having to deal with memories. Michael and Pat were close in age to Kevin and Kathy, and they got along well. The next day we all climbed into the old Chevy station wagon that we'd purchased for occasions such as this, and with picnic doings, drove to Waimea Bay. Later that day, they left for a sightseeing trip to Maui and the Big Island before returning home.

In early 1979 Christine, Moreland, Leah, and Lyle came. All together in the station wagon, we toured the island and picnicked again at Waimea Bay. By now, we knew of special places to take guests for brunch, lunch, or dinner, where views of Honolulu, Diamond Head, and the ocean were wondrous. A few months later Don Ray's family came, and we had the itinerary down pat!

Although perhaps not consciously aware of it, our closeness to family and friends augmented our theme of being at "home" in whatever "house" we might find ourselves in. We knew having family and friends visit was a stabilizing force for our children; that they could see how meaningful family is, and that friends are precious.

Shop 6

After commuting to Hickam Air Force Base for almost a year, I was able to get a clerk-typist position on Schofield Barracks at Shop 6, a supply and maintenance area just about five minutes from our house. It was a godsend—one of the best work experiences ever—and I was close to home! The guys I worked with, all civilians who had those wonderful-sounding Hawaiian and Oriental names, made me feel like a queen. It was a rare day that I didn't have an orchid or another flower of some kind on my desk!

Kathy Finding Her Way

I had to leave for work in the mornings before Kevin and Kathy left for school. I trusted them, and when Jim was in the field, as he often was, they took his car, which helped. Kevin had his driver's license, and Kathy had a driver's permit.

I was still working at Hickam AFB and Jim was in the field one morning when I got into the sedan to go to work. *Strange*, I thought, *I don't remember parking this far forward yesterday.* I glanced at the speedometer, and because I'd filled the tank with gas there at Schofield Barracks after work the day before, I knew the mileage exactly. Now there were sixty miles more! *Oh, dear*, I thought, *what's going on?* Kevin and Kathy were getting ready for school, but because of my work situation, I had no options; I had to get to work. The first thing I did at work was call and make sure Kevin and Kathy were in school. Mr. Koga assured me they were, and I felt better, but I knew there would be a scene when I got home!

I confronted them both, and Kathy came forth with her story. She had sneaked out of the house (her bedroom was right on the front), picked up her friend Holly, they went to Honolulu; she came home and sneaked back into the house. I didn't know a thing until I found the car the next morning. Kevin knew nothing; in fact, he was appalled. Upon learning what happened, Jim was upset but even more disappointed. He talked with Kathy as I had done trying to make her understand that her behavior was unacceptable. Needless to say, she was grounded big time! This began some difficult times for us. I understood she was a teenager trying to find her way, but she seemed to have a poor self-image. Neither Jim nor I could understand it, and we talked with Kevin. "All the boys think Kathy's beautiful. I heard some guys talking about her one day. One said he'd like to ask her out, but he wouldn't because she was so pretty. He was sure she'd never want to go with him."

Yes, she was a very pretty girl, and I couldn't understand why she seemed discontent. She loved pretty clothes, so I tried to teach her to sew. Well, she was very upset when I insisted she rip out a crooked seam and re-sew it! I refused to discuss it. To finish the work she'd have to come to me for help, and eventually she did.

When Kathy was grounded, it was as hard, if not harder, on us than it was on her. I couldn't be home every day and watch her every move. We tried giving her boundaries. Making things difficult too was the fact that Kevin was having so many successes and never gave us trouble. He was content to come home, read, watch TV, or have friends over to play pool. She thought we were partial to him. Their relationship, so cute when they were little, had deteriorated. Sometimes he aggravated Kathy to a point of exasperation and that is probably what happened the time Jim heard Kevin yell, and looked to see Kathy chasing him with a butcher knife! He immediately put a stop to that and lectured them both. When I heard about this, I was heartsick. I could not believe things had come to this between them, our beautiful precious children that were the joys of our lives. Jim and I had lived by the age-old Biblical adage that "if you show your children the path they will not depart from it." Jim tried to console me with stories I'd not heard about his younger days, and after all, he'd turned out all right. I laughed a bit at that, but I also reminded him that he was a guy and it was different for girls. He also told Kathy that she needn't try to put stuff over on him, because most of it he had invented! But this time we decided we had to get some help. I talked with our chaplain and learned we were eligible for counseling through the military medical system. He set it up, and once a week for about six weeks, we all went together for counseling. Each week we talked about things going on in our lives. Jim and I were honest about our relationship, and we were happy with our marriage. We knew we made mistakes now and then, but we discussed things and if those discussions got a bit heated, which they could especially about money, we worked things out. It's called respect for each other. The biggest problem for us now was financial difficulties. Kevin and Kathy were honest in their opinions about things, mostly dismay at not being able to buy more "stuff," but they were content at home except that Kevin thought Kathy acted silly and she thought he teased her too much. Otherwise, they didn't seem too worried about anything. Finally, the counselor said he'd like to talk with each one of us alone. After that, he said he didn't think we needed to go on with counseling because what we were doing as parents was good and to keep doing it. He also revealed that he'd asked Kathy what the most important thing in her life was. Expecting her to say her friends, cheerleading, or going to the beach, he was pleased when she told him that her family was most important. That was unusual for her age, and he felt like she would be okay, but for us to continue to set boundaries and do the best we could. I wish someone had told me then what I heard later, that problems between parents and children during the teenage years just might be God's way of making the eventual parting easier!

We tried, muddling along, enduring sassy outbursts and rudeness. Once when Kathy was upset with me, she packed her overnight kit and started to the door. I was close by.

"What are you doing, Kathy?"

"I'm leaving this place! I hate you! I'm going to stay with Holly!"

"Kathy, you are not leaving this house. There's no better place in the world for you than right here with us. We're your family; we love you."

She bolted toward the door, but I grabbed her and held tight. She squirmed and tried to break away, but I wouldn't let go. I held her until she melted in my arms. We both cried. When I dared to loosen my hold, she went to her room and stayed there for a long time. I was saddened the incident had occurred, but I was not about to let her even think for one minute that she wasn't wanted. When Jim came home and I told him about it, he said, "Well, good for you. I'm afraid I might've let her walk right out of the house." But, I knew his heart and if she had left, he would have done everything in his power to find her and bring her home. Fortunately it never came to that. Even though there was an occasional outburst from her about one thing or another, she never attempted to leave home again. What she seemed to want to do more than anything was spend time at the beach! The kids loved the beaches; they were so assessable, and it was hard to resist the temptation to go. They were both strong swimmers and had taken water safety classes, so we were comfortable they wouldn't be reckless. Kathy, did however, skip school to go to the beach more than once. One day, Mr. Koga called Jim to tell him that Kathy was missing her final tests. Kevin had told him he was pretty sure he knew where she was. Jim went by the school, and as Kevin had finished his tests, he went with his dad to one of the North Shore beaches. Sure enough, they found Kathy and

Holly stretched out, soaking up the sun. Kathy jumped up and wrapped her towel around her legs when she saw her daddy.

They gathered their things and Jim took them back to school. Kathy passed her tests; nevertheless, she was grounded ... again.

Kevin McGraw, left tackle.

Kathy McGraw, sweet sixteen

Wrestlers and Cheerleaders

Kevin had begun wrestling in Georgia and loved it, so he was happy Leilehua had a wrestling program. He traveled to several high schools on Oahu for matches, and went to a tournament on

Maui. Jim loved the matches, and yelled and cheered for Kevin while I sat there with my heart in my throat and my stomach knotted. Kevin did well, and we were very proud of him.

Kathy tried out for varsity cheerleader her junior year. She was good, but if she made it, she'd be the *only* blonde in the group. Sadly, we weren't optimistic because we'd already seen some reverse discrimination. Kevin was never bothered by anyone because he was a big guy, but Kathy was a mighty cute little blonde and, apparently, a threat to some of the local girls. Most of the teachers were locals as was the cheerleading sponsor who had the last say in who was selected.

Jim went to pick her up after tryouts and took a flower lei. He was there when she learned she was not selected.

"I'm proud of you for trying," he said as he placed the lei on her shoulders and hugged her.

"It's all right, Daddy," she said letting some tears escape. "The other girls were better than me. They deserve to be the cheerleaders."

When Jim told me that it touched my heart. How I hurt for her—I understood because I'd been a cheerleader and at the time it was so very important to me. What annoyed me was the appearance of obvious discrimination, but we wouldn't dwell on that. We could only pray that our own spirits would never dwell in that abysmal arena.

Leilehua Mules

Because of his size, Kevin played on the offensive line. The smaller, quicker boys, mostly of Oriental heritage, played in the backfield. He was disappointed, but he did well at left tackle, and knew his attitude would make the difference. The Mules were very good. We loved watching them play in their quaint stadium and at all of the away games. The Mules won the district championship, but lost the state championship to the Waianae Warriors.

At the end of the season, names of players who made Hawaii All-State appeared in the Honolulu newspaper. Kevin's name was among those listed as "Honorable Mention, All-State." He was happy, and because football had been such a large part of our family life, even before we had children, Jim and I were very proud! Any success our children had warmed our hearts. They were the joys of our lives.

Graduation

Graduation in Hawaii was unique. Kevin's graduation ceremony in May of 1979 was outside; the weather was warm and humid. Families and friends bought flower leis from vendors that lined the street outside the stadium. The leis, made of plumeria, carnation, orchid, jasmine, and other flowers, were placed on graduates to wish them well. Those with many friends and loved ones there had to hold their arms straight out to keep the leis from falling off! *Interesting*, I contemplated, *that our children were born in Italy, and now Kevin was graduating from high school in Hawaii. What a life!*

Kevin applied to attend Northern Arizona University at Flagstaff, and he was accepted. We were happy because Jim was pretty sure he'd be reassigned to Fort Huachuca after three years in Hawaii, and our family would be close together.

In July, Kevin flew out of Hawaii to return to the mainland for college. I didn't want to believe it, but I knew it was time for this dear child, now a fine young man, to leave. Even so, I felt an enormous relief that there would no longer be fusses between him and Kathy! She and Jim had told Kevin goodbye that morning before they both had to leave for work. Jim hugged me because he knew the day would be hard. It was a poignant moment. We knew our family would never be quite the same.

One of Kevin's friends went with he and I to the airport to see him off. Because the flight was delayed more than once, we were there a long time. As the two boys chatted and I watched them, memories kept coming back. I thought about the time his bike hit a rock in the street and the resulting fall chipped one of his front teeth. He'd cried not because he was hurt, but because the tooth would never be the same. I remembered the sadness we all felt when he learned his eyesight would keep him from being a military pilot. After that he had no interest in trying to go to West Point. I remembered watching him make a speech at a Boy Scout function once and being so pleased at how well he did and at the audience's response. Now he was leaving and I could only rely on my faith, as my prayer had always been for guidance to equip our children with the proper tools to meet their life's travels.

Abbi, Pandy and Puppies

In late spring 1979, Abbi turned fourteen. We knew we wouldn't have her long, so we found a male Sheltie for Pandy so she could have puppies. The mating was successful, and in May she delivered five puppies. We kept one, our Princess Uilani Aloha, which in Hawaiian meant "Princess from Heaven." We called her Lani. Abbi played with the puppies and seemed to heartily approve of them, but after a short illness, she died on July 5.

Schofield Barracks had strict regulations about burial of pets, and our only option was to have post engineers handle it at the post dump. All we could do was watch in deep sadness as she was placed in a shallow hole. Kathy threw a lei to rest on this dear, sweet pet that had been such a wonderful part of our family. We sobbed as the operator of the huge earthmover covered her with soil and gently smoothed it over.

It was hard enough to see her go, but the indignity of this burial broke my heart. As Jim and Kathy and I turned and walked away I thought, rightly or wrongly, *of all the inconveniences, burdens and sorrows associated with military family life, this has to be one of the worst!* Upon our return home the joy of having the puppies helped. Life goes on.

Aviation Detachment, Wheeler Army Airfield

Jim received outstanding OERs at the 197th at Fort Benning, and at the 125th in Hawaii. It was really a shame that they weren't enough. Signal Corps Branch told him that if he'd change his MOS (military operation specialty) from Aviation to Cryptology he'd likely get promoted. Jim had done some cryptology work in Italy, but it was not his thing. All he wanted to do was fly.

After eighteen months, Jim was assigned to the U.S Army Aviation Detachment at Wheeler Field. It was known as a VIP unit because much of the flying was to take dignitaries—senators, congressmen, military officials, and such—from Oahu to the other islands. They also brought mail to and from the Big Island, as well as transporting servicemen and their dependants who were assigned to outer islands so they could shop in the commissaries and exchanges on Oahu.

Jim's date-of-rank placed him in the position of Detachment Deputy Commander. He was checked out in both the Huey helicopter and the fixed wing U-21, which was the Army's version of the twin-engine Beech King Air. The U-21 was no problem, but it had been four and a half years since he'd flown a helicopter. He didn't have need to fly the helicopter much, but flew many hours in the U-21 from island to island. He loved it, and often spoke of the beauty of the islands. He told one time about being in a helicopter with an extremely talented pilot who hovered over a mother whale and her baby. It was quite a sight and he loved it.

"You know what?" I looked at him, squinting my eyes.

"What now?" he responded, seeing the look on my face.

"When I come back in my second life, I'm coming back as the Army Aviator, and you can stay home all the time!"

"Okay, whatever." He laughed and gave me a hug.

Jim was so happy to be flying again and his attitude revealed it. Even though he flew a lot, sometimes leaving early and getting home late, he was home more because this unit didn't participate in field exercises. At least he was home almost every night and I didn't feel the burden of having to do so much by myself.

"Eagle Six"

That summer, a new Lieutenant Colonel took command of the aviation detachment. Jim remained Deputy, enjoying the work and flying. One day after this new boss returned from a trip to the mainland, the First Sergeant came to Jim and told him he had something to show him. That night, Jim came home and told me he needed to talk. "Frances, I don't know what to do. Top showed me a travel voucher the boss put in for reimbursement. It's fraudulent."

"My word. What's it for?"

"It seems the boss asked one of the NCOs to drive him to the airport in a military vehicle and then pick him up again. That NCO even helped him with his bags, but then on the voucher the boss claimed expenses for driving his *own car and for tips* for a bellhop to handle his *and his girlfriend's bags.*"

"That's *terrible!*"

"I think so too, and they want me to do something about it. I just can't believe he thought he could get away with something like that, especially when so many people see every voucher."

We both knew what a terribly sticky situation this was—Jim might be accused of having "sour grapes" because he hadn't been promoted.

"Will you pray with me?" I asked. "All we can do is ask for guidance."

"Yes … thanks."

We joined hands and prayed for guidance to handle this ugly situation.

Jim didn't do anything right away, and the first sergeant asked him about it every day. He knew these fine men were looking at him to do something; they all knew what would happen to *them if they filed a fraudulent travel voucher!* Jim knew the ramifications of setting things in motion for justice to be done. It was a very distressing situation for him.

After about two weeks, Jim garnered the courage to take the papers to his boss who was the Schofield Barracks Commanding Officer with jurisdiction over Wheeler Army Airfield. The colonel couldn't believe his eyes, and asked Jim if he was sure he wanted to pursue this. Jim told him that with the NCOs looking at him, he felt he had no choice. So, the Colonel forwarded the paperwork through appropriate channels to the Commander of U.S. Army Forces in Hawaii. Soon, Jim was called to the Deputy Commander's office at Fort Shafter.

"Major, do you know what this means?" he asked.

"Yes, sir."

"Do you realize that if we take action, this Lieutenant Colonel could be relieved of his command? I don't think we can do that to him."

"Sir, do you know something I don't know?" Jim asked.

He watched as the Colonel hesitated, and appeared to be very uncomfortable.

"Well, no, Major," he finally said. "But this is a very bad situation."

"I realize that, sir, and I'd rather not be involved; but I am, and I have some mighty fine soldiers looking at me to do something about it."

"I see, Major. Well, okay, that'll be all."

It was not long before that boss was relieved of his command. Because of Jim's rank, he was now in charge of this very visible aviation detachment. It was not the way he would ever want to become "Eagle Six."

It had been a very distressing the situation, and I prayed for everyone involved. It was a relief then to see how well Jim was accepted as the unit commander, and I could tell he really was liked when his secretary kept sending home Hawaiian recipes that she thought I might like!

A Call from Arizona

Jim hadn't been Eagle Six long before he told me about answering a call from the Airfield Commander at Fort Huachuca.

"Good morning, Major. How are things in Hawaii?"

"Great, sir. We call it paradise!" Jim responded.

"I guess you do. Well, Major, the folks at Signal Branch told me you might be ready to come to Fort Huachuca."

"That's where I want to go from here, sir. What's the deal?"

"Well, you fly the Mohawk and the U-21, and I need you here."

"That's fine with me, sir. When do you need me?"

"Last week," he said.

Seems this man needed to leave his assignment earlier than

expected, and he was trying to find someone to take his place as Airfield Commander.

"Whoa! That's quick, sir. If branch approves, how soon do you think I'd get orders?"

"Well, branch told me if I found someone, they'd cut orders as soon as possible."

It was late October. Jim soon received orders to report to Fort Huachuca on December 1. We hadn't expected to move quite so soon, but I was resigned to the fact it would come eventually, and after all that we'd been through in recent months, I was ready. Kathy was confused about it at first and didn't say much. I called Mother and Daddy to let them know that we'd be moving to Arizona again, and we'd be there for their anniversary!

I didn't think a lot about it at the time, but finally recognized that indeed, their prayers had been answered. The Lord does work in mysterious ways. Jim, although regretfully, was a part of carrying out a needed justice. We wondered if his boss, fully aware of the awkward situation, had somehow been instrumental in seeing that we were able to leave Hawaii quickly. He didn't say anything; Jim didn't ask, and we will never know. What the Colonel and his wife did do for us was host a farewell party in their quarters not far from ours. They asked us for the names of as many of our friends as we wanted so they could invite them. Many of our friends came to say farewell—friends from the Signal Battalion, neighbors, and even friends we'd known at other assignments. Everyone was dressed in the usual tropical attire, and there was so much food, mostly prepared from local recipes. The officers Jim worked with gave him a plaque that had his name, rank, a set of Senior Aviator wings, all of his medals, the dates of his time there, and with two Hawaiian figures attached to denote the time in Hawaii. It was the most beautiful plaque we'd ever seen! The gathering was a wonderful closure to our time in Hawaii.

Wrapping Things Up

Of course I did dread the actual moving; it was always frustrating and tiring, and Kathy didn't want to leave Hawaii—she wanted to graduate from Leilehua! We understood, but couldn't see leaving her there. Then, her friend Holly invited her to stay with her until graduation. We visited with Holly's mother who was willing, and she showed us their charming home in Wahiawa from where the girls could walk to school. All seemed well, and we agreed to send money every month for Kathy's stay. But, oh my, how scattered our family would be! I was fearful of so many things that could go wrong in a situation like this, but since Kevin left, Kathy had really settled down, and because she wanted to stay, she eagerly acquiesced to our conditions. Jim and I discussed the situation. She had her job in an ice cream parlor, and she was making her grades. Also, Holly did not have a car—there was comfort in that! They would have to take "The Bus" which was the island's free transportation system, anywhere they needed to go, so we agreed together to let her stay. Of course she would be flying out with us because of the fiftieth anniversary celebration, and there was always the chance she wouldn't want to come back alone. If that happened we'd gladly work it out.

Jim shipped the Pontiac in time for it to be in Long Beach, California, when we arrived. We had a VW Bug we'd traded the station wagon for, that we shipped just before we left.

I don't know how Jim managed to do all he did while we lived in Hawaii. He not only completed the non-resident C&GSC course, but he also worked toward a Master's Degree. He was in his last semester when he got orders, and was granted permission to take final tests early. He eventually received his diploma, but missed the graduation ceremony. It wasn't a major concern at the time.

Leaving Kathy Behind

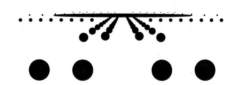

We left Honolulu at 11:00 p.m. on Sunday, November 18. We landed at LAX at 5:00 a.m., but had to *try* to make ourselves comfortable in the terminal and wait until 8:00 a.m. for the rental car concessions to open so we could rent a car and pick up our doggies. They were so happy to see us! We drove to Long Beach, got our car, transferred the luggage, pet shipping crates, and other traveling necessities, and then returned the rental car. We needed gas and more cash for the trip, so we drove to El Toro Marine Air Station near Long Beach, where cashing an out-of-state check would be no problem. It was cold, and because we had no coats coming from Hawaii, we had to buy some. I also found a dress and high-heels for the anniversary celebration, but we found nothing to Kathy's liking. The clothes were so different from what she was used to in Hawaii.

Finally, out of LA on I-10 and then I-40 up through Barstow and Needles, we were on our way to pick up Kevin. Snow was falling in Flagstaff when we arrived in mid-afternoon. The cold air was a shock to our systems! It seemed an eternity since we'd seen Kevin, and he looked so good. We were all together, and he and Kathy were even civil!

Travel was slow because the highways were beginning to ice, and patrolmen were everywhere. Until the weather evened out

Jim followed eighteen-wheelers, and we got to Winslow to spend the night. Up and out early the next day, we drove to Albuquerque. While getting gas, Jim determined it was not safe to travel to Amarillo on the tires and decided to have them replaced.

As it happened, our friend Marge Rita was living there with her sister, where they operated a dress shop in downtown Albuquerque. We wanted to see her, but would've settled for a phone call; however, when we realized we'd be there to have the tires replaced, Jim dropped off Kathy and me to visit with her. Reeling from the divorce, she was trying to make a new life, as well as a living. We learned that Joe had married a woman he'd met years earlier in Korea. We were sad for Marge, but with a beautiful Christian spirit, she told us she looked to the future prayerfully. We knew this pretty lady with a talent for singing and playing the guitar would be okay.

And, another blessing—Kathy found a dress. Sometimes things work out...

We'd lost two hours of travel time, and even though we'd called to tell her when we'd arrive, we got there later than Grandma, now eighty-one, thought we should have. She said she was glad to see us anyway. Ghern was there, and we spent Thanksgiving all together. It was good to learn that Standard Oil had transferred him from Wyoming to Hobbs, New Mexico. He'd now be much closer to Grandma.

While there, Jim had a call from the commander of the U.S. Army's Electronic Proving Ground at Fort Huachuca to let him know that he would be assigned to EPG because he was a Mohawk pilot. Seems they needed him worse than the airfield did.

"Probably what really happened, Frances," he confided to me after we went to bed, "was the post commander found out I'd been passed over and didn't want me as airfield commander."

"I'm sorry, sweetheart. That makes me sad, but you'd rather fly the Mohawk, wouldn't you?

"You've got that right! I don't care to ever again have all the headaches that go with being a commander."

I knew he hated the circumstances, but that he would live above it. I was proud of him.

The Fiftieth Anniversary

On Friday, we traveled to Clovis to Mamaw and Papaw's. We could only be there two nights, as Kevin had to get back to college on Monday.

Mr. and Mrs. Chester Ogden's fiftieth anniversary: (left to right) Royce and Sammye Ogden, Jim and Frances McGraw, Moreland and Christine Martin, Chester and Medah Ogden, Shell and Melva Denison, John and Cynthia Van Auken, and Doyle and Marilou Ogden

The elegant celebration held in their church's Fellowship Hall on Saturday, November 24, was exactly fifty years after their wedding. All six of us Ogden kids were there, one great-grandchild and, all but one of sixteen grandchildren. Mother and Daddy were so humbly proud. That evening, we visited more while eating at a favorite local restaurant, and on Sunday morning, we gathered for brunch before everyone had to say good-bye. We sang "Happy Birthday" to Kathy—it was her seventeenth birthday. That afternoon, we put her on an airplane bound for Denver where she'd catch a nonstop flight back to Hawaii. Mamaw was upset.

"Mother, we have to do this for Kathy," I told her. "We'd rather not, but she wants to graduate from high school there, and we've made arrangements that we think will be fine."

"Well, I don't like it. She seems so little and so young to be making that trip alone."

"I know, but we just have to hope and pray that everything will be all right." I saw her moistened eyes as she looked away. I felt a sorrowful numbness.

As soon as Kathy was on her way, we headed west to get Kevin back to Flagstaff. On the way he came down with fever and sore throat—tonsillitis again. He was miserable and slept a lot. We hated to leave him.

"I'll go to the dispensary first thing in the morning," he said. "They took care of me before, and I'm sure they will again." We remembered when he'd arrived at NAU back in August he'd planned to try out for the football team, but that first week he came down with another bad case of tonsillitis. When he felt well, he was too far behind.

We called Kathy. She'd made her trip fine, and she was excited to be back in Hawaii. We talked with her thereafter at least once a week.

2352 Golf Links Road, Sierra Vista, Arizona

We drove from Flagstaff to Sierra Vista and talked about it being the first time we were without one or the other of our children since Kevin was born in 1961. We found ourselves lavishing a lot of attention on Pandy and Lani. Lani, now six months old, was one of the most beautiful Shelties we'd ever seen—one of the smartest too. She was small enough to nestle between Jim's headrest and his neck. He loved it!

We checked into a motel before going to see Don Ray and Mary Beth. The next day, we visited Bob and Joyce Stachel in their lovely new house. After visiting a while, they'd have nothing else but for us to stay with them while we were waiting on quarters, or until we found a place to live. We hesitated, but they insisted, as they had three bedrooms and den with all the amenities, even a swimming pool. We were fond of Bob and Joyce, so we agreed to give it a try, *but we would pay our way*. Joyce, a real estate franchise owner, and Bob, now retired from the army and well-entrenched in commercial real estate, were busy. We wouldn't be holding hands all the time.

During that last week of November, Jim signed in at EPG. He learned because of his date-of-rank, he'd be overseeing the Aviation Detachment that provided infrared radar surveillance with the Mohawk, and the testing of other electronics. We had ample time to find a place to live.

In the meantime, I went to the Civilian Personnel Office (CPO) and turned in my SF-171 to renew my career with the Federal Service. There was nothing available right away, but I eventually interviewed for a couple of positions and accepted one as secretary to the Fort Huachuca Public Affairs Officer (PAO). That was where the post newspaper, *The Huachuca Scout*, was published, and since I'd studied journalism in college, it seemed right up my alley.

Townhouse at 1300 Carmelita

We thought about buying a house, but interest rates were high, and inflation rampant in late 1979. A quality house only two-thirds the size of the one we'd built in Georgia would cost almost twice as much. Joyce, the real estate specialist she was, showed us that we could qualify for an FHA loan with a small down payment. She showed us some townhouses under construction; we liked what we saw, and decided to purchase one that had everything we needed. At that time, almost all new construction was Southwestern in architecture with white or grey adobe brick walls and red or brown brick trim. We were very comfortable with it. The townhouse had two bedrooms and two large baths; the living room was a little small, but had a beautiful fireplace in the corner. The modern kitchen was U-shaped and between a breakfast area and the dining room. There were large windows in each room, and a sliding glass door onto the patio. The view of the mountains was incredible!

We were excited when the loan was approved, and the builder let us move in just before everything was finished. Bad move. Our excitement was short-lived. We came in from work one day to see that the builder had laid concrete for a large patio and had extended the roof to cover it. We had explicitly not asked for that, as it would add a considerable amount to the loan, and Jim reminded the builder. He replied that it was part of his deal, and we'd have to pay for it. Jim told him we'd move out before we'd pay for something he knew we didn't want. The builder called his bluff! Well, now we were in a pickle. Joyce came through again, telling us that the FHA loan folks felt we were right to not pay for something we hadn't asked for, and that the loan application would be voided without fault. She found us a nice house to rent, and we immediately moved out of the townhouse.

1257 Mesquite Street

Here we were, both trying to get adjusted in our new jobs, and we had to move. This time the army *didn't* pay for it. We rented a U-Haul truck and spent the weekend packing, moving, and unpacking. We really were weary, but the rent house was nice and more comfortable than we could have imagined. Also of Southwestern architecture, the house was just a few years older. There was a curved drive up to the large carport with storage area on the front; there were three bedrooms, two baths, kitchen/dining room combination and a comfortable living room. There was nothing particularly striking about the décor, but our furniture, pictures, curtains and drapes made it seem like home. One of the best things, though, was the covered patio on the south side. The west end was shaded with honeysuckle, and a swing there made our after-dinner times of sharing coffee and dessert very pleasant. This was actually where we began that tradition because of the ambiance, and it was now just the two of us. We could have lived there comfortably for a long time, but the house was not for sale. Joyce wouldn't let us off the hook about buying a house. She knew we qualified for an FHA loan, and encouraged us to build. We wanted our own home, so we talked with a builder and showed him the plans for the house we'd built in Georgia. We scaled the plans down to what we could afford, and began the deal. I loved the building process; Jim did not, but he went along with me. We chose a corner lot not far from the rent house. It sat up higher than other lots on the street and we had a nice view of surrounding mountains. We decided on a Southwestern style with red adobe brick and olive green trim. Again, we had three bedrooms, two full baths, and a large step-down great room with fireplace and French doors out onto the rear patio. We had a separate dining room and a breakfast area. We made the kitchen a little larger than the one in Georgia, but we did without a game room. In our bathroom, of course, there were two lavatories. We were a working couple and enjoyed so much having the "his and her" areas for getting ready for work each morning. In our bedroom we had corner windows installed and I found that I could lie in bed at night and gaze at the stars before falling asleep. It was nice.

We had beautiful tile from Mexico installed in the entry way. We chose a beige carpet throughout that wouldn't clash with anything, and we had kitchen carpet (mode du jour) installed. In the meantime, Jim and I attended real estate classes. We were quite sure we wanted to retire in Sierra Vista, and although Jim hoped to continue flying as a profession, if one or the other of us could get set-up selling real estate, then things might work out. By the time we returned to Hawaii for Kathy's graduation, we had our licenses, I had sold a house and had earned enough to pay for my real estate expenses.

Kathy's Dilemma

We called Kathy often and she called us. She was in her last semester of high school, still working, and we sent the agreed upon money to Holly's mom.

After about six weeks, Kathy called to say she was moving out of Holly's house.

"What's going on, Kathy?"

"Oh, Mom, it's just awful here. Nobody does anything but me. You know we talked about me doing my share of the work while I'm here? Well, they must think I'm the maid!"

"Nobody else does anything?"

"No! Mom, you know you taught me to clear the table and get the dishes in the dishwasher. Well, I do that, and everyone else just leaves the kitchen and goes to watch TV or something."

"So you're really going to move?"

"Yes. Do you remember Anna Canencia, the girl that Kevin took to the prom?"

"Yes, I remember Anna."

"Well, she's invited me to stay with her family. We talked with her folks, and it's okay because they have an extra room since one of her brothers moved. They're a real nice family."

"I'm sure they are, but we'll have to talk with them. Can you give me their phone number?"

And so Kathy moved in with Anna's family. She had a warm experience there, and appreciated the Canencia family. We did too, and still do!

NAU Football

Kevin went out for football during spring training at NAU, and invited us to come up for the spring game. This time he showed us the campus, and what fun it was to see others call out his name as they passed by! He was known and well liked.

The football game was incredible, and a nice warm-fuzzy for Jim and me. Kevin played tight end, and the blocking skills he'd learned early-on proved invaluable. The team made the winning score following his beautiful block! We loved it all, and were so proud of him.

Graduation in Hawaii

Jim, Kevin and I flew to Hawaii to attend Kathy's graduation. She met us at the airport. I ran to her and hugged her as tightly as I could. She appeared somewhat rumpled, and I was puzzled because she'd always taken pride in how she looked. She later told me she was worried that we wouldn't be glad to see her because of the problems she always caused. But when we all hugged her so close, she knew she was still part of our family. She also said she was ready to come home with us.

We stayed in a cabin at the Army's recreation area at Waianae

Beach, and enjoyed the low-key rural setting. We also visited with the Canencia family that had helped Kathy. They were a beautiful family of Filipino heritage, but American in every sense of the word.

Kathy's graduation ceremony was much like Kevin's, and we took pleasure in seeing so many kids that we'd known before. We were proud of Kathy, and she looked gorgeous! She seemed proud of us, and she kept telling us how glad she was that we were there. She realized now that she belonged with her family, and not alone in Hawaii.

The time came to leave, and we wondered if we'd ever come back. The soft Hawaiian music on the airliner intercom system brought feelings of melancholy, and even sadness. The time had passed so quickly. None of us had much to say on the flight to the mainland.

Back at home, we were a family again, and things seemed normal—Kevin and Kathy fussed at each other. Dismayed, we encouraged them to grow up and understand they had no other siblings—they were all they would ever have. They both enrolled in school at Cochise County Junior College, got summer jobs, and helped around the house. They made new friends and delighted in seeing some kids they'd known in the early seventies. Toward the end of the summer, Kevin had a talk with his Dad.

"Dad, I've decided not to play football."

"Oh? I thought you enjoyed playing."

"I do, Dad, I really do. I love the game, but I think the best thing for me to do is concentrate on my studies. I want to make something of myself, and I want my college education."

"I'm proud of you, son, and if that's what you want, then go for it."

"You're not going to be upset if I don't play football?"

"Not in the least. It's entirely up to you. I didn't ask you to play, did I?"

"No, but I wanted to show you I could make it, and that's why I went out in the spring."

"Well, you didn't have to do that for me. You played a great game, and we really enjoyed watching, but I'm even more proud of you for wanting to make your grades and make something of yourself. I'll always be proud of you."

Kathy enjoyed her summer classes so much that she enrolled in more classes that fall. She was beginning to realize that she liked learning—a new world was opening for her.

1140 Tacoma Street

We moved into the new house just before Thanksgiving. It was not as uptown as the one in Georgia, but it was in a nice neighborhood and had what we wanted. The kitchen was a little bigger and we now had a microwave oven. The large two-steps-down great room with wood-burning fireplace was wonderful!

As a teenager, Jim had learned to lay carpet while working with his brother, Ben, in Amarillo. He still had his carpet tools; in fact, we had carried them all over the country every time we moved! He always installed the carpet himself, if needed, everywhere we lived. Now he even sewed together different colored sample pieces—off white, blue, brown and beige—for our bathroom. I loved it, and because he worked so hard I appreciated it that much more! While he worked, and I was his little helper, we recalled the times in college during our first year of marriage when he made extra money laying carpet. It had helped so much when he wasn't playing football. He seemed to enjoy the physical labor and was still so strong that he could muscle the carpet and tools around very well.

Flying the Rivers

Jim loved flying the Mohawk so much that I teased him about it being his mistress! Actually, I loved the stories he told when he came home. An interesting aspect of the job was his opportunity to fly over much of the United States. One of EPG's missions was to fly over rivers and take pictures with infrared cameras to learn what flood potential there might be. They also flew over many government installations to determine if unusual amounts of heat were being released. These seemed strange missions to me, but Jim explained it. During the Carter administration, military budgets took a big hit, and not only were promotions hard to come by, but so were aircraft parts and supplies. The Coast Guard was given the job and money to determine flood control and excessive heat-emission problems, but they didn't have the flying capability, so they contracted out the jobs to the U.S. Army. Jim flew the length of many major rivers and loved every minute!

And, because he was a helicopter pilot, he was on a stand-by list of those called to fly medevac. He came in one day later than usual.

"I just got back from flying a medevac," he said somberly.

"Oh dear. Was it a rough one?" I asked.

"When we landed on the hospital helipad, two medics brought a newborn boy in a portable incubator onboard. The attending doctor told us to hurry because the baby was sinking fast."

"Oh, my word!"

"He was the most beautiful new baby I'd ever seen, but they told us he was having difficulty breathing. It took us twenty minutes to get to the hospital in Tucson, and I was so thankful for one of the smoothest, most gentle landings I've ever made in a helicopter."

"You must have been praying," I said.

"I was."

Later at dinner, Jim seemed preoccupied. I asked him what he was thinking about.

"I can't get that baby off my mind. I hope he's doing okay."

Flying the Learjet

In 1980, the price of oil was high, and exploration of this indispensable energy product was profuse. Oil companies and related industries prospered and many bought aircraft and hired pilots. Jim often landed at airports throughout the country and saw corporate jets. Visiting with the well-paid pilots made him envious. He wanted every opportunity to get a good flying job when he retired, so *somehow* amidst all the turmoil of our lives, he managed to take a week's leave to California to get a type rating in the Learjet. He accomplished the mission, and thanks to his flying skills, our future looked good.

Thanksgiving with Family

For our Thanksgiving trip to Texas and New Mexico, Jim rented a Cessna 182 from a flying club and we took off, flying first to Flagstaff to pick up Kevin, and then across eastern Arizona and New Mexico. We flew over Lake Sumner, and then over Fort Sumner about twenty miles south.

"See, there it is, Frances, there's the farm," Jim said as he lowered the aircraft as much as he could over the valley.

""Yes, I see it! See kids, look! There it is! That's where I grew up!"

"Ohhhhhh!" Kathy squealed as we circled over the pretty farmland.

"This is so neat!" Kevin said.

"There's the barn, and the windmill, and the chicken houses."

"Yeah, it's the farm all right," Jim said. "I recognized it right away when I flew down the Pecos River last month. I was surprised I could pick it out so well myself."

"Oh, Jim, this is so neat," I said. "Thank you so much!"

"Not a problem," he said as he smiled and began climbing to continue the sixty-mile trip to Clovis. Mamaw and Papaw met us at the airport. There were great hugs all around!

The next day as we prepared to go to Lubbock for Thanksgiving dinner at Christine and Moreland's, Jim and Papaw talked. They decided it would be nice for Mamaw to fly with Jim and the kids, and I could drive over with Papaw. Great idea! Mamaw really enjoyed seeing Jim do what he loved best.

On Friday, we flew to Amarillo. Ghern and Mike were at Grandma's also. After we'd visited a while, Grandma told Jim that a high school buddy, Bob Conley, had asked him to call.

"You know Bob's doing pretty well," she said. "He has his own oil company and making a lot of money. He still brings his tax return for me to make out for him and Juanita."

"Is that right? When we saw them in Hawaii he was acting so rich that I figured he'd have some high-falutin' accountant doing that now," he teased.

"No, I still do it. He wants you to call him. He wants to know when you're going to retire."

Jim called Bob. He and Juanita wanted us to come out Saturday evening and bring the kids.

Visiting the Conleys in their lovely home in affluent Southwest Amarillo was special. Their two girls, Kris and Robin, were delightful and chatted happily with Kevin and Kathy. Bob and Juanita were gracious hosts, and the time warm and comfortable.

Bob told Jim that his company, Spur Petroleum, was doing well and that they expected to buy an aircraft soon. He wondered if Jim would retire and join his company as chief pilot. Jim told him he'd have to talk with me because we'd just moved into a new house and we really wanted to live in Arizona. Bob said he'd be in touch.

Sunday morning we were up and out early to get Kevin back to Flagstaff and then on home. Flying was special, and to be able to cover the miles we had to in order to enjoy our families during that short holiday time seemed incredible!

We returned to our jobs and busily prepared for the holidays. There were festive unit functions, and gatherings in friends' homes. We played poker at Bob and Joyce's house and bridge with Don Ray and Mary Beth. Mary Beth found a score pad that we'd used years before when she and I were learning to play. We decided to keep a running score of our Bridge games from then on. Jim and Don always beat us, but we had fun. While we were playing, Jim mentioned to Don Ray that Bob Conley had talked with him about coming to work in Amarillo. Don had a fit!

"Don't even think about that! You're going to retire in Arizona and live here close to us!"

"That's what we really want to do, Don, but I've been checking out flying jobs here in Arizona, and there just aren't any."

"I thought you were going to sell real estate," Don responded.

"Yeah, I know, and that's okay for Frances, but it's not my thing, Don. I want to fly."

Don looked at me, but I had no response. I winced and shook my head. He looked at his longtime friend. "I know you like to fly, but do you really want to move again?"

"No, but I've got to go where the job is. We love Arizona and being here by you guys, but I want to fly. I even checked with

CPO, and they say there are no flying jobs expected to open up in the near future at Fort Huachuca. And, on top of that, if I did go to work for Federal Service, I'd lose half my military retirement pay."

"How's that?" Don asked.

"Well, when I got my Regular Army commission back in '67, it was supposed to be my ticket to Command and General Staff College and other Army schools that would set me up for promotion, but you know how that turned out. Anyway, if you're an RA officer and you retire and go back to work for the government, you have to give up half your retirement. Otherwise, you're "double-dipping," and there's a law against it. It's a crock of course, because if you're a retired Reserve Officer that doesn't count, and you get both pay checks in full."

"My word!" Mary Beth exclaimed. "That's not right."

"No, that doesn't seem fair," Don said.

"It's not, but that's the way it is. So, I've got to be on the lookout for a good flying job somewhere. I hope we don't have to move, but we may have to." They couldn't believe that we'd even think about moving again. There was that possibility, but I hoped that a flying job would come along so we wouldn't have to. I knew Jim was tired of the military scene; getting passed over every year was not fun. We talked about things as we jogged— still for two miles, at least three times a week. According to the experts, it was a good time to talk because if we were running too fast to talk, we were running too fast!

Bob Conley called and asked Jim to join Spur Petroleum as Chief Pilot.

"We don't have an airplane yet, but that's why we want you. We figure you'll have the best idea of what we need for the job."

"You mean you'll want me to help you buy an airplane?" Jim
d.

I couldn't hear Bob, but I really tuned in to what Jim was saying when I heard that so I ran to our bedroom to pick up the phone.

"That's right. In the meantime, we'll get you trained as a landman so you'll be busy when you're not flying."

"Does a landman still do the same thing these days?" Jim asked.

"Same as always," Bob answered. "You'll check land records at courthouses to determine who owns property, and then we'll talk to them about leasing so we can drill on it."

"That's what I thought," Jim said. "I'd really like to do that."

Jim had studied geology in college with the dream of working in the oil field, but his time in the military changed all that. Now he had a chance to get back into it. He was excited, but when he told me what Bob offered to pay, I was disappointed. I thought he was worth more; and besides, I was aware of what corporate pilots earned.

"But, Frances," Jim said, "the company will train me to be a landman, and that's a lot. They'll pick up that tab."

I didn't know how to respond. I was in so much turmoil about picking up and moving again, and moving of all places to Amarillo, where it was cold and windy in the winter, and hot and windy in the summer. Besides, I wasn't too keen on living close to Grandma. I didn't mind going to visit every once-in-a-while, but to live close by again, I just didn't know if I could do it. I immediately felt guilty. I knew living close would mean a lot to her. *What kind of a person are you, Frances?* I admonished myself. *She doesn't have that many more years. The least you can do is help out where you can.*

And so I agreed to the move, Jim made preparations to retire from the Army, and we put our pretty new house up for sale.

In February, we flew to Amarillo to look for a place to live, this time in a flying club Cessna 172. We left in early afternoon, thinking we could get to Clovis before dark. We flew northeast of Deming between the Continental Divide and the Rio Grande River to go north and around White Sands Proving Ground. Suddenly we could see clouds gathering over the mountains. Jim was puzzled. Weather was not predicted when he'd made the flight plan.

"These clouds probably won't last long," he said. "We should be able to get past them."

The small plane lumbered along as we went into the clouds. It was dark and noisy. Jim pulled out a flashlight and began looking at the wings.

"What are you doing?" I yelled above the engine noise.

"Checking for ice on the wings," he yelled back.

I shuddered as the aircraft managed the turbulence with its own shudders. We could see flashes of lightning. My knees were shaking. All of a sudden, Jim turned the aircraft to the left. I couldn't hear him, but I could read his lips, "We're going back!"

We landed in sunny Deming, but we could see the dark clouds to the north. We paid to park the aircraft and for a motel room, but that was small compared to what could have happened. I called my folks to tell them we'd go on to Amarillo and then come back by to see them.

When we crawled into bed I told Jim that I was so glad he'd turned back. He said he was too. We slept well that night.

The next morning in Amarillo, Bob Conley met us at the airport and took us by the office to meet everyone, including a realtor and investor in the company who took us to look at houses. We found a house that was nice enough, had all we needed, and the price was right. We made an offer contingent on our house selling in Arizona. Grandma was happy.

We then flew to Clovis to see Mother and Daddy. They were also happy that we'd be much closer.

"What are Kevin and Kathy going to do?" Mother asked.

"They plan to finish this semester, and then transfer either to West Texas State or Texas Tech," I told her. "Kathy's staying with Bob and Joyce until school's out."

"I'm glad they don't want to stay in Arizona."

"Yeah, and they're excited about moving to Texas. It feels like home to them."

They saw us off at the airport, and we headed toward Carlsbad. Flying over Portales and the ENMU campus where we'd met twenty-three years earlier was fun. Then, facing a strong headwind as we flew west, Jim realized we couldn't make it to Carlsbad without refueling. He radioed a change of flight plan to land in Roswell. About halfway there we were flying along, bouncing in the wind, *when all of a sudden my right-side window flew open!* I about jumped out of my skin, but without conscious thought to do so, I reached out, grabbed the handle, pulled the window in, and locked it. Jim was impressed that I didn't panic. I read his lips over the noise, "Good job, Frances! Bess 'um heart."

Army Retirement

At home, we geared ourselves for Jim's retirement and the move. I was in turmoil about leaving our house and Arizona, but conflict among others at my workplace actually made it easy for me to leave my job. Jim asked for nothing special for retirement, except to fly his beloved Mohawk one last time. It was a hassle because there was no real mission to justify the flight. His boss relented, though, when Jim asked him how much the traditional retirement parade he was entitled to would've cost the unit if he'd asked for it. And so, he was able to take his Mohawk for a few hours to fly over Arizona ... one ... more ... time.

We were graciously bade farewell by Jim's unit and my office, and received special gifts typical of retirement. For me, it was bittersweet. I felt Jim deserved so much more.

Our house sold, and the purchase in Amarillo went through, except the people wanted to stay there until school was out. We had to be out of ours by April 1, so Jim called Grandma and asked if we could stay with her for the months of April and May. She was willing, of course.

On March 31, 1980, we were packing out of our house when the news came that President Reagan had been shot. We were in shock. The pace of the packers slowed, as did our work to clean the house. Finally, when we were assured the president was in no great danger, the job was done, and we were on our way.

We got to live in that sweet house 119 days.

The Crazy Years

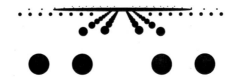

Studebaker Street...Again

Grandma's house number changed from 610 Studebaker to 920 Studebaker and to 920 West Studebaker during the years 1959–1981. While we lived in Italy, zip codes came on the scene; those did not change.

We settled in with Grandma, paid rent, and helped where we could. Pandy and Lani were good little dogs, and she seemed to enjoy them. She was amused, though, when Jim and I got up early three times a week to go jogging. The streets there were rough, so we drove about half a mile to Wonderland Park to jog on the vast picnic area trails. This was about the only time that Jim and I were alone. We talked and planned. He was excited about his job, and our future looked bright. Right now, though, I needed a job. I was told the only federal service entities in Amarillo were the HUD office and the VA hospital. That wasn't true, but neither appealed to me, and I didn't bother to check it out. In the meantime, Bob Conley told Jim that a law firm in their building needed a secretary. One of the attorneys, Art Baker, was a childhood friend of Jim and Bob. I interviewed for the job and took a typing test. I messed up the typing test and was sure I wouldn't be hired; however, I got a call from Art to come in.

He asked me more questions and said they'd like to hire me as their receptionist. I accepted, thanked him, and told him I was surprised they'd hire me because of my typing test.

"We were more impressed with the spelling test," Art said. "Bob Sanders said that he thought anyone who spelled 'judgment' correctly could do the work."

Interesting, I thought. I had no conscious realization that the spelling should be judgment or judgement! I checked the dictionary and learned the spelling is optional; nevertheless, at the law firm of Sanders, Kiser, and Baker in Amarillo, it was spelled judgment.

I was paid much less than what I'd earned with the government, but the idea of working near Jim appealed to me, and it meant we didn't need another car. Also, the work activity and clients revealed these three attorneys, Bob Sanders, Sam Kiser, and Art Baker to be dedicated Christian men. Bob was also the federal magistrate.

Soon, Spur Petroleum provided Jim with a much-appreciated company car, and Jim had a new experience keeping up with expense records. He asked me to open a second bank account to keep his expenses separate from our household account.

7416 Jameson Street, Amarillo, Texas

The folks we'd bought the house from asked to stay there another month. That was a hardship for us, but not as hard as it would've been for them to move out with small children. It wasn't bad until the kids came. It really taxed our space to have two more adults in the house plus two more cars in the driveway. Grandma didn't mind; she seemed happy we were there.

While there, we attended the Pleasant Valley United Methodist Church with Grandma. The following spring my brother-in-law, Shell Denison, now an ordained minister, came from San Jon, New Mexico, as pastor! What an interesting turn of events.

Kevin got a job at nearby Tascosa Country Club as a life-guard, and Kathy began working at Dillard's in downtown Amarillo. They were happy and made new friends.

Finally, it was time to move into our house. Although it was fairly new and in quite a nice neighborhood, it wasn't an eye-catcher from the street. It was a brown brick with brown trim. We thought we'd fix it up with a different trim color as soon as we could. It had three nice bedrooms and two full baths even if ours did have just one lavatory. The entrance floor had beautiful, colorful tile, and there was a one-step-down into the large, paneled living room that had a fireplace in the corner. We missed having a separate dining room, but the eating area was roomy and we did have a breakfast counter. The utility room was between the fully-equipped kitchen and large double-car garage.

The three months we waited versus the two we'd expected had been long. Now we could finally have some semblance of the lifestyle we enjoyed. The transactions of selling and buying a house were benign, and there was even money left over—enough to manage joining the small Tascosa Country Club where we could play golf with the Conleys. The prospects for Spur Petroleum to do well and for us to prosper were good. Why not? Why couldn't it be our turn to reap the benefits and at the same time live close to our families? We transferred our membership to St. Paul United Methodist Church. *It seemed we were where we were supposed to be.*

That fall, Kevin transferred to Texas Tech in Lubbock. Kathy lived at home and attended classes at West Texas State in Canyon. Kevin dreamed of being a lawyer and majored in political science. Kathy took basic subjects, not yet knowing what she wanted. Jim enjoyed studying to be a landman, and in order to stay proficient in flying, the company paid for him to lease an aircraft for a few hours now and then. They had not decided when to buy an aircraft.

During football season, Jim officiated high school games throughout the Panhandle. I attended some of the close-by games, but most Friday evenings I spent with Grandma. We'd shop if she needed to, and then go eat catfish at Long John Silver's.

Spur Petroleum had some good drilling operations in place. Bob and his partner kept expecting any day to see the "big one" come in that would keep their investors happy, put their small company on the road to success, and set us all up for a long time to come. We couldn't help but get caught up in the excitement as we watched other oil companies thrive. Bob and Juanita had plans to build a fine new house and encouraged us to do the same, so we had some plans drawn. We also traded our Pontiac for a big Chrysler New Yorker. Why not?

Matters of the Heart

In early April 1982, Jim went for one week to Oklahoma City to a landman school. Later that month, Bob and Juanita celebrated their twenty-fifth wedding anniversary with a reception in their home. It was a nice evening with many Borger folks there that Jim hadn't seen in years. We enjoyed visiting, but Jim drank too much. I'd not seen him that way in a long time. I was embarrassed and told him the next day that it would not be pretty if he let it happen again. I meant it, and although I didn't pay too much attention at the time, he began pulling away from me. One morning about the middle of May as we struggled to share the single lavatory in our bathroom, our eyes met, and I didn't like what I saw. When he was dressed, he announced to me that he wanted a divorce. I was stunned and thought, *Well, what in the world is this?* I looked him straight in the eye and said, "Jim McGraw, you can't do better." I knew he heard me, but he didn't respond and soon left in his company car.

It was hard to get through the day and of course I was quiet. That evening Jim came in and proceeded to pack, removing his underwear from the chest of drawers and clothes from the closet. I couldn't believe my eyes. I sat on the bed and watched every move he made, just knowing that he'd come to me, hug me, tell me he was sorry for what he'd said that morning, and I'd say it's okay, and everything would be all right. But he didn't. He carried his suitcase to the car then came back to get his shaving kit. I tried to talk with him, but his only response was in answer to my question about where he was going, and that was he didn't know where he'd be. Throughout all of this I did not cry, I was numb.

What I didn't know then was that Spur Petroleum was in trouble, as were many oil companies. OPEC had suddenly lowered the price of imported oil so that drilling in America was now too expensive. Bob had told Jim the company could no longer justify a pilot and that he'd have to let him go the end of June. I talked with the Conleys and the lawyers I worked with about our situation. They were all stunned because Jim and I had seemed devoted to each other. I had thought so too.

I beat myself up pretty good trying to figure out what in the world had gone wrong. I wondered if he'd finally thought my exasperation with his mother was too much, or my moodiness when there was so doggone much to do with all the moving, or when the money was tight. But wait a minute! He had always seemed to understand those things, and besides, he's the one that left without explanation! It really made me mad that he wouldn't talk about it, but the worst part was, my heart was breaking.

It was strange seeing Jim in the hall at work, and one time we found ourselves on the elevator together ... alone. Neither of us spoke. Then one day he asked me to join him for lunch at Tascosa Country Club. He was growing a mustache and no longer had the short military haircut. He seemed strangely cavalier in explaining that he had always loved me, but sometimes people change, and he had changed. He thought that perhaps I too should make some changes in my life. He said he'd be leaving soon to find a job in Oklahoma City because there were a lot of oil, gas, and aviation companies there. He figured I'd have plenty of help from family, friends, *and* the lawyers I worked for that I "seemed to care so much for."

I couldn't respond and we parted quietly, coolly. It had never been my nature to overreact, to yell and scream, or even to cry if I was upset. I tried hard to always give the benefit of the doubt and let a situation unfold before I took any action. Now, as usual, I had to let things settle for a while to try to understand, but the more I thought about it, the more upset I was. I was *pissed!* I couldn't recall even using the word before, but there was no other word that accurately described my feelings. At home, I was alone with unfamiliar thoughts. How dare him! What about our long-term commitment and all that we'd shared? I had so many questions, but always drawing on my spiritual foundation, I prayed for understanding and strength.

I talked with the lawyers I worked for. They were dismayed as they had thought Jim and I were devoted to each other. They heard so much of this type thing every day from clients and were terribly disappointed that yet another marriage was in trouble. I sought comfort from the other girls in the office and they were so kind. One had been divorced and shared her story with me, but all of this was so foreign to me. I was miserable.

Jim came by in a couple of days with a small U-Haul truck, loaded his recliner, the portable TV from our bedroom, and a few more things from the garage. I was thankful Kathy was working and Kevin was already back at Tech and were not there to see this. I knew they couldn't believe what was happening either. I asked questions, but he wouldn't talk with me. Then, finally, he announced he was headed for Oklahoma City. Barely able to get the words out, I asked, "What are you going to do for a car?" I knew he'd have to turn in the company car.

"I'll buy another car. I'm sure Mr. Standley will loan me the money."

Ah, yes, Mr. Standley, our banker—he'd been *so* helpful through the years.

Telling the Family

My heart was heavy and I had no idea what to do. Kathy still lived at home and was finishing the semester. She acted strangely and would hardly talk with me, but we went to church together and both shed tears as we sang and prayed. Kevin was stunned, so I went to Lubbock to try to explain to him what was happening. We joined Christine and Moreland at their kitchen table. What I learned was that Kevin had already talked with Jim, and that he told Kevin that he might not understand now, but that he would some day. Moreland was sure there was something here that didn't meet the eye.

"Well, if you're concerned about me, Moreland, I can tell you that I have been faithful to Jim. That is *not* the problem!" It was the truth.

Kevin burst into tears. I wondered if Jim had, in trying to rationalize, told him I'd been unfaithful. He soon composed himself, and we talked more. Christine and Moreland assured me they'd help any way they could.

I drove to Clovis that Saturday afternoon to explain the situation to my folks. How I dreaded this! They'd always cared for

Jim and were perplexed, to say the least. We sat at the dining table and talked for a long time. I assured my folks that I loved Jim, that I didn't understand why he was gone and that I wanted him to come home. Daddy asked me to go to church with him the next morning. Mother wasn't feeling well.

I told him I'd love to go, and he reminded me it was Communion Sunday. I asked him what he meant because I was perplexed at his tone, and I assured him that I always appreciated taking communion. He answered that it was his opinion that a lot of people take communion when they haven't cleansed their hearts of hate and haven't asked for their own forgiveness, "and then they become literally, physically ill," he said in a slow and deliberate tone.

I'd never heard anyone talk about communion that way. All of a sudden I realized that he, like Moreland, was trying to learn just what part I might have played that caused our problems. He would never come right out and ask me if there was someone else in my life. When I explained that there was no one else, that I loved Jim and wanted him home, and that there was no hatred in my heart, he said he thought it would be okay for me to take communion. His words remained with me and I don't think I've ever taken communion since without thinking about them.

Figuring Things Out

Bob and Juanita asked me if there was someone else in Jim's life. I told them I didn't think so; at least I'd never had a reason to think so before.

Jim had never been a ladies' man. We both had always had a lot of female friends and usually they were wives of his friends. I'd never seen him flirt or anything close to it. He'd always been so good and made me feel like he loved me more than anything.

I was totally surprised and shocked at his actions. I kept recalling the tender moment when he'd asked me to marry him; how upset he'd been when he'd struggled with the words "according to God's holy ordinance" when we repeated our vows and his gentle kiss after those vows. Then when we were horseback riding on our honeymoon, I heard him behind me singing softly something about a pretty woman's love. My heart had flipped then; now it was hurting. I longed so to talk with him and remember these things with him! I wanted to remind him of the joy we'd felt the day, finally, after all of our hard work, when he graduated from college and I pinned on his gold Second Lieutenant bars. Oh! I didn't understand why he wasn't running back to me!

But, the more I thought about it, the more I realized something unusual was going on. I was puzzled at Jim's change. We'd always had a love affair, we had always needed each other, and we always worked out our problems. I called Don Ray and asked him if Jim had called to talk with him about us. I felt Don Ray would be the first person he'd call if something was wrong that he needed help with. But, no he hadn't called him. We talked awhile and he told me he thought something was going on because it was pretty strange that Jim wouldn't talk with me about our problems. I agreed, but I sure couldn't find out if he wouldn't talk with me.

Jim finally did call to say he was staying in a boarding house and didn't have a phone, but he'd call me now and then. I thought it strange—no phone or address to give me. Then one day the bank statement for Jim's expense account came in the mail. I hadn't used it, but it was a joint account with my name on it, so I had no qualms about opening it. As I looked through the checks he'd written, I saw one to a florist there in Amarillo. Since I hadn't received any flowers, I called the florist to see what the check was for. I had to be careful—I knew I had to set up the query. A pleasant lady answered the phone.

"Hello, my name is Fran McGraw, and I need to get some information from you."

"Sure, what is it you need, Ms. McGraw?"

"Well, we sent some flowers to some friends recently, and I have our check here, but I can't remember the address that we had them delivered to. Would you happen to have that on file?"

"Sure, Ms. McGraw, I'll see what I can find for you. What's the date on that check?"

I gave this sweet-sounding lady the date, and she put me on hold for a moment.

"Oh, yes, here it is. That was for one dozen roses sent to..."

She gave me the name of the person, the address, and the telephone number. *My, my*, I thought, *how easy is this!*

As I dialed the number, I was amazed I had the courage. A woman answered.

"Hello," I began. "My name is Fran McGraw, and if you'll bear with me here a minute, I'll explain why I'm calling. You see, I'm not crazy, and I'm not going to yell at you, but I believe my husband may be there with you, and I'd just like to know what it is you have that can undo a twenty-five-year marriage."

"Uh, well, uh," she sputtered. "Just a minute, Jim is here. Talk with him."

So, I talked with Jim right then and there. He explained to me that he was staying in this woman's house because she was helping him out until he found a job, and besides that, she had a fourteen-year-old son, and that nothing was "going on."

"Jim, I don't care if anything's 'going on' or not, but I do think you need to come home so we can talk about things. There are things we need to get squared away if you're going to stay in Oklahoma."

"Well, Frances... well okay. I'll call you later today."

Jim did call me later to say that he'd moved out of the woman's house and into a motel until he could find a place to live. Seems this gal was really upset when she learned I did not want to end our marriage!

Later that week when Jim called again, I told him I was going to drive to Fort Worth to visit my brothers and that our friend, Karen Smith, was there visiting Tommy's parents. I wanted to see her too.

"Well, you know we don't have any money."

"*Well, of course I know we don't have any money, Jim!* That's the biggest concern I have, but I'm going to go see Karen. Why don't you come down and meet me there?"

"No, I won't do that. I've got to keep looking for a job, but I'll be in touch."

I took off work Friday afternoon and drove alone to Azle, just west of Fort Worth. I joined Karen and Kelli at Tommy's folks' home and spent the night there. It was the first time I'd seen her since Tommy died. I tried to tell her about Jim and me, but she didn't seem to want to hear it. She kept talking about how things had been since Tommy died, and told me about another fellow she was seeing. Now I didn't want to hear about that—I was too caught up in my own sad situation. But we did talk a lot about friends and family. I enjoyed the time with her, and cherished her friendship. The next day I visited Doyle and his family, and then spent Sunday night with Royce and his family. It was strange talking with them about our separation. My brothers didn't say too much and even though I assured them otherwise, I figured they, too, wondered if it was all my fault. They both offered their sympathy and hoped that things would be all right, and of course if I needed anything to let them know. Early Monday morning, I began the three-hundred-mile trip back to Amarillo and made it in time to get to work that afternoon. It was June 28, our twenty-fifth wedding anniversary.

All the way, I kept conjuring up memories. I remembered our first anniversary and that I was so disappointed when a difficult carpet laying job way out in the country caused Jim to get home too late and too tired for any celebration. Then on our second anniversary when he was at Fort Hood for an ROTC summer camp, I'd gone with my folks to Albuquerque to see Melva and her family. On our return trip to Fort Sumner, we stopped in Santa Rosa at the very same café on Route 66 where we'd stopped to have dinner on our wedding day. I had wondered then if we'd ever get to celebrate an anniversary! I also remembered that somewhere among my things there was a paper on which I'd written down what we had done on as many anniversaries as I could remember. The seventh he was in flight school, the tenth and thirteenth he was in Vietnam, and we'd celebrated the twentieth at the Cannon Club on Diamond Head with our friends the Gordons and Reillys. Big celebrations didn't mean a lot to me; I preferred quiet dinners in out-of-the-way places, but it was sad to think about how nice Bob and Juanita's had been just a few weeks earlier, and we would never experience anything like that. Oh, what a romantic fool I was!

Jim called to say he'd come home that Friday night if it was all right because he thought we needed to talk. As calmly as I could, I told him I thought we needed to talk too. He had car trouble and arrived later than planned. We were both tired and didn't talk much. In fact, I was upset that he had not called to say he'd be so late. I didn't say anything, but I was grumpy. He said he was tired and that he'd sleep in Kevin's room. I told him no, that he was still making the payment on the house, and that it was still his house. I told him that he could sleep on his side of the bed, and I'd sleep on mine. I was surprised that he agreed. He went to bed first, and I followed when I thought he was asleep. He wasn't, and soon you couldn't tell whose side of the bed was whose.

The next day he got a tee time at a municipal golf course. It was not like the country club where we could no longer afford membership, but hey, it was a golf course. And strange as it was after the events of the past six weeks, we enjoyed the time together. We didn't dwell on the lack of manicured greens and fairways, nor did we miss the fancy clubhouse.

Jim told me how sorry he was for the mess he'd gotten us in, and that he really wanted to come home. He thought he could find a job in Amarillo, but he'd have to return to Oklahoma to get his things and tie up some loose ends. I told him it would be nice if he found a job in Amarillo, but if he found one somewhere else that was okay, I'd go with him. He was still apprehensive about how I'd deal with him being home. I told him that of course I had always loved him, and that I remembered the Marriage and Family class at ENMU when Professor Tibbets talked about this very thing happening in marriages. He told us girls in the class that if it ever happened, that we should just give it a little time, and that more than likely our guy would come right back home to us. Jim thought it pretty amazing that I'd remembered that, but he still wanted to know how I was going to handle his filing for divorce. I told him I didn't know he'd filed for divorce because I never got any papers. He thought that was strange and I did too. I asked him if he was sure he wanted to come home so we could try to work things out between us. He assured me that he did, so I told him that the subject of his time Oklahoma would not be brought up unless he brought it up. I'd give him that because he was my man, but I wasn't going to take anymore crap from him. He said he understood, but I most certainly knew he'd recall my statement if I ever brought up the subject! I remember only one time that I did, inadvertently. He raised his eyebrows, not menacingly, but I knew he remembered what I'd said, so we moved right on to another subject.

Jim eventually explained to me about meeting a very nice lady at the landman school in April, and that they hit it off very well. She was divorced from an Air Force fellow and was impressed that Jim was retired military. He thought she was probably "just looking for benefits." Nevertheless, *she had made him feel very good about himself.*

As for the divorce papers, Kathy told me later they were delivered to the house. She signed for them. When she realized what they were, she tore them to pieces and put them in the trash. The law firm that sent them didn't follow up.

We renewed our jogging three times a week. Jim was very attentive to me, and one time he said, "You know, Frances, while I was in Oklahoma, I kept thinking about you and what you said to me that morning when I told you I wanted a divorce. It just kept ringing in my ears."

"Oh? What was that?"

He pulled me close and let his chin rest on my shoulder. "Well, you looked right at me and told me that I couldn't do better. You were right."

I tried not to and didn't want to, but I grieved for a very long time that this had happened to us. Even though we got on with our lives and shared some very special times, it took awhile for that sad feeling to go away.

Looking for Work

We were thankful for military retirement because jobs were scarce. Everyone associated with the once-lucrative oil industry was looking for work. Flying jobs were almost nonexistent, but Jim did freelance some and made some medevac flights, and football officiating brought home a small check every week. He applied for other jobs, but I knew his heart wasn't in it. We put our house up for sale, and sold the Chrysler. We made do with the sixteen-year-old Chevrolet that Jim bought in Oklahoma. There was no eating out, no movies, no Sunday brunches, no pizza called in, and we juggled bill paying. We were still making payments on the kids' cars and paying for their insurance. Both in Lubbock at Texas Tech now, they worked for their spending money and were good troopers. Somehow, we managed to keep a good credit rating.

Around December 1, Jim saw an ad in the Amarillo paper for a pilot. The job would be flying a twin-engine Cessna 421 for a rancher-oilman in the town of Spearman, north of Amarillo. He went for an interview, flew the aircraft to Colorado and back with both the owner and current pilot looking on, and was hired. His boss told him that he'd had seventy-five applications for the job ranging from a former airline pilot in Houston to a cowboy in Denver, but that his demeanor and flying skills made the difference—along with the fact that he was a Texas Panhandle boy! I was aware of all those things and not at all surprised that he'd been hired. I was also so very relieved, even though it would probably mean another move. With the new income, we were able to buy a small new car for me. Jim rented a tiny apartment in Spearman and came home on weekends.

Finally, our house sold and things seemed to be looking up, except for my questions about where were we going to live, what about my job, and how were we going to pay for a move ourselves. We rented a U-Haul truck, Kevin and Shell helped us move, and we put everything in storage. Melva and Shell invited me to stay with them at the parsonage until we decided what to do. Their offer was much appreciated because I couldn't find it within myself to stay with Grandma. She had called me when Kathy told her that Jim was in Oklahoma, and she said some unkind things. She told me she was going to cut Jim out of her will and leave everything to Kathy. When I asked her why she left out Kevin, she said that she didn't like men and most of them didn't like her. *Oh, I was livid! Her own sons and grandsons were men for crying out loud, and as if she had so much to leave anybody anyway, for goodness sake!* I couldn't care less about any money, but I was hurt that she thought along those terms. I simply removed myself from her emotionally, and it took a while *and* a lot of prayer to get over it. A few weeks later, she called me to see if I would come help her call friends who had given her checks for income tax work. She couldn't find them anywhere. So, I went over to help and called these people. They were everyone willing to write another check and send to her. I helped her look for the checks she'd lost, but they were nowhere to be found. It was all coming together now. Since the previous Thanksgiving she'd made some interesting statements about "people living in her attic that the government had planted there," so we knew now she was on her way to dementia. It was hard to see her that way.

The time with Melva and Shell was good. I sang in the choir alongside Melva, and I especially enjoyed hearing Shell preach. He'd "been there, done that" as the saying goes. He and Melva had trouble early in their marriage and he was gone a long period of time. When he returned he wanted to be with her and their children, but he was fixated on making money and tried numerous get-rich-quick schemes. There seemed to be constant turmoil in their lives. When he answered the call to preach he was a partner in a gold mine venture. "From gold mining to soul mining," he said, and he understood God's grace.

Jim called one day to say the bank in Spearman wanted me to come for an interview. I did and was hired, but I hated to leave the law firm. I enjoyed the work and the people who had been so good to me.

"Fran, you're not a legal secretary," Bob Sanders said, "but you did everything the other girls did when we needed you. We sure hate to see you leave, but we're glad you and Jim are doing okay."

I appreciated his comments, and left with so much respect for those three fine attorneys. My last day there was March 11, 1983, my forty-fifth birthday.

1025 Townsend, Spearman, Texas 79081

Spearman, population 5,000, clean and prosperous, was in the heart of the Texas Panhandle. We liked it. We found a charming two-bedroom house that would accommodate us for a while, although we had to cover up some of our things and leave them on the patio. Our plan was to save what we could and eventually buy a house...again. Jim's boss and his wife were gracious and included me on trips when there was room. One trip that Jim remembers was taking this wealthy Democrat family to Austin in January 1983 for the inauguration of Mark White as Governor of Texas.

With good snow in late March, skiing was fantastic at Angel Fire, New Mexico. Don Ray, Mary Beth, and boys Jim and Jon, came from Arizona and joined us there over Spring break. It was a good getaway for Jim and me, and time with the Martins was special.

During this time, Kevin and Kathy were having a hard time deciding where they were "from," as they had no hometown. One time, a young man at Tech asked Kathy where she was from.

She answered, "Spearman, I think."

"Hey," he responded, "you can't be from Spearman because that's where I'm from!"

We laughed about that, and hoped their ties to Amarillo and Clovis were strong enough to give them identity and roots, even if they hadn't finished high school at either place.

Around May 1, and just out of the blue, Bob Stachel called. He wanted to know if Jim would be interested in coming back to Arizona to help him start up a commuter airline.

"What in the world is that all about?" I asked.

"Since the deregulation of the airlines, the industry is wide open," he said. "There are several small airlines starting up all over the U.S., and some are doing very well. Bob says he and some others are backing a fellow that's been flying from Sierra Vista to Tucson in a Cessna 182, and they want to get a bigger aircraft so they can haul more people."

"What does he want with you?"

"He'd like for me to come onboard as a pilot, probably chief pilot, and with my aviation experience, he wants me to help in getting the certificates they need."

"Certificates?"

"Yeah, you know the FAA has to certify all the airlines. They have to meet all kinds of requirements to fly passengers."

I had no idea what he was talking about, nor did I have any idea that I would eventually learn a lot more about some other kinds of *aircraft certification!*

"Bob wants me to meet him next week in Wichita, Kansas, to talk with the Beechcraft folks. If I can get off from my job here, we'll take a couple of days and go to Kansas. We'll find out what he's talking about."

All I could think about was Arizona!

We met Bob in Wichita. He and Jim visited the Beechcraft plant to learn about acquiring an aircraft. A few days later, Bob called and wanted Jim to come look things over, so he took his Fourth of July time off to drive out. The prospectus that Bob presented was well done, and there were a number of eager, high-profile investors. While there, Bob offered Jim a job that would pay him more than what he and I both were making in Spearman, plus moving expenses! He wanted us to come as soon as possible. Jim left his car and flew back to Texas.

Our moving back to Arizona didn't set too well with Grandma, Mamaw, and Papaw, but we had to do what we thought was best for us. Kevin and Kathy were okay with it because they loved Arizona too. Jim's boss hated to see him leave, but he was not forthcoming when Jim told him he'd need a raise to stay in Spearman.

So, back to the U-Haul place for another truck to load up all we owned again. This time, Kevin and Kathy came to help. Soon we were on our way, me following in my little Pontiac. We'd already said our good-byes to our folks, so we traveled west to Logan, New Mexico; Tucumcari, Santa Rosa, Vaughn, Carrizozo, and through the Lincoln National Forest to Ruidoso, where we spent a couple of hours with Aunt Winnie and Uncle EJ in their retirement home. We traveled to Alamogordo, stopping to get gas at Holloman Air Force Base, and then over to Deming, Lordsburg, and finally, once again we were in Arizona. It was all so familiar, and how we loved it!

Arizona Townhouse

Bob and Joyce had a townhouse waiting. Ironically, it was very similar to but larger, and just across the street from the townhouse we'd tried to buy, but moved out of in 1980. This time we had a big garage, three large bedrooms, and room to accommodate our furniture. What joy to have the space! There was a long hallway with our master bedroom and two baths on the right and two bedrooms on the left. The open living room, dining area and kitchen with a breakfast bar were at the back. A large pantry accommodated "stuff." We moved right in and getting settled wasn't very hard at all. There were large windows and we had a nice view of the Mustang Mountains. It seemed so much like home. It was good to be back, and good to be near Don Ray and Mary Beth.

Huachuca Airlines

Jim began immediately working with Bob to get the airline started. Sadly, in the short time it took us to move, the fellow who'd asked Bob to help him get the airline going pulled out and took his airplane with him! So Bob and other investors worked a deal with an airline based in Utah, to borrow a Beech-99, a twin-engine turbo-prop twenty-passenger aircraft. Jim was excited to fly it, and it was perfect for the trip to and from Tucson. I began working for the airline also, and I learned to write airline tickets, screen passengers for security, and bring in the aircraft to a parking place when the maintenance supervisor was not there. I soon became Personnel Manager and supervised three other employees. I wrote salary checks for two other pilots and maintenance folks, paid the bills, and kept the books. Jim and I enjoyed working together while discovering the ins-and-outs of the airline business, such as it was. We worked our tails off and rarely saw each other. Jim worked with the FAA flight standards folks in Phoenix, and eventually obtained an airline certification for Huachuca Airlines.

But something was wrong. Fort Huachuca was not supporting the airline. The military side did, but the civilian side did not. We learned there was animosity between that realm and the Stachels. Some investors pulled out while others got testy about their money, and rightly so. Our dismay increased when the airline bank account got so low that we had to use $1,000 of our *own money to put gas in the aircraft!* Suffice it to say that Jim was in such turmoil that when he learned Rio Airways, a commuter airline based in Killeen, Texas, needed pilots, he applied for a job. Rio was the Delta connection for regional flights that connected to Delta flights at DFW Airport. In late January, Jim flew to Killeen, just outside of Fort Hood, for an interview and was hired immediately.

Well, here we were in *Arizona* again and the job was in *Texas.* We'd been through so much in the past year and a half, and this mess was not fun. Jim packed up his Chevy to leave, and I was dismayed at his aloofness. He told me I could come to Texas if I wanted to.

"If I wanted to? What do you think I'm made of, Jim McGraw?"

"Well, everybody here loves you and you've done such an outstanding job that I'm thinking you don't want to go with me."

I assured him that I certainly did not want to be in Arizona without him, and that I understood his frustrations. Most of all I thought we should be together and I hoped he wanted that too. He said he did, and that he would call me as soon as he could. He wanted to know if we still had our savings account and I said yes, that I had guarded it carefully. We embraced and he was gone.

Oh, I did not want him to go away again! That old numb feeling came back and I was like a zombie trying to figure things out. I wasn't worried about him leaving *me* so much, but I was worried about him leaving so abruptly that it had left everyone else with the airline in a tizzy. They were kind to me and of course I continued working, but it wasn't a pleasant situation.

He called often and was very upbeat about Rio Airways. The last week in February he managed time off to fly to Tucson, helped me pack up things in *another* U-Haul truck and off we went to Texas ... again ...

In the meantime, Kathy had transferred to the University of Arizona for the fall semester, and wanted to stay. She had a good job in Tucson and shared an apartment. *The poor child,* I thought, *here she came to be close to us, and we're leaving her a thousand miles away again.* She had a good head on her shoulders and worked hard; even so, it was hard to leave her.

We said farewell to Don and Mary Beth. They were sad for us, but tried to understand. Sadly, we didn't leave in good stead with Bob and Joyce. We couldn't help that. We felt they'd been less than up-front about the situation with the airline; however, we took responsibility for our own lack of investigation before we'd moved out there. It was a hurtful situation, and we hated that it ruined our friendship.

Townhouse on North Seventh

I followed Jim back to Texas to a town called Copperas Cove on the west boundary of Fort Hood. Jim had run into friends we'd known in Hawaii, Guy and Jenny Evans, who now had the Century 21 Real Estate business there, and they helped him find a brand new two-bedroom townhouse. We arrived late on the second day, pulled a mattress off the truck, and spent the night on the living room floor. Strange as it was, Don Ray came to Fort Hood on a TDY assignment the very next day and offered to help us unload the truck on that Saturday. What a blessing, as two of the folks who were with Don came to help too! They said they'd much rather be doing that than lying around a motel. There *are* angels in this world, sometimes in strange disguise.

Now this townhouse wasn't in the nicest of areas, and it seemed half the size of the one we'd just left in Arizona. Two *small* bedrooms and the one bath were upstairs and a small living room, kitchen and eating area were downstairs. There were no drapes or blinds, so I had to deal with that. Thank goodness for the sets of curtains and drapes with rods and brackets that had moved right along with us. Of course some had to be altered. My sewing machine was humming once again.

Rio Airways and Fort Hood

Jim did well at Rio Airways and earned everyone's respect. He made friends, as he always did, and worked as hard as I'd ever seen him. He was soon familiar with all the routes Rio flew from the Dallas hub. The farthest west was San Angelo, Texas, farthest north, Oklahoma City, and farthest east, Fort Smith, Arkansas. They also flew to Beaumont and Corpus Christi.

In the meantime, I took my SF-171 to the CPO on Fort Hood and applied to get rehired by the government. Six weeks later, I had a clerk-typist position and worked with engineers in a test and evaluation environment.

By that time, Jim was promoted from first officer to captain with a nice raise. He settled into the training department, where he found his niche as an instructor pilot. He worked long hours and was often gone on weekends, but *he was happy*. We saw that we could think about buying a house now. Oh, that ever-elusive house!

Of course I'd been in touch with our folks and told them we were doing well, that we were quite happy and we weren't going to leave Copperas Cove anytime soon! Mother and Daddy had been helpful and encouraging and wanted to see us. They managed to come the first weekend in May, but it just so happened that was the weekend that Ghern and Jim had to move Grandma's things out of her house in Amarillo. Nita had taken her to Houston to live with her. Grandma, age eighty-six, was suffering serious signs of Alzheimer's, and could no longer care for herself.

My folks stayed just the weekend, as Daddy wasn't feeling well. He wanted to see places where he'd lived as a child—places like Gatesville, McGregor, Moody, Leon, Speegleville, China Springs, Valley Mills and Crawford. We drove a lot and saw a lot that day, but it turned out to be one of the hottest days recorded for May in Texas—104 degrees! It was very hard on them. Daddy showed me his mother's grave in a beautiful country cemetery in Crawford and the general area where he was born that's now covered by Lake Waco.

I showed Mother and Daddy some of the houses we'd looked at. The one we liked best was in a treed neighborhood, just across the street and down a ways from the high school football stadium. I told them we had enough money to make a decent house payment, but I didn't know how we were going to manage a down payment. It might take us a while to save enough. Daddy said that maybe he could help us if it wasn't too much. I couldn't believe my ears! Here my dear Daddy, who'd been through so much himself, who'd rarely had an extra dime for anything, was offering to help *me!* We hugged and my tears flowed.

603 Manning, Copperas Cove, Texas

We bought that three-bedroom brick house that I'd showed my folks, and moved in the first week of July. What a joy after living in the small townhouse! It was a pale green and off-white brick, with a two-car garage, and nice attic space. The front entrance, between the carpeted formal living and dining room areas, had parquet flooring. It took you to the carpeted den that had a fireplace on the back wall. To the left were two nice-size bedrooms with a full bath between. Both bedrooms had nice large windows that helped the rooms seem airy and sunny. The alley-style kitchen was open to the dining room and had a breakfast area at the other end. Alongside the kitchen and behind the garage were our master bedroom, shower bath, and nice closets. With Jim's encouragement, I paid a decorator to make special curtains for the breakfast area and drapes to cover the sliding glass window. We dug into boxes and pulled out panels and drapes we'd used at other places for the dining and living rooms. Little by little, it seemed like home. My boss's wife gave me some African Violets that I placed in front of the living room window. They flourished there, multiplied, and were such a joy to us!

We had signed a note to pay the down payment money back to my folks, and each month I sent them a check with a letter of assurance that we doing well and were happy in our new house. Later that summer I flew to Lubbock as a non-revenue-space-available passenger—the benefit of Jim being an airline employee. Kevin picked me up at the airport, and we drove to Clovis to join Mother, Daddy, Christine, and Moreland for a trip to my hometown for a high school reunion. Several of my 1956 classmates were there. I was happy that our tall, good-looking son was with me. It was fun to show him off. Then, during the assembly, Daddy was given an award for his service as a school bus driver many years before. It was a nice tribute, and one he didn't expect. He made an acceptance speech and stated it would probably be his last time to ever come to a reunion in Fort Sumner. It disturbed Christine and me, but we rationalized that it wasn't really that uncommon for Daddy to say something like that. Exactly two months later on the morning of Friday, October 5, 1984, the ringing phone awakened us. Jim answered. It was Christine, and she wanted to speak with me. "Frances, Daddy had a heart attack last night, and he didn't make it," she said softly. He and mother came to Lubbock yesterday, and we went out to eat. He saw some folks he knew and got up to talk with them when his right leg collapsed. He told us we'd better go home so he could lie down. We did, but the pain in his leg didn't get better, so we had an ambulance take him to the hospital."

"So Mother was there with you all the time?"

"Oh, yes, she was very upset and couldn't wait until we got to the hospital to make sure he was taken care of. He was admitted right away and taken to the ICC floor. We know the doctor who saw him, and he told us he'd watch him closely. He suggested that we go home and try to get some rest. So we told Daddy bye about eleven. He told us he would "see us in the morning.""

"*Ohhh,*" I whimpered.

"But the call came about one o'clock that he had died. The doctor said he had a blood clot in his leg that traveled to his heart, and that's what caused the attack."

And, so, my dear daddy was gone.

Jim asked about the call. He sat on the side of the bed, his head in his hands. We were so saddened by this sudden event. I could hardly move, but I managed to call my boss and get ready to go to the airport. Rio Airways gave me another non-revenue-space-available ticket from Killeen through DFW to Lubbock and I was on my way. Jim came on Saturday morning. We knew Papaw hadn't been feeling well, but I suppose we were afraid to acknowledge that. It's hard to accept those things when you're so fearful of losing someone you love. On the flight to Lubbock floods of memories came to me and I welcomed them. I remembered the tears in Daddy's eyes on my wedding day when, after the preacher's question as to who was giving the bride away, he answered, "Her mother and I," and then kissed me softly on the cheek. As hard as it was to let Daddy go, the doctor gave us a lot of comfort. He told Mother and Christine that when he realized he was in distress and was working on him, Daddy said to him that he needn't work so hard, that he was ready to go. There's so much comfort in knowing your loved one is at peace at the end. Even so, I knew I would miss him, but my thoughts turned to my mother. She had been ill much more through the years than Daddy, and I had thought she would probably go first. She would need all her children's emotional support. Later, I recalled their visit to Copperas Cove and to the places of Daddy's childhood. It never occurred to me then that he was probably aware that it would be the last time he saw those places. All of Daddy's children and their spouses, and all the grandchildren except Keith, who was in England, and two little great-granddaughters, were there. It meant so much to Mother. She told me later that the mail had come just before they left Clovis, and that when she cleaned out the pockets of Daddy's jacket, she found the opened letter I'd written. They had deposited our check before leaving town. How thankful I was that he'd read my letter that day that included my thoughts on how happy we were and how we loved our house!

Texas Tech Graduation and Jobs

Kevin graduated from Texas Tech in May 1984 and we were so proud. Kathy flew from Arizona, and it was good to be together again.

Kevin didn't want to apply for law school right away. He expected to have a job soon, but it didn't materialize because of the real estate slump that summer. He was very unhappy. Jim asked if he'd be interested in working at Rio Airways because they always needed good help. Kevin thought he would, so he came to stay with us until he could get his feet on the ground. He trained as a ticket agent and was good at it. He became a favorite in the terminal, and it wasn't long until the competition,

American Eagle Airlines, hired him away, and then promoted him to station manager at the Waco Airport. He was happy to finally be on his own!

Then Kathy came home for Christmas. She liked being there, and asked if she could stay with us and transfer to a nearby college. One of the reasons she liked it was the fellow she'd gone out with, Alan Evans. Alan was the son of Guy and Jenny Evans, and he and Kevin had played football together in Hawaii. He was now an Army Lieutenant waiting to go to flight school. We liked Alan a lot.

Jim flew to Tucson and brought Kathy and her Sheltie, Sheena, back to Texas. We had plenty of room, and it was good to have her with us. The doggies got along fine.

Kathy soon had a job at a restaurant, where she made good money. She also enrolled in college at Mary Hardin Baylor University in Belton, a few miles east of Killeen.

Lieutenant George J. Misek and Miss Nancy Jeanne Harder

Kathy and Alan soon had a falling out, and she met Lieutenant George Misek. We could remember his name by associating it with the Bible characters Shadrach, Meshach, and Abednego from the story of the fiery furnace. He said it was more like "Meeshek," and that it was Hungarian. He told us about his parents coming to America in 1956 when his father was nineteen and his mother was sixteen. They'd fled Hungary during the revolution against Russia, and although both were from Budapest, they met each other in America. His father had done very well as a machinist, later establishing his own company in southern California. The eldest of three boys, George was athletic and fair with gray-blue eyes. He played golf, but had no interest in aviation at all! He and Kathy dated for several months, they were engaged and then married in May 1987. We'd grown to care for George and he seemed devoted to Kathy even though he seemed much too serious all the time. Also to us, they seem too sarcastic in their discourse with one another, and when I gently called them on it, they both assured me they were okay, it was just their way of communicating. *Hmmmm*, I thought, even though I was content that Kathy had married a soldier. George was educated, well read and loved the military. He expected a full career. He was adamant in his desire to put a stop to those "commies" that had caused his parents such pain and sorrow. I knew they would have struggles with a life in the military, but Kathy was aware of the trials as well as the many benefits. Kathy continued college and worked part-time. Not long after they married, George was promoted to Captain.

Bride Kathy and her daddy

In the meantime, Kevin met lovely Nancy Harder in Waco. Nancy was home for the summer after graduating from Southwest Texas University in San Marcos. The eldest of three girls, she was dark-haired, blue-eyed, tall, and slender. Her parents, Bud and Joyce Harder, originally from Kingston, New York, settled in Waco when she was a child. Sadly, Nancy's father, Walter "Bud" Harder, died from cancer the summer she and Kevin met.

Kevin was soon promoted again and moved to American Eagle Airlines Headquarters in Irving, Texas, near DFW Airport. Nancy returned to Southwest Texas and took a year's course to become a paralegal. The next spring they were engaged, and they planned a December wedding.

As they made their plans, Kevin asked George to be a grooms-man, and told him that he'd be expected to wear a tuxedo. George balked. He would wear his dress blue uniform because it served as his formal attire. That didn't suit Nancy because she wanted all the men's attire to match. Kevin called me to say that the situation was causing problems between him and Nancy. Seems she had checked with an ROTC instructor who told her that George could wear a tuxedo—he did not have to wear his dress blues. I told Kevin to tell George that he'd really like him to be in the wedding but he'd have to wear a tuxedo, and that if he couldn't do that, then he'd ask someone else. And that he did. Kathy was dismayed, but George was unyielding. He wore his dress blues to the wedding, but was not in the wedding party. Jim was torn about this. He understood how George felt, on the other hand it was Nancy's wedding and we thought she had a right to have it the way she wanted. It put a strain on these two couples' relationship; nevertheless, our children's beautiful church weddings, seven months apart, were joyful.

Kevin had recently been hired by American Airlines for a position in crew scheduling—this time a management position. They lived in Arlington, and Nancy worked in Dallas as a paralegal.

Mr. and Mrs. Kevin M. McGraw

Atlantic Southeast Airlines

The relationship between Rio Airways and Delta Airlines deteriorated, and Jim could see the writing on the wall. He wanted to fly, so he applied for a pilot's position with Atlantic Southeast Airlines (ASA). ASA was a successful and growing commuter with headquarters in Atlanta, and Delta was placing them at DFW for commuter routes that Rio could no longer handle. ASA hired Jim in October of 1986, and he had to go immediately to Atlanta for training. We were relieved to learn then that he'd be based at DFW, and was therefore able to commute from Killeen. In October 1987, he was promoted to Chief Pilot, ASA, DFW hub. I was extremely proud of him! His boss, however, wanted him to move closer to DFW. *Oh, no! Not another move!* But, things were looking up. Jim's salary had increased, and we knew if we sold our house, we could handle the move.

Chief Pilot, Atlantic Southeast Airlines, Dallas Hub

19 Crestwood, Trophy Club, Texas

When flying in and out of DFW Airport, Jim could see a golf course community called Trophy Club, on Highway 114 just east of Roanoke. It was only fourteen miles from the airport. We looked at several places, but the charm of this community and its proximity to the airport kept calling us back. Soon we had a full-price offer on our house. One catch, the folks wanted it in one week! We counter-offered for ten days. It was accepted, and what a time we had! But we were able to make a similar offer on the house we wanted in Trophy Club. Offer accepted, and that was that! This house was white brick with a red tile roof, and it satisfied our fondness for the Southwestern design. The driveway on the right side of the house curved into the double garage at the back. Because of our dogs we'd have to close the gate every time we came in or out, but that was okay, we could manage that!

I had already contacted the Federal Aviation Administration in Fort Worth about a job, and I was told to report on Monday, April 11. We loaded all we had on a really big U-Haul truck this time, and we managed, with George and Kathy's help, to get it done. We stayed with them for a week in Killeen until we could move into the house in Trophy Club. Sometimes things work out!

On Sunday, April 10, 1988, we moved to Trophy Club, and by nightfall we were almost moved in. The house was a large one-story with three big bedrooms, two and a half baths, an extra room off the utility room behind the garage that served us well as an office, and huge living room with a ceiling-to-floor rock fireplace with bookshelves on either side and opposite the front door. To the right of the fireplace on the side wall, sliding glass doors opened to the patio. The formal dining room to the left of the front door opened to the alley-style kitchen and breakfast area that had a built-in desk and shelves. I remember making the statement while standing in our vaulted-ceiling living room with huge wood-burning fireplace, *I don't know what the future holds, but today I am happy.*

We eventually afforded membership in the Trophy Club Country Club and enjoyed countless hours of golf, "Bridge," and other social activities. When the Trophy Club United Methodist Church was built, we transferred our membership there. We developed lasting friendships with the Obergs, Shanahans, Heberts, Sheplers, Kellys, Crosswys, Askews, Springers, Shirley McDonald, and others.

Still Jitterbugging in 1990

The Settled Years

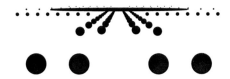

FAA—Airway Facilities

How I hated to go to work the next morning, but that's what I had to do—my new boss said they needed me desperately, and they did. The airline business was booming, and so much was required to keep planes in the air flying safely to and from every destination. I learned about the facilities needed to support the airways in order to maintain a safe and efficient national airspace system. It was fun to tell Jim about my work as an administrative assistant among engineers. Sometimes he'd chuckle and comment on how amazed he was that I understood so much about his flying. I loved it!

Surrounded By Family

That spring, Mother came to stay with us for a while, and told me she believed she could live with Jim and me. I suspected that she had told all my siblings the same thing; nevertheless, it pleased me that she said it. We would have loved having her with us. She was so comfortable to be around, and I had teased Jim through the years that he had married me for my mother. They shared a wit and sense of humor that almost made me jealous.

One thing interesting about our move to the Fort Worth area was that Doyle now lived in Lake Worth, Royce stilled lived near Burleson, and Christine and Moreland had settled in southwest Fort Worth! Now, four of the six Ogden Kids lived within forty-five minutes of each other! It was special to get together often. Cynthia and John still lived in Atlanta, and Melva and Shell were in Lubbock.

Jim's sister, Nita, and new husband, Jerry, still lived in the Houston area where Grandma McGraw was in a nursing home. Her Alzheimer's had progressed so that Nita could not take care of her.

In May of 1988, Kathy graduated with honors from college. We couldn't have been prouder! She and George then moved to Georgia, where he attended the Infantry Officers Advanced Course. After Christmas, they moved to Fort Carson, Colorado. She was pregnant with our first grandchild.

Scary Times

During the holidays, Mother began to have mild strokes and was hospitalized off and on. By late spring 1989, she was able to come and again take turns staying with the four of us in Texas. Sadly, while at Royce's, she fell and broke her hip. She was hospitalized for some time following hip-replacement surgery.

In June my mammogram revealed problems, and a biopsy proved cancer in the left breast. Jim and I were scared beyond belief. My options were to endure chemotherapy and radiation, or have a mastectomy. The doctor explained that if I had to have breast cancer, the kind I had was the "best." It was estrogen receptive, there was medication to block estrogen, and it did not spread as quickly as other types. When the doctor finished, he left Jim and me alone. Jim sat beside my bed, we held hands, and we cried.

"Jim, I don't want to do chemotherapy and radiation. I don't want to be sick, and I've seen how sick it's made others. How do you feel about me having a mastectomy?"

"Frances, that's your decision. If that's what you want, I'll support you." He leaned back in the chair, looked at me seriously, and said, "Frances, I didn't marry you for your boobs." Then he grinned. "But maybe for your legs." We both laughed, and everything was okay from there!

On June 23, I had the mastectomy. Jim's love and support was strong and comforting. It wasn't any harder to keep on going than it ever had been. I also had support of friends at work, at Trophy Club, and family—especially Christine, as she had endured the same thing ten years earlier. She'd done very well. My own spiritual foundation assured me that my future was in the Lord's hands.

During this time, Jim had his second cataract operation. He'd had the first on his left eye a year earlier, and had done very well. Both times lenses were implanted surgically, and he could see well without glasses! After seeing his mother and both his brothers forced to wear heavy, thick-lens glasses, he knew what a blessing it was for him. Now it was his turn, and with the benefit of modern medicine, he could continue flying!

We supported and cared for each other during this time, being especially thankful that we were settled in beautiful surroundings and close to family. My two brothers, a sister and mother were close by, and I wondered how it had all come about. I was reminded once again that the Lord does work in mysterious ways.

Mitchell McGraw Misek—1989

On Saturday, September 17, 1989, we had a call from George that our first grandson had arrived! Jim and I took leave and headed for Fort Carson, Colorado.

Jim drove back to Texas, but I stayed a few days and flew back. What a joy to be grandparents of a beautiful baby boy, *and* to see Kathy's maternal instincts surface so well! I was fifty-one and ready for grandchildren, thankful that I could live to see at least one. Kathy was almost twenty-seven and ready to be a mother. Jim's only problem, he said, was that he now had to sleep with a grandmother! Little Mitchell was precious, and we tried not to make too much of it in front of George, but he looked so much like Jim. We were very proud grandparents.

Law School

With Nancy by his side, Kevin began law school at South Texas College of Law in Houston in August. Nancy worked as a paralegal nearby, so they were able to see each other often. We saw them only at holidays because he had to study so hard. What a joy to attend his graduation in May of 1992, and then learn he had passed the Texas State Bar Exam on the first try! It was also exciting that Nancy was expecting their first child in December.

More Scary Times

In the fall, Jim made a visit to the urologist. He learned his enlarged prostate was squeezing the urethra, and that his bladder was probably damaged. His only option was to have a surgical procedure to chip away at the prostate to allow a full urine flow. The surgeon told him afterward that his bladder looked like that of an eighty-year-old; but thankfully, it would not get any worse. Jim recovered quickly and resumed flying and all of his normal activities. Again, we were thankful for modern medicine and God's blessings.

In December, I had breast implant surgery, but by late the next summer it had to be replaced, as it became very hard. Including Jim's cataract, prostate, and my breast-related surgeries, we'd been under the knife seven times within two years. Not much fun, but we were grateful we were fine otherwise. We'd often heard the statement that *life was not fair;* but being the ever-hopeful optimist, I would add, but *we've had our share.* Jim would smile and agree.

Medah Iva Hutchisson Ogden (1906–1990)

Mother's hip replacement surgery had to be redone. She was in and out of the hospital and not well. The two hip surgeries took their toll, and she began to wither away. After developing a staph infection and being admitted to the hospital in October of 1990, she suddenly passed away during early morning hours—exactly six years and six days after Daddy died. None of her children were with her at that hour.

I was still asleep on that Saturday morning when Christine called to tell me mother was gone. Not only was I sad that mother was gone, I was mad at me! I had planned to go see her after work the evening before, but I was so tired after a long work week, that I turned toward home instead of the hospital which was several miles away and in the opposite direction. *I'll go see her early in the morning,* I told myself, *I won't be so tired then.* That wouldn't have been so bad except I hadn't seen her for the last month. When she developed the staph infection, Christine told me her doctor said that no one with a fresh wound should come to see her. I had just had the new breast implant, and had not healed completely. Aware of my anguish, Jim told me to stop beating myself up, that we didn't know Mamaw's time was so close, and that there could very well be a hidden blessing there because I might have been very disturbed about her condition and wouldn't have wanted to remember her that way. Could be; nevertheless, I've always felt sad about it.

Mamaw had more love and caring in her little finger than most folks have in their entire bodies. Our hearts were broken, but we also knew how she had suffered. We took her to Clovis for the funeral in the church she loved and she was buried alongside Daddy in Lawnhaven Cemetery.

At Thanksgiving the year before, all six of her children and most of her grandchildren gathered in our home to celebrate the day. It was a happy occasion, and also a joy to know that Mamaw had held at least one of our grandchildren.

Our second grandson, Michael Scott Misek, was born on March 25, 1991, at Fort Carson, Colorado. Two beautiful grandsons! We were blessed! Like Mitchell, Michael had blond hair and brown eyes, and a wonderfully happy countenance. George's mother came as soon as he was born and I went up later to help. I had no problem that Mike wasn't a girl; I loved little boys and we were getting them!

Kevin had been out of law school six months and had a position with a law firm in Houston when our third grandson, Benjamin Walter McGraw, was born December 6, 1992. Ben also had blond hair, but he had big blue eyes. We could hardly believe it! We now had three beautiful grandsons!

We waited until the following weekend to go see this little guy so Nancy could have some special time with her mother for a few days. Then it was a little weird to see our son, our child that we had such vivid memories of when he was born, holding his own son. I wanted to say *now you know how I feel,* but I didn't. The moment was his and I surmised that he probably already knew how I felt anyway.

It seemed that everywhere we were our focus was family, and that was good, whether we were with my family nearby or visiting Jim's sister's and Kevin's families in Houston. We traveled to see them and Grandma as often as we could.

That Christmas Kathy and her family came as they were moving to Fort Irwin, California, where George had been reassigned. They'd be farther away from us, but they would enjoy being closer to his parents who lived near Disneyland.

In September we flew to California for Mitchell's fourth birthday. While we were there we all went to see George's parents in Placentia. We four grandparents really enjoyed being with and watching those two little boys. They had so much fun at Knott's Berry Farm and Disneyland! It was good also to see Kathy so radiant. She was expecting their third child in December, and of course they were hoping for a girl. She told us that after the baby was born they would be eligible for a larger set of quarters there on Fort Irwin. She was so excited at the prospect of living in a one-story house after dealing with all three bedrooms upstairs where they lived now. I was so tempted to tell her to forget about moving if they didn't have to—it is so disruptive and time consuming! I'd had plenty of experience there, but I had to bite my lip and remember this was their decision, not mine.

On our anniversary that year, I told Jim that we'd been married thirty-six years and we'd had thirty-six different mailing addresses.

"You have all those addresses?"

"Sure do."

"Wow, thirty-six moves..."

Seems someone in our family was always in the moving

process. In October, Kevin took a position as Assistant City Attorney for the city of Waco. He and Nancy bought a house in nearby Speegleville on the west side of Lake Waco—very near where Papaw was born in 1907. I seem to always have to connect things like that—family, you know. Nancy's mother, Joyce, and her husband, Joe Huddleston, lived nearby. Their family gatherings always included Joe's three sons and families, Nancy's two sisters, Kim and Suzanne and their families *and* Jim and me.

Aircraft Airworthiness Certification

In the summer of 1990, I had been selected for a secretary position in the FAA's Southwest Region Aircraft Airworthiness Certification Office. I worked in support of airworthiness certification engineers. I learned that *anything* anybody wants to attach to an aircraft must first be certified to be airworthy.

In time, I was promoted to a Technical Publications Writer/ Editor position and had responsibility for publishing a quarterly newsletter that was viewed in airworthiness certification offices nationwide. It was the most satisfying work I'd ever done. I was given full reign to gather and edit articles, plan the design of each issue and see that it was published timely. The opportunity to participate in the FAA's quest to keep the skies safe was incredible. After all, I had a personal stake in safe skies!

Between 1992 and 1996, I was a member of a process improvement action team. We traveled to certification offices near Boston, on Long Island, in Atlanta, Wichita, Chicago, Denver, Seattle, and Long Beach, California. Three times I traveled to New England. I was proud to be a part of it and enjoyed the travel. Jim remarked that I didn't need to come back in my second life as an aviator; I was getting to travel enough in this lifetime!

During his time as Chief Pilot for ASA, Jim also traveled

a lot, mostly to Atlanta, or wherever a conference was held. I accompanied him on occasion, and sometimes we managed to play golf. Twice he had the opportunity to fly to Brazil and ferry back new aircraft.

Amye Agnes Johnson McGraw (1898–1993)

The last time we saw Grandma, Jim tried to talk with her, but there was no sign of recognition, and we could not understand her jabber. It was heartbreaking—she had been so strong physically and mentally. She passed away on July 12, 1993, one month and six days before turning ninety-five. Her memorial service was in Pasadena near where Nita, Jerry, E'Laine, Revena, and their families lived. Kevin, Nancy, and Ben came from Houston. Kathy flew from California, Ghern came from Kerrville, and Carol and Richard and two sons, Mark and Eric, came from Laredo. Nita and Jerry accompanied Grandma's body to Amarillo and Jim and I joined them at Llano Cemetery, where she was buried alongside Grandpa. Nita said that she hoped Grandma didn't mind the flight from Houston to Amarillo. Jim answered that yeah, Grandma sure didn't want anything to do with flying unless it meant we were flying home to see her! We all chuckled because it was true. She was quite a gal. It was a blessing now to know she was at peace. Grandma outlived two husbands, two children, three grandchildren, and almost all of her friends.

Now all of our parents were gone. We reflected on the blessing it had been to have had them so long. Now, we took great pleasure in watching our grandsons, and we were also looking forward to another one. We agree with whoever it was that said, "even though we lose loved ones, when a child is born, it is God's opinion that the world should go on."

And the world will go on! Our fourth grandson, Maxwell

Ogden Misek, was born December 20, 1993, at Fort Irwin, California. During birth, the doctor heard a loud pop and said the baby's collar bone was broken. It was a scary moment, but he recovered very well and seemed none for the worse. Maxwell had dark hair and eyes the color of his dad's. Kathy told us that she and George were a bit sad when their third child was not a girl, but when they heard the doctor say he had a broken collarbone, somehow that didn't matter anymore, they just prayed that he'd be okay. George came to pick me up at Orange County Airport just a few hours after Max was born, and Jim came then for Christmas. I was able to help Kathy with everything and George's folks came for Christmas dinner. What doting grandparents we were!

Four beautiful grandsons! Mitchell was four, Michael was almost three, and back in Texas, Ben was one year old, and now we had Max. I love little boys!

Family portrait, 1995

When George was promoted to Major, they moved into larger quarters—but not for long, because in 1996 he was reassigned to Fort Hood, Texas. We were all in Texas again! He and Kathy bought a house in Harker Heights and Kathy took a position teaching English at Killeen High School. They were close by then when Kevin and Nancy's second boy, Bradley Reid McGraw, was born February 10, 1997, in Waco.

Bradley was a big seven pounds, four ounces, and twenty-one-and-a-half inches long. Just as I arrived at the hospital, I saw a nurse take him away, and Kevin told me she was taking him to the neo-natal ICU. His lungs were not fully developed, and he could not breathe properly. *Our hearts were in our throats! It was scary to see him with tubes and monitors attached!* Nancy was with Bradley most of the time and was able to save her milk until she could feed him. When we went in to ICU to see him, we had to scrub our hands and arms and put on masks and smocks. He was so beautiful even though he was asleep every time we saw him. One nurse talked about the other children in that ICU, and told us how tiny some had been when they were born, and that still, some of them might not make it. It was very sobering. The doctor assured us that because Bradley was a big boy, he would be fine. They expected him to lose some weight and he did; but after ten days, he was home and progressed normally. I asked the doctor if it was a genetic thing because of my brother's two children who'd had the same condition when they were born. He said there was nothing to support it being genetic, but for some reason it seemed to run in families. We thanked God for Bradley's progress and for our five incredible grandsons, well knowing that there is a time to live and a time to die.

Shell D. Denison, Jr., 1936–1997

In 1997, Shell was pastor at the First United Methodist Church in Seminole, Texas. He began to have breathing problems that spring, was treated for bronchitis, but by July he was very ill. A longtime smoker, Shell succumbed to lung cancer on August 10. Jim couldn't get off work, so I traveled to Seminole with Royce and his family. Two services, one in Seminole and one in our home church in Fort Sumner, were comforting. Shell and Melva's son, Barry, now a pastor himself and living in Israel, gave the eulogy at both services. What a fine man Barry had grown to be—the child that had been born just four weeks before Jim and I were married. Shell was laid to rest in the Fort Sumner Cemetery alongside members of his family. Melva gave me a tape recording of the services, and when Jim and I traveled to see her a few weeks later, we listened to it on the way. It was nice closure. Even so, the reality of our own mortality loomed before us. We talked about where our final resting place would be. As Jim was eligible to be buried in a national cemetery, we decided on the one in Dallas where we could be together.

Planning to Retire

Because of FAA regulations, Jim had known for some time that he'd have to retire when he turned sixty-five in February of 2000. We had been so grateful that commuter airlines rules were different, and that he didn't have to retire when he turned sixty as did the "big guys" that flew for major airlines. We began making plans for his and my retirement, as I'd be eligible for social security when I turned sixty-two in March of 2000.

We bought a membership lot at a place called White Bluff, a golf course and residential development on Lake Whitney, about halfway between Fort Worth and Waco. We thought about retiring there. In the fall of 1998, we put our house up for sale, and surprisingly soon (when I was in San Diego for computer training, of course), we had an offer we could accept. I had to leave the training one day early to get home in order to put things in timely order. The buyers wanted our house by November 1, so we found a place in southwest Fort Worth to rent, and best of all, we wouldn't have to store our furniture. We had lived for ten and a half years at 19 Crestwood—longer than we'd lived anywhere, and my goodness, we sure had accumulated the *stuff.*

5233 Fallworth Court, Fort Worth

Kevin, Doyle, and Royce helped us move out of the Trophy Club house and into the rent house. That hasty move was exhausting!

Both our commutes to work from there were not bad, mostly freeway, and it was fun to be close to Christine, Moreland, and the Hulen mall. We were also closer to White Bluff and traveled there often on the weekends to play golf and make plans for a retirement home. We also thought it neat to be closer to Kevin and his family.

At White Bluff, we upgraded to a lot on number eleven fairway on the Old Course. A huge live oak tree would shade part of our patio and deck, and other trees were perfect for a tree house for our grandsons. We thought we'd died and gone to heaven! We contracted to build a house that'd be within our means—a two-story, three-bedroom, two-and-a-half baths, just 1,812 square feet. The foundation was laid on Jim's sixty-fourth birthday, February 16, 1999. We arrived after the workers were gone for the day, and marveled at what a difference the foundation made in the looks of the lot. One problem was that this lot had an eight-foot slope and meant that we'd have to have stairs up to the patio. While we were thinking about a storage barn for the lawn mower, tools and such, we decided to build a deck alongside the patio, and build it so that we could have a storage place underneath. It worked and we love it.

"Retired, Not Expired"

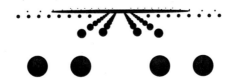

85 Trailwood Drive, White Bluff
Number 35 A, Whitney, Texas

During the week before the house was ready the last week of July, Jim had carpal tunnel surgery on his left wrist. The surgery went well, and using a brace to protect his wrist, he could help with the move. We had quite a convoy for the move—my sedan, Jim's RX-7, Kathy's van, George's pickup, Kevin's pickup—all loaded to the gills, and in front of the big truck we'd hired for all the big stuff. It was very late on Saturday, July 31, when we finally fell into bed.

It wasn't long before we were told our address would have to include the section number. Thus, we were now at 8521 Trailwood Drive.

Kathy and her family spent that first week with us in our new house. George had been assigned to Fort Buchanan, Puerto Rico, and they were on their way to live there for three years. Kathy was excited about the adventure and wasn't concerned at all about another move; in fact, she welcomed it, hoping that hers and George's now fragile relationship would improve. She told us they had been to counseling and, "at least George was saying all the right things." We were dismayed but not shocked that they were having problems. We had seen too much cynicism and sarcasm in their relationship. She told us that when she wanted to begin taking the boys to Sunday School, she talked with George about it. He had been raised Catholic so Kathy had lovingly agreed to raise their boys Catholic. Now she wanted him to help her. Her heart was broken, though, when he told her to take them wherever she wanted to, he didn't care. She felt betrayed, and decided to take them where she was familiar with what they would learn. She began going to the Protestant Chapel services and Sunday School. She would not have her children miss having a foundation to lean on!

George had already shipped his big pickup truck to Puerto Rico, so they left their van with us to sell or keep; however things worked out. We also agreed to keep their Golden Lab called Hannah, and kitty, Gary. I knew I would miss them and their sweet boys, but I was much too involved in our new life situation to worry about them. All I could do was pray.

We absolutely loved our house. The red brick had some blue in it, so we painted the siding white and the trim blue, and what we ended up with was a red, white, and blue house! Jim built a white picket fence, put out bushes and plants, and put down sod in the front and side yards. He had a tall, sturdy flagpole placed in the front yard so to fly his flag every day. We left the backyard natural, but removed the stickers and vines. When it rains, the native lantana blooms.

We'd been in our house about six months, when there was a horrible fire about a quarter of a mile from our house. It began at a campfire on the lakeshore and moved quickly. We could see the smoke and flames, and it was so scary. We watched as the White Bluff Volunteer Fire Department did their thing to keep it from spreading to the two-story house just three vacant lots from us.

Jim stayed close to the firemen, and I began packing the car with precious things! Thankfully, the fire was abated before morning. It was a good introduction to volunteer firemen and how they worked. We attended monthly meetings, and both became part of the support team whenever firefighters are called out. This was right up our alley as far as volunteer work was concerned, and Jim was soon asked to be on the volunteer fire department board of directors. Two years later, I was elected secretary.

We also became active in the newly formed White Bluff Chapel, an interdenominational Christian fellowship. We share the same life values as most of our golfing buddies, and find our chapel family to be the most giving and beautiful we've ever been a part of.

After living at White Bluff about three years, a five-digit address system was put into place. Our "911 locator" address was now 21085 Trailwood Court. We were weary of sending out address changes.

Retirement Number Two

Jim retired from ASA in December of 1999. Kevin, Nancy, Ben, age seven, and Bradley, almost three, joined me at the ASA terminal so we could see Jim bring in his last flight. We saw his safe landing and taxi to the tarmac. We watched as airport firemen, using hoses from fire trucks, made an arc of water over the aircraft as he taxied in … one … last … time. He closed out his final flight and climbed off the twin-engine turbo-prop 30-passenger Brazilia airliner. The firemen gathered, saluted him, and gave him the traditional certificate among the cheers and applause of many coworkers. It was an emotional time—it didn't seem possible thirty-five years had passed since he gingerly climbed upon that stage at Fort Rucker to accept his wings. I was very proud of Jim, and as I followed him in my car for the two-hour trip to White Bluff, the thought occurred to me that we might have missed it all if we'd not held on to our marriage. I wondered if we could have come this far if we'd stayed apart. We'd been together now for forty-two years, and I was pretty sure that we'd be together for as long as we could. Jim had lived his dream and could enjoy a pleasant retirement; I was about to finish my career, and then, oh my goodness, we'd have to put up with each other every day!

I retired the last day of March 2000. My friends gave me a farewell luncheon and then a reception on my last day at work. I received many generous gifts. I loved my work, but I couldn't wait to be at home all the time, and also get out on the golf course. I was also ready to give up the one and a half hour, seventy-five mile commute to and from the north side of Fort Worth!

Now fully retired, Jim helped form the White Bluff Men's Golf Association, and became its first elected president. I joined the White Bluff Ladies Golf Association, and became its second elected president. We learned that we were just as busy as ever with chapel, fire department meetings, property owner potluck dinners, Bridge parties, and golf. Golf was the best outlet because Jim played with his buddies and I played with the gals. We always shared with each other what happened on the golf course; we knew how the other one felt if the game went poorly. Occasionally we played in couples golf tournaments, and when we went anywhere, we carried along our golf clubs. I was so glad that he had suggested I learn to play golf back in '68!

But golf wasn't our entire world. After all, we lived just a quarter of a mile from Lake Whitney.

That summer we received the proceeds from our sold membership at Trophy Club Country Club, and promptly bought a pontoon boat. Jim had always enjoyed the water, but I was a land lubber. I had a lot to learn. We practiced launching the boat then returning it to the trailer. I was to back the trailer into the water so he could just drive the boat onto it. It took me a few tries to get the concept, but soon I was right out there with the best of them. It was fun; we invited family and friends to join us, and we had some good outings. We even joined other White Bluff boat owners for Friday night get-togethers. Problem was we didn't want to afford keeping the pontoon at the White Bluff Marina. Others complained of the cost and how dirty their boats got and that they were constantly cleaning them, etc., etc., so we put ours in a storage place a few miles away. That meant Jim had to go get it, bring it to the dock, launch it, then we had to load it up afterwards, clean it, take it back to storage and make sure it was covered well, and on and on it went. It finally got to be too much and we sold it. Nice thing was, we got as much for it as we'd paid for it! But, we decided you really need to be rich to do the boating thing, or be a lot younger than we were. Golfing was a better deal for us.

Life Changes

For Thanksgiving, Jim and I flew to Puerto Rico to be with Kathy and her family. We felt blessed to be able to fly non-reve-nue-space-available on Delta. We so enjoyed the time with them in their beautiful quarters at Fort Buchanan, but we sensed the same turmoil in their lives. Kathy had their quarters decorated so well; the boys' schools were close by, and Kathy was able to get a job teaching soldiers so they could get their GED diploma. But, the sad thing was, Kathy told us, George did not expect to get promoted again, and it was tearing him apart. The Army was his life. At least he didn't have to worry about the Regular Army Officer-Reserve Officer thing that Jim did, and he knew he would get to retire after twenty years, but he was not a happy camper. He retreated in his unhappiness to the computer and began shutting Kathy out. She wanted so much to have a relationship like her folks did, but it was not to be. We urged her to keep trying, hoping things would change.

Finally, in January of 2002, she and the boys came to stay with us until she could figure out what to do. She enrolled the boys in school and set out to see where she and the boys could settle. But, oh my, Kathy was an animal lover and brought three stray cats and two stray dogs back from Puerto Rico! I believe taking care of the animals was Kathy's way of dealing with things when George was so far away emotionally. When she was making arrangements to fly the animals to Texas, the ASPCA offered to pay their way. Seems there are a lot of stray animals in Puerto Rico that are not taken care of, and this was a good way to take care of five of them! We had quite a time at our house with our Taffy and Hannah and now, five more! Fortunately we had a fenced yard. I thought it was a bit above and beyond the call of duty, but Jim was an animal lover, too, and he helped take care of them. The three boys were good to help. They loved the animals.

George followed about two months later. He had orders to spend a year in Saudi Arabia, so Kathy wanted to settle near us for the year. They purchased a home in Cleburne, just thirty miles up the road, and she began teaching eighth grade English at Cleburne Middle School. George went to Saudi Arabia, and upon completion of that year, decided to spend time in Egypt for another year. Kathy explained to us that their marriage was over, and that she was filing for divorce. We were saddened, but for whatever reason, these two people just fell out of love with each other. Part of it was Kathy's outgoing personality that made George uncomfortable, and his expecting her to conform to his wishes much as his own mother conformed to his father's wishes. Also, George was gone from home a great deal, as is the way of the military so much of the time, and Kathy had learned to be independent. She took care of the bills, checkbook, house and cars, yet George wanted her home all the time to do his bidding. Once he was in his recliner and asked her to get him a beer. She promptly told him to get his own beer! She thought he could do that himself when she had children to take care of, meals to prepare, clothes to wash, and on and on it goes. Sure, he worked hard, but not so hard that he should expect her to wait on him at home.

We tried to get George to communicate with us, with Kathy's blessing, of course, but he would not answer our emails. They were divorced in May of 2004. When George returned from Egypt, he lived in Grapevine, Texas, so he could see his boys often. Then, in January of 2005, he was sent to Iraq to serve one year. We continued to keep in touch with him and sent care packages while he was in that hellhole. Upon returning, he was assigned to a unit near the Pentagon in Virginia—sadly, a long way from his boys.

Fortunately, U.S. Army rules are that divorced parents must pay child support. That was a big help to Kathy; nevertheless, we watched as she had to sell the big house and buy a smaller one she could afford. She gave her boys a good home, and they always went to Sunday school and church. George was in touch, every so often.

In the meantime, Kevin took a corporate attorney position with Protection One, a home and business security systems corporation, and they moved from Waco to McKinney, about thirty miles north of Dallas. It now took two hours to get to their house through Dallas traffic. We didn't mind though, as they purchased a beautiful new four-bedroom house with all the amenities, including a huge game room over the garage. The school at the end of their street was wonderful for the boys. Best of all, Nancy could stay at home and be a full-time mom!

Life was moving along for our children and their families and we were thankful to be as close as we were—as Jim said, "close, but not too close."

Ever thankful for all our blessings, Jim and I both played golf on the morning the airplanes hit the World Trade Center. What a shock to come in from the peaceful golf course and learn that terrorists had attacked our country! We were stunned along with the rest of the world, and listened to President Bush speak to our nation. We were comforted and felt assurance that our country would seek out the cowards who had planned and pulled off the hideous terrorist attack. Our lives changed. We also became well-acquainted with cable news channels. We had little patience for those airport security and FAA folks who were not professional in their work. We'd both had some experience along those lines and we believed there were things that could have been done to prevent at least some of the tragedy. Our hearts went out to innocent flight crews, passengers, and those on the ground. We talked a lot about it, and Jim tried to imagine having to deal with something like that in the air. Under the same circumstances, he felt there was probably little that could have been done differently. The very idea that an airplane he loved could be used on purpose for such terror and destruction was very disturbing. He was ready to sign up to go to war right then and there, if the Army would have taken him!

We were in such turmoil over the terrorist attacks for a long time. But, even though we will always have to be watchful, we slowly began to see things and people in the world that are beautiful, and good, and peaceful. Life goes on.

And so, there was much joy when, in 2002, Kevin told us he and Nancy were going to have another baby! We hadn't expected this as Kevin was now forty-one, and Nancy was thirty-nine, but the pregnancy was planned, and they were *very* happy. Blake Patrick McGraw came on December 18 and what a blessed event! He weighed seven pounds, thirteen ounces, and was twenty inches long. When Kevin called to say he would be born soon, Jim was working as a marshal for a golf tournament and couldn't go right away, but I jumped in our van and scurried up there! I had never been able to be there at the moment of birth of any of our grandsons, and this time I might make it! We already knew he was a boy and that was just fine. I hurried as fast as I dared, but darn that Dallas traffic, I arrived just minutes after Blake was born. Ben and Bradley were there grinning from ear to ear, and Nancy too, not to mention Kevin! He took me to the room where the nurses take care of the newborn babies, and we watched through a big window as the nurse cleaned out his ears and nose. As she turned him over once we could tell it startled him and he jumped, reaching out with his arms as if to try to catch himself. It was so cute! He settled quickly and it didn't seem to bother him at all. I told Kevin he had a good one there. He smiled proudly and nodded his head in agreement. We love little boys!

Jim calls his six grandsons his "six pack." They are precious to us and being around them is joyful. One thing I tell my friends now is, "I am finally surrounded by men, they love me, and it's okay with Jim!"

Our children are settled in their communities and churches. There is joy and thankfulness in watching our grandsons grow and progress under the nurturing hearts and eyes of their parents.

Left to right: Kevin, Jim, and Bradley McGraw, Mike and
Max Misek, Ben and Blake McGraw, and Mitch Misek

Conclusion

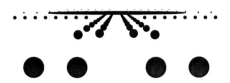

In 2007, we celebrated our fiftieth year of marriage. We've survived—perhaps with not a lot of accumulation of things, but for the most part, we've had a good time. We've reflected on our time together and some of the things that, perhaps, have helped along the way:

- We established our marriage on a spiritual foundation.

- We remember the reasons we got married in the first place.

- We set goals and learned how to discipline ourselves when our impulsiveness took over, as well as when we faced misfortune and had to redirect our lives.

- We dedicated our children to God, asking his guidance as we directed their way.

- We valued and honored our parents, respecting them for the strength that they revealed in their life travels.

- We cherished friendships and understood how precious they are, understanding that we could help each other when things got rough along the way.

- We first got to know each other on a dance floor, and

we continued "dancing" even though we "got out of step now and then."

- We chose a common interest that we both could enjoy, together or apart.

- We have always delighted in the joy that touching brings.

On the occasion of our fiftieth celebration, we were astounded at the number of friends and family that came to honor us, as well as the cards, letters, photos and mementos that our daughter had collected from those who could not attend. We humbly remember our son and our daughter and their families making it the sweetest commemoration we could have ever hoped for! Everything was memorable; the flower arrangements designed from our wedding pictures, the cake so similar to the one on our wedding day, the incredible h'ors d'oeuvres, the slide show of our fifty years together. Then, there was the joy one grandson had sharing the day with his new girlfriend, the *inadvertent* fire the other grandsons caused in the parlor of the conference center, and to the littlest grandson being so excited to get to go across the street, walk across the railroad tracks, and then later watch a train go by!

Remembering is good. It is golden. It is joy. Memories of these special times, places, people, and things are just as sweet as all of those safe landings.

Jim and Fran McGraw celebrate their fiftieth wedding anniversary

Epilogue

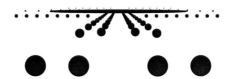

A blessing on the occasion of the fiftieth wedding anniversary of Jim and Fran McGraw, June 28, 2007 from Kevin McGraw.

Dear Lord, we gather today in loving celebration of the marriage and family of Jimmy Jon and Frances Elizabeth McGraw; also lovingly known as Jim and Fran, Mom and Dad, and Grammy and Papa Jim.

Who knew that fifty years ago, on June 28, 1957, when they said their vows to each other, it would last at least fifty years, let alone a lifetime. Only you, Lord.

Especially in this day and time of throw-away relationships and convenient love, only you could have known that theirs would last this long and still be going strong, and for that, we are all truly grateful.

We are so grateful for the beautiful example that they give us every day of how a strong marriage should work, and of how, as the Apostle Paul taught us in his letters to the Corinthians, a marriage should be the model of your Son, Jesus, the groom, and his bride, your church. As Jesus and his church lovingly serve each other, so do Jim and Fran.

Lord, as we close this blessing, we humbly ask your special blessings on those friends and loved ones of ours, both here and far away, who for whatever reason, will never have the opportunity to reach this milestone. As we consider that fact, Lord, you make us mindful of the true and special blessing that you have bestowed on those whom you have allowed and will allow to experience this wonderful moment. Jim and Fran are truly mindful of this, as are we all, and are humbly thankful that, against all odds, you have allowed them to be together today to enjoy this moment.

So, as we join with them in celebration today, Lord, we realize that everything happens according to your great and wonderful plan, and rejoice that our family has been able to play a small part in the realization of that plan. So today, in honor of this special marriage, I would humbly ask all those present to join with Jim and Fran, Mom and Dad, Grammy and Papa Jim, in re-dedication of their marriage and their families to your service and to your ultimate glory. In everything we do, Lord, let us remember to glorify you. We ask these things in the awesome power of Jesus' name, Amen.

To my parents as they celebrate their fiftieth year of marriage,

From Kathy Misek

I want to say how blessed I feel that I have two parents who love each other and are committed to honoring their wedding vows. Though times have not always been a piece of cake, over the years they have always shown a deep consideration and tolerance for each other that I think is amazing—as a matter of fact, it is in their ability to nurture and appreciate their relationship that I see their greatest strength.

My dad reminds me somewhat of George Bailey in *It's A Wonderful Life*. My dad may not have been a pro ball player or gone on to be a general of the army—although he and my mom have gotten to experience some amazing things—but it is in his relationships that he has truly risen above the best and lived an exceptional life. He still keeps in touch with his closest friends, and still loves and appreciates my mom dearly. And, I love him for that.

And in my mother, I have been so blessed to have her patience and easy way. I don't remember her ever being grouchy or mean when I was a child. She has always been so eager to do what comes along, and so prayerful in the good times and bad.

So, to both my parents, I want to congratulate them on their fiftieth anniversary and say thank you to them for being such good role models and for showing me that true love most certainly does exist! I love you, Mom and Dad.